Towards a Productive Aesthetics

Historical Materialism Book Series

The Historical Materialism Book Series is a major publishing initiative of the radical left. The capitalist crisis of the twenty-first century has been met by a resurgence of interest in critical Marxist theory. At the same time, the publishing institutions committed to Marxism have contracted markedly since the high point of the 1970s. The Historical Materialism Book Series is dedicated to addressing this situation by making available important works of Marxist theory. The aim of the series is to publish important theoretical contributions as the basis for vigorous intellectual debate and exchange on the left.

The peer-reviewed series publishes original monographs, translated texts, and reprints of classics across the bounds of academic disciplinary agendas and across the divisions of the left. The series is particularly concerned to encourage the internationalization of Marxist debate and aims to translate significant studies from beyond the English-speaking world.

For a full list of titles in the Historical Materialism Book Series available in paperback from Haymarket Books, visit: www.haymarketbooks.org/series_collections/1-historical-materialism.

Towards a Productive Aesthetics

Contemporary and Historical Interventions in Blake and Brecht

Keith O'Regan

Haymarket Books
Chicago, IL

First published in 2021 by Brill Academic Publishers, The Netherlands
© 2021 Koninklijke Brill NV, Leiden, The Netherlands

Published in paperback in 2022 by
Haymarket Books
P.O. Box 180165
Chicago, IL 60618
773-583-7884
www.haymarketbooks.org

ISBN: 978-1-64259-786-8

Distributed to the trade in the US through Consortium Book Sales and Distribution (www.cbsd.com) and internationally through Ingram Publisher Services International (www.ingramcontent.com).

This book was published with the generous support of Lannan Foundation and Wallace Action Fund.

Special discounts are available for bulk purchases by organizations and institutions. Please call 773-583-7884 or email info@haymarketbooks.org for more information.

Cover art and design by David Mabb. Cover art is a detail of *Pomegranate*, mixed media on William Morris fabric (1998).

Printed in the United States.

10 9 8 7 6 5 4 3 2 1

Library of Congress Cataloging-in-Publication data is available.

For Nadra

∴

Contents

Acknowledgements IX

1 Introduction 1

2 Brecht and the Now 20
   1   *Mann ist Mann*: The Right Question and the Precision of Time 23
   2   The Knowing *Johanna* 38
   3   *Kuhle Wampe* and the Good Answer 48
   4   Concluding Brecht to 1933 60

3 Blake, Opposition, and the Now 63
   1   Blake and Romanticism 65
   2   Expect Poison, Demand Movement 69
   3   Innocence's Opposition to Experience 88
   4   Conclusion: The Future in the Present 101

4 Brecht, History and the Productive Past 108
   1   And the Cart Rolls On ... *Mutter Courage* and Learning from Those Who Don't 112
   2   The Religion of the Now: *Galilei* and the Knowing Science 129
   3   The Chalk Lines of History: *Der Kaukasische Kreidekreis*, Productivity and the Past 139
   4   Concluding the Historical Brecht 150

5 Blake, *Milton*, and Historical Redemption 154
   1   Blake Contra Newton 155
   2   The Importance of What Is Missing 161
   3   Filling in That Which Is Missing 167
   4   Milton's Entrance 171
   5   Blake *Labouring* in History 179
   6   Brecht, Blake and the Uses of History 192

6 Conclusion 196

Bibliography 207
Index 228

Acknowledgements

This book's origins begin with my doctoral work at York University. I was incredibly fortunate to write my dissertation in the Graduate Program in Social and Political Thought, in an environment defined by political commitment and intellectual generosity. While it is difficult to ascertain a specific genesis for long-form projects, many of the ideas expressed in this book spring from discussions with the sincere and imaginative thinkers I have had the fortune to meet. Many of the conversations developed herein were born after graduate seminars had officially ended and yet continued in the welcoming homes of scholars such as Himani Bannerji and Aijaz Ahmad. I am immensely appreciative for the kindness, patience, and rigor that they both showed in the earliest stages of this project, and for both steering me away from a much more conventionally academic project. Likewise, this project is unthinkable without the guidance, reassurance, and downright decency of David McNally. It is hard to imagine a scholar-activist more perceptive and considerate, and he remains an outstanding mentor in influence and action. I am also heavily indebted to the support, questions, and comments of Ian Balfour, Scott Forsyth, Susan Ingram, Esther Leslie, and of course David again, that have helped shape this document.

I have benefitted from sustained access to Brecht's Archives in Berlin. Numerous research stays there were made possible through generous financial support provided by the Canadian Centre for German and European Studies, the Deutscher Akademischer Austauschdient (DAAD), Freie Universität Berlin, York University, and through research grants cumulatively won over decades through the collective efforts of union activists at CUPE 3903. Raj Virk and Sheila Wilmot were cheerful guides in accessing those later funds. While in Berlin I was assisted by the incredibly supportive staff at the Bertolt-Brecht-Archiv and the Staatsbibliothek zu Berlin. Thanks to Sebastian Budgen for his easy early communications about the project, and to the detailed editing work provided first by Greg Sharzer and then Danny Hayward. Their careful assistance between these sentences has been of immense value.

While they have helped me on other projects before, during, and after this text's production, Professors Baus, Bell, McKenzie, and Sufrin have provided opportunities, soft shoulders and unflinching support. For this and many reasons besides I owe them a debt of significant gratitude. Likewise, I consider myself incredibly fortunate to work with so many brilliant graduate students through York's Writing Centre. Listening, reading, discussing, and developing new ideas with a wave of critically minded scholars has kept me humbled and hopeful. Their energy and boldness of thought has meant the world to me and helped me grow in innumerable ways.

Special thanks to the friends who have helped sustain, nourish, and, let's be honest, put up with me. They include Greg Sharzer, Emily van der Meulen, Rob Heynen, Todd Gordon, Jackie Esmonde, Susan Bender, Seth Clarke, Steve Tufts, and the late but still powerfully resonant Mary-Jo Nadeau. A big shout-out to all my fellow picketers on the Glendon line. Your solidarity over the course of several strikes kept me motivated and my confidence boosted. My sisters Kim and Tracey have offered regular reminders of the goodheartedness of our mother, Alice, who passed during this text's earliest stages. My partner Nadra's parents Susan and Qadeer have been wonderful entries to my life, and their tenacity and willingness to help whenever and wherever they can has served as a great model. Her family have been as welcoming as can be hoped for. Nadra's two children, Razia and Ruby, keep me youngish and laughing, even if they prefer to do so by reveling in every new grey hair that appears.

Finally, to Nadra, her third reference here and most definitely my charm. Her love, compassion, and energy have aided me immeasurably throughout this project. She has kept me grounded and offered encouragement, lightness when it was needed, and humour always. This is dedicated to her.

CHAPTER 1

Introduction

This book originates from a desire to understand how materialist and non-materialist cultural texts interrogate the politics of production in oppositional ways. The absence in the academic literature of a full consideration of the aesthetics of production has resulted in a turning away from or devaluing of the connections and determinations that exist between cultural forms and their political-economic and social underpinnings, within a tradition of aesthetics that seeks to understand the social landscape which propels it and makes it possible, and to respond in consciously oppositional ways. This has predominantly encouraged a forestalling or avoidance, especially in and following the age of postmodernity, of an interrogation of or conversation with oppositional aesthetics.[1] For those that do try to take seriously the fundamental social contradictions of the day, too often these interventions eschew an engagement with the actual political situation and respond with old answers to new questions. This appears often when framed by a realist poetics that presents contemporary audiences with a conception of veracity and devotion to totality[2] that does more to obscure than illuminate. Even more importantly, it negates the role of agency by assuming objectivity in making cultural politics. As Fredric Jameson defines it, 'traditionally in one form or another the central model of Marxist aesthetics as a narrative discourse ... unites the experience of daily life with a properly cognitive, mapping, or well-nigh "scientific perspective"'.[3] This form of cultural politics does not begin from below and of the now, for which the oppressed and exploited must be integrated producers of the text. Instead, it reproduces the textual dynamics of the society it is trying to change.[4] In contrast, the works of Bertolt Brecht and William Blake, two of the most oppositional cultural producers, articulate an aesthetics wherein the moment of the now is the *sine qua non* of an aesthetics of production.

Drawing from Walter Benjamin's 'The Author as Producer', an aesthetics of production encourages a debate around the way cultural work relates to its own

---

1 The literature maintaining this critique is extensive, but most important here are Eagleton 1996; Harvey 1990; Jameson 1991.
2 The primary exemplar of this tradition is Lukács 1962. A less intellectually sophisticated version is found in Caudwell 1973.
3 Jameson 1994, p. 104.
4 See in particular the discussion of the forms of realism in Fischer 2010.

society. Benjamin's text does not ask 'What is the *attitude* of a work to the relations of production of its time?', but rather 'What is its *position* in them?'.[5] This comment raises serious, formal questions about the forms of production and the role of cultural production in the function of literary analysis. Cultural production has a long pedigree, and one of its clearest definitions is put forward by Pierre Bourdieu in his *The Field of Cultural Production*. He writes that: 'The space of literary or artistic position-takings, i.e. the structured set of the manifestations of the social agents involved in the field – literary or artistic works, of course, but also political acts or pronouncements, manifestos or polemics, etc. – is inseparable from the space of literary or artistic positions defined by possession of a determinate quantity of specific capital (recognition) and, at the same time, by occupation of a determinate position in the structure of the distribution of this specific capital. The literary or artistic field is a field of forces, but it is also a field of struggles tending to transform or conserve this field of forces'.[6] Bourdieu's concept of forces moves discussion away from mere 'influence'[7] to the larger forces at play within a given literary text as well as a larger field of play that both structures and makes possible the production of literary and cultural documents. In this regard, the 'superstructure' is, as Terry Eagleton notes, 'a relational term' in that it 'designates the way in which certain social institutions act as "supports" of the dominant social relation'.[8] An emphasis on cultural production puts the question of 'literary technique'[9] more firmly in relation to its technological and political determinants: what was possible, or deemed possible, at what time in literary history, and also what questions were being raised, or even being occluded, that necessitated an aesthetic response. This begins a form of investigation that sharply contrasts the literary text's relation to its own '*Jetztzeit*' or '*time of the now*' and history. This is a sincere political question[10] and encourages the further question as to what form of response a cultural producer is committed.[11] A central point of departure where much of this work has run into obstacles is on the distinction between what the Welsh literary critic Raymond Williams terms oppositional and alternative cultures.

In his 'Base and Superstructure in Materialism and Culture', Williams states that the degree of difference between oppositional and alternative cultures is

---

5   Benjamin 1978, p. 222.
6   Bourdieu 1993, 30.
7   Bloom 1997.
8   Eagleton 1991, p. 83.
9   Benjamin 1978, p. 222.
10 Benjamin 1978, p. 223.
11 Here I am using Theodor Adorno's formulation, in contrast to 'autonomous art'. See Adorno, 'Commitment' in Adorno et al., 1998, pp. 177–95.

INTRODUCTION 3

subject to what he terms 'constant historical variation'. Clarifying his historical moment but also expressing a more generalisable perspective, Williams continues:

> Thus, the effective decision, as to whether a practice is alternative or oppositional, is often now made within a very much narrower scope. There is a simple theoretical distinction between alternative and oppositional, that is to say between someone who simply finds a different way to live and wishes to be left alone with it, and someone who finds a different way to live and wants to change the society in its light. This is usually the difference between individual and small-group solutions to social crisis and those solutions which properly belong to political and ultimately revolutionary practice. But it is often a very narrow line, in reality, between alternative and oppositional. A meaning or a practice may be tolerated as a deviation, and yet still be seen only as another particular way to live. But as the necessary area of effective dominance extends, the same meanings and practices can be seen by the dominant culture, not merely as disregarding or despising it, but as challenging it.[12]

Despite the fact that this distinction is nearing its half-century mark, its prescience for our times should not be underestimated. As it stands now, there is no dearth of alternatives to the existing order of capitalism. Indeed, the so-called linguistic turn in the social sciences has witnessed an extraordinary heap of 'deconstructions' of the cultural logics of capitalism that, although they attempt to rid societal formations of the consequences of systemising thought, most often characterised as totalising, have done little to aid in the struggle against one of the deepest entrenchments of capitalist power on an ever-increasing scale. As E. San Juan Jr. notes in regards to contemporary cultural studies, 'an emancipatory discipline producing testable knowledge cannot go beyond textualism without rejecting methodological individualism and its framework of idealist metaphysics. Linguistic analysis needs to be supplemented with a critique of ideological structures'.[13]

David McNally, in his *Bodies of Meaning: Studies on Language, Labor and Liberation*, has spoken to the inability of contemporary trends in aesthetic theory to deal with societal structures. He writes, 'For the new idealism, there is no way out of the linguistic forms of thought or the social relations characteristic of

---

12 Williams 1980, pp. 41–2.
13 San Juan Jr. 2002, pp. 234–5.

Western capitalist society'.[14] These anti-systemic oppositions rule out the problematics of opposition, even if not always intentionally or even willingly. All that remains are pockets of activity rather than any conception of a sustained challenge to the system's logics. The institutional order may still be capitalism, but imagining a world beyond it is seen as risible. Indeed, we have entered a period of 'Capitalist Realism', as Mark Fisher has termed it, wherein a systemic, 'aggravated and chronic'[15] logic dismisses any notion of opposition beyond the 'alternative'; as such, systemic opposition appears as the greatest affront in academia.[16] For this reason, Williams' distinction is indispensable for a committed materialist criticism.

In this text I will be arguing that Blake and Brecht represent high points of oppositional cultural production. In terms of their impact throughout the history of oppositional cultural practice, few authors have wielded such a great influence in determining the major questions, if not always resulting in the same answers, that subsequent producers have posed and grappled with. They are two of the most significant archetypal producers of oppositional aesthetics: the strategies they employ – for Brecht read distancing effects, gestural politics and Epic Theatre, and for Blake read an explosive verse full of inspiration and messianic energies – have become models for a variety of expressions of the complex social realities faced throughout the history of the left.

In this text I hope to compare the two authors to examine how both exposed contemporary modes of oppression and exploitation in direct connection to the moment of the now, coupled with a Janus-like vision of the past. For the latter, they discarded the reproduction of an accurate historical reality and sought something much closer to Walter Benjamin's famous analysis of an historical materialist approach to history. When we accept that, as Benjamin notes, 'There is no document of civilisation which is not at the same time a document of barbarism', the mode in which we look towards and examine the past alters. In this context, a cultural producer operates in a space where the need for response is most keen. Yet rather than reproducing historical truisms, that is truths that do not sufficiently examine the terrains of history and the contemporary, the oppositional project proceeds differently, focussing not only on how historiography has occluded projects and movements from below, but

---

14   McNally 2001, p. 7.
15   Fisher 2009, p. 7.
16   Works helpful in illuminating this process are Dworkin 2007; Ebert and Zavarzadeh 2008; Ebert 2009. Two historical critical texts in this regard are Wolin 1992 and Hodge, 'Labor Theory Of Language: Postmodernism and a Marxist Science of Language', in Mas'ud Zavarzadeh et al. 1995, pp. 252–70.

how the lessons of such repression of past struggles colours and shapes those in the present. As Benjamin notes in 'Theses on the Philosophy of History': 'A historical materialist therefore dissociates himself from [barbarism] as far as possible. He regards it as his task to brush history against the grain'.[17] Benjamin's argument is responding to a vision of progress that had haunted progressive forces in German Social Democracy, and therefore had eliminated their ability to challenge the immense resources and, it should be emphasised, capabilities of capitalist forces to defeat opposition head-on or co-opt it.[18] Nevertheless, an overriding belief in a slow progression of victories that would eventually produce a greater socialist victory had led the working-class movement into a position of existential and practical inactivity. In response, Benjamin postulated that what was necessary was not a return to reassuring truths, often specifically a-historical arguments about progress and stability, but a much fuller reckoning with the role that experience plays in articulating a revolutionary politics or a 'radical moving-forward'.[19] Susan Buck-Morss, commenting on the introduction to Benjamin's essay in her *The Origin of Negative Dialectics*, expresses this new form of historical investigation as follows: 'Now in this new methodological introduction Benjamin had stressed precisely the opposite moment, in which truth emerged only by the setting up of a critical distance between the material and the interpreter, and that meant standing at the present edge of history, on the dividing line between "now-time" (Jetztzeit) and the possibility for a radically different future. From this perspective history could not be affirmed or rationalized'.[20] Benjamin tries to cleave open new pathways of responding to our time, and his insights are reflected in Brecht and Blake's aesthetic strategies and politics.

There are two forms of temporal engagement that Brecht and Blake express. First, we have a specific conception involving lived experience. This develops from a deep understanding of the period through which we live: a balancing of the ways in which that living could be structured differently, and a reckoning with what that differently ordered society would require on the level of social political forces and at the level of ideological reconceptualisation. This relies on a Janussian moment found between the present and a 'radically different future', for better or ill. The present's newness, as opposed to capitalism's fake newness (the newness of the commodity, of false-novelty, old wine

---

17 Benjamin 1968, pp. 256–7.
18 For a detailed discussion of Benjamin's essay and its fragmentary nature (and how this reflected his political thought) see Benjamin 2013, pp. 162–202.
19 Richter 2016, p. 113.
20 Buck-Morss 1977, p. 169.

in new bottles), is an entire mess of congruent and discordant impulses, concerns and motivations: capital is constantly remodelling and refashioning how we experience the world in its own image. However, these structured moments of indeterminancy are always informed by history and constrained in innumerable ways. This must be understood in order to construct a counter-hegemonic force. In response to this conflagration, Blake and Brecht argue for a political engagement with the deeper ideologies and structured ways of thinking that operate in the interstices of indeterminacy in the contemporary political moment. This is the moment of the now dealt with in Chapters 2 and 3.

The second engagement occurs in a similar Janussian temporal space but occurs between a collision of past and present. This moment, following Buck-Morss, happens on the cusp of one's historical position and the historical past writ large. Yet this is not a matter of precisely understanding one's history and then drawing the links between the two. This would reproduce the folly that Benjamin warns us of as the past takes on a far more malleable and plastic form in the hands of the artist. The incitement or impulse driving the artist releases its potential against the current disasters, as opposed to locking it down and containing it, making it safe. The emphasis is far less on merely understanding an historical moment, but rather on imagining what can be usefully made of the past for the changing needs of the present. We move from history as 'not so much a past reality as an unrealized possibility'.[21] In this regard the present is still Brecht and Blake's focus, but during their own moments of historical loss, such as the ultimate failures of the French and Russian Revolutions, they transport historical periods, singular moments or figures for their own purposes. The knowledge and use of history provides a refuge in that it offers a way of engaging with the contemporary moment that places emphasis on the agency of working class movements and their connected cultural producers to both counter and halt the feeling and actuality of a crushing inevitablilism that marks capitalism's dominance.[22] Its potential is uncapped and open to exploration and experimentation. Brecht and Blake shift away from a concept of the now and of history that negates this potential; in their

---

21   Levine 2014, p. 5.
22   As regards the relationship between the powerful Messiah and the knowledge that comes of the Messianic impulse, Benjamin Britt notes: 'There is agency first of all in critical awareness, which Benjamin cultivated through a variety of philosophical and aesthetic categories, and which he eventually related to a politicized conception of the Messiah. This Messiah is not subject to human control, but awareness of the Messiah is not possible without awareness of tradition, which survives in modern culture' (Britt 2016, p. 135). Useful also in this regard is Martel 2012.

INTRODUCTION 7

place is a highly productive and ultimately responsive theory of aesthetic practice. The emphasis on a responsive aesthetics necessarily involves a complete and thoroughgoing rejection of capitalist ways of thinking, in particular those forms of rationality which do not engage anything outside of this manacling frame. Responsiveness in this aesthetic realm shifts discussion from a 'setting right' or a mere retooling, to an understanding and correction of this twisted logic. The recognition of this complexity explains in part the lamenting tone of Brecht's poem/song 'In Praise of Communism' from *Die Mutter*. 'It's just the simple thing / That's hard, so hard to do'.[23] The acknowledgment of getting there, and the problem of merely reproducing unexamined thinking underlies Brecht's criticism of Lukács: 'Even those writers who are conscious of the fact that capitalism impoverishes, dehumanizes, mechanizes human beings, and who fight against it, seem to be part of the same process of impoverishment: for they too, in their writing, appear to be less concerned with elevating man, they rush him through events, treat his inner life as a *quantité negligeable* and so on. They too rationalize, as it were'.[24] The question of responsiveness was clearly haunting Blake's poetry and visual aesthetics, and his concern was more central than with his contemporaries. Questions of reception and of how to provide a total artwork framed his confrontation with the degraded political environment in which he worked. Without completely giving in to this experience, he sat in conversation with the spaces and ideas that existed for creating oppositional cultural work that could be useful, at the same time thinking through previous forms that could exist again, by occupying a space not necessarily outside but rather on the other side of this degradation.

This book mobilises the works of Brecht and Blake to rethink the role of the artist in the contemporary moment. As aesthetic and political interventionists, they organised their works around the double strategy of working through the time of the now and, when necessary, used history as a device to reinforce and clarify their conception of and relation to their now. This cultural response stresses a sophisticated relationship between the audience and the producer.[25] Such a relationship centres upon the notion that the moment of the now must

---

23   Brecht 1978b, p. 28.
24   Brecht in Adorno et al. 1998, p. 68.
25   Two critics have noted the response that both Brecht and Blake wish to draw. Firstly, Neil Larsen has described the interaction between Audience and Play in Brecht that 'bringing into juxtaposition, not disparate images or objects, but rather the disparate attitudes towards *actions* on the part of the dramatic characters themselves, on the one hand, and on the part of the audience, on the other' (Larsen 2001, p. 196). This sug-

always be the focal point of the aesthetic, and that this moment is in every instance haunted by history and the defeats and victories of oppressed groups and the working class.

Blake and Brecht have often been placed on opposite ends of the spectrum of oppositional aesthetics. It is particularly tempting to literary theorists of all persuasions to erect a binary which places an impassioned Blake, with his visions of Angels in trees, etc., against the cold, emotionless and almost hyper-rational Brecht. Yet while this comparison may contain a kernel of truth, it risks an unproductive dualism. Rarely have there been two oppositional cultural producers so convinced of the virtues or merits of a belief in production as Brecht and Blake. This is important because the nature and viability of productive aesthetics is frequently under question. The French philosopher Jacques Rancière, whose ideas helped to redefine the political reading of cultural and literary texts,[26] has cast doubt on art's potential to create. He argues in an interview in the influential art magazine *Artforum*:

> In the time of politically engaged art, when critical models were clearly agreed upon, we took art and politics as two well-defined things, each in its own corner. But at the same time, we presupposed a trouble-free passage between an artistic mode of presentation and the determination to act; that is, we believed that the 'raised consciousness' engendered by art – the strangeness of an artistic form – would provoke political action. The artist who presented the hidden contradictions of capitalism would mobilize minds and bodies for the struggle. The deduction was unsound, but that didn't matter so long as the explanatory schemata and the actual social movements were strong enough to anticipate its effects. That is no longer the case today.[27]

Rancière's argument implies that oppositional aesthetics could not have significantly altered the world in which they inhabit. While there is a partial yet obvious truth to this, to argue that art alone could not change the world ignores the unique and complicated relationship between cultural production and social struggle. Just as E.P. Thompson argues that 'class happens',[28] so too does the

---

gests a conversation and activity that is also argued by John H. Jones in relation to Blake's *Milton*: 'Blake wants his readers to form their own responses to the poem, each of which would recreate the poem anew' (Jones 2010, p. 178).

26   See principally Rancière 2006; Rancière 2010; Rancière 2011.
27   Rancière 2007, pp. 258–9.
28   Thompson 1982, p. 8. Still one of the most useful theoretical texts on the connections between society and cultural forms remains Williams, *Culture* 1981. E.P. Thompson's later

making of culture. There is no easy causal relationship between oppositional culture and effect, but to deny one altogether would be to miss the larger point regarding social and cultural interactions and formations.

In what follows, I have three broad, overarching objectives. The first is, through a series of close readings, to suggest how the logic of the texts leads towards a subversive criticism of their society's dominant ideologies (particularly in Chapters 2 and 3). This criticism involves the mobilisation or renewal of lost history which is carried out to highlight the contradictions that are increasingly apparent in these dominant ways of understanding the past, and the present (Chapters 4 and 5). I provide an account of the intensity and sophistication which each author brought to the pursuit of connecting their work with the deeply changed political and social environments that defined their more overtly historical work. Each had to grapple with fundamental transitions at all levels of their social formations and think through how this changed terrain could be reflected, given that each author wanted to make an impact with their plays and poetry that would continue the artistic pursuit of responding to the struggles in their society.

My second objective is to highlight the central role of experience and experimentation, and the potential of determining human action, as core structures in the authors' work. As they have become institutionalised, Brecht and Blake have been treated as isolated cultural producers. As of yet there is no full length study of the two,[29] yet both authors emphasised the role of reception and how to encourage an active reading of their works, and an active readership more generally. Their goal was to help initiate and develop a way of seeing the world from an oppositional perspective so as to recognise and promote an understanding of art that does not stop at the point of production, but locates the audience as capable creative producers themselves. In this way, experimentation and reserving a space to maintain and produce a critical gaze is not just a positive trait in their work but a necessary condition of its greater logic. The artist's experimentation should mirror that of the artist's productive readership.

---

edition of his text on William Morris, Thompson 1976, is a further attempt to articulate the detailed historical connections between the art and politics.

29   One recent exception to this can be found in Piccitto 2014. This text offers some connections between Blake and Brecht as regards similarities in promoting active spectatorship, but is not a comparative study. Despite the contention that Blake constructs 'a Brechtian alienation that jars us out of our complacency' (Piccitto 2014, p. 54), there is too little substantive engagement with Brecht's theatrical theory, as evidenced in the critically unspecific notion of Brechtian alienation.

My third objective is to place Brecht and Blake together as exemplary figures of oppositional cultural practice. While the two wrote at very different conjunctures, I aim to pull from each a mode of criticism and practice that seeks to empower useful analysis that is geared towards an oppositional aesthetic that is itself ultimately productive and resistant. This is a move towards a theory of literary production of each that not only explores the role of aesthetics in creating new forms of experiences and expressing nascent ones but is also directly attuned to the key problems of oppositional movements. Therefore each chapter shows how opposition to exploitation and oppressions is a driving force in the two authors' works. It is important to understand and reflect on the particular characteristics and determinations of the dominant ideologies that seem particularly indomitable.[30] Yet failure to explore how one can challenge these (even if the ultimate goal begins with the admirable goal of encouraging the reader to take the contradictions upon themselves and act politically) is insufficient for both Brecht and Blake.

Chapter 2 will focus on Brecht's earlier works, up until shortly before his exile in 1933. This section will highlight first of all the key motifs working within these works: the ways that new in/human ways of being were situated during Weimar. Brecht saw himself living during a period of remarkable transition in the class struggle and examined the possibilities that this heightened conflict would offer for a transition to socialism. From this, he sought to work through the tensions of this period, following the logic that open class struggle had for art, while also considering how these could be translated on stage and film. Yet because of the particular logic involved in this creation, especially regarding the Expressionist focus on the new individualities that capitalist modernity produces,[31] this necessitated an aesthetic response beyond what theatre and the dramatic arts had hitherto articulated. The response from a political aesthetic perspective was to stretch out to other newly and often formally unexplored media and incorporate them into his overall aesthetic strategy.[32] Most relevant in this regard is Brecht's *Mann ist Mann*.

Chapter 2 will address the scant attention given to this early work by teasing out the key contradictions of the play. The purpose is to locate the political and cultural tendencies dominating during Weimar that were fundamental for the development of his aesthetic. In *Mann ist Mann*, Brecht is working out the rela-

---

30 One of the most fully conscious attempts to sketch out these relationships on the level of theory is provided by Eagleton 1976, pp. 44–63.
31 In a useful response to this process and its gendered content, Pollock argues that '… no critic has fully recognized the extent to which Brecht develops the emergent but stalemated figure of the "New Woman" in late expressionism' (Pollock 1989, p. 85).
32 A helpful text here is Mueller 1989, in particular pp. 1–21.

tionship involved in a temporal-political question: the modern worker's ability to respond as an individual to capital's remodelling of the worker to fit its own desired image,[33] and the theatre's capacity to respond politically and aesthetically. This process involved experimentation on a scale almost unparalleled in Brecht's career as well as extensive revision beyond anything that Brecht would later perform. This is absolutely indispensable in framing the problematics of change that Brecht diagnosed in the societal reformation of the new human as determined by capitalist contradictions.[34]

This chapter will not only delve into the contradictions and internal and external workings of one play. This chapter will also present a continuum of practice in Brecht's pre-1933 works, using the reading of *Mann ist Mann* to develop a better understanding of this new society and the changeable human who is without options. The conclusions that Brecht came to from his work on this play informed his highly productive and much acclaimed work of the period from 1929–33. This work provides a more confident socialist alternative to the concept of changeability and proposes a productive way beyond the twin evils of Capitalism and Fascism. *Kuhle Wampe* and *Die Heilige Johanna der Schlachthöfe* are answers to the specific nature and mode of production of meanings and processes of meaning-making that Brecht so brilliantly displays in *Mann ist Mann*.

What shall be made clear throughout this chapter is that Brecht framed his work as a response to the contemporary moment.[35] His attention to experimentation underlies his commitment to an understanding of the *Jetztzeit* –

---

33   This has also been misrepresented, or at least misunderstood. 'Brecht's enthusiasm for the transformative, revolutionary potential of the commodification process in modern society may seem naïve today, considering the homogenising, totalising effects of global capitalism and the apparent limitations of collective as well as individual resistance and activism. But Brecht's positive evaluation of the capitalist labour process has to be understood within the framework of Marxist thought, which considers the economic system of capitalist society only as a transitory, indeed necessary, stage towards a total functional transformation (*Umfunktionierung*) of life' (Gritzner 2015, p. 67). While Brecht was indeed fascinated by the ability of capital to change the conditions of labour relations for its own interest, this was not due to a resigned acceptance of capitalism's benefits, but an attempt to work through the system as it is, rather than one would want. In a similar way, Brecht wrote to Lukacs: 'Is there no solution then? There is. The new ascendant class shows it. It is not a way back …. It does not involve undoing techniques but by developing them. Man does not become man again by stepping out of the masses but by stepping back into them'. This is the response against 'capitalism in its fascist phase' (Brecht in Adorno et al. 1998, p. 69).
34   Squiers and Roessler 2011, pp. 119–33.
35   This '*usefulness*', as Jameson notes, 'would have delighted' Brecht (Jameson 1998, p. 1).

the moment of the now. This stands in contrast to what several of the key studies of Brecht have sought: as Anthony Squiers notes, 'to provide formalistic approaches'.[36] This approach implies an extraction of and derision for the political impulses of his work, framing him as an innovator of the purely aesthetic: chiefly in conversation with and opposed to the Aristotelean tradition. However, this chapter argues that these strategies were part of a larger political-cultural moment that saw the audience member as a producer of the text itself and a producer of the means of future cultural and social production. As such, Brecht's work before 1933 moved towards a consistent whole which is responsive to his own society's political and economic culture, and that also attempted new methods of engaging his audience to encourage oppositional forms of thinking in them.[37]

Chapter 3 turns to William Blake. This book places Brecht and Blake side-by-side in Chapters 2 and 3 to highlight how each explored the time of the now, albeit at an earlier point in their careers and without reference to history. Alongside any discussions of the contemporary moment will necessarily be a discussion of the role of experimentation in Blake's works. Experimentation here does not refer to a narrow definition of 'trying new things' but to a greater ontological framework that Blake made known in his work, typified in the opening line of David Erdman's collection, that 'As the true method of knowledge is experiment, the true faculty of knowing must be the faculty which experiences'.[38] My entrance into Blake's writing will be his most common entry point for modern readers, the cycle *Songs of Innocence* and *Songs of Experience*.

Although written a few years apart, the chapter will read the two song cycles in conversation with each other, because they offer a unique dialectical examination of Blake's England. Blake constructs two opposing forms of living in the world, both built around the response to a potential fulfilling and nurturing form of life. In the song cycle, Blake produces a yawning excoriation of the logics of contemporary capitalism, 'a world in which the mind and the senses are completely ensnared by fallenness'.[39] Unlike Brecht, however, Blake's references involved a specific lived relation to God in the world which could never truly be disentangled from inter-personal lived relations and likewise from the natural world of which we are a part. The problem for Blake was that the dom-

---

36   Squiers 2014, p. 14. The studies referred to include Willett 1977; Bentley 1999; Esslin 1969.
37   In this way Brecht invites us 'to act as a political *subject* rather than be exploited as a political *object*' (Shookman 1989, p. 459). For an examination of Barthes's treatment of Brecht, highly recommended is Carmody 1990, pp. 25–38.
38   Erdman 1988, p. 1.
39   Williams 1998, p. 26.

inant forces of his day were attempting to poison the waters that made life so creative and nourishing. Blake understood the political power of God in the world, especially as the dominant ideologies of his day sought to consolidate their power and manacle the freeing nature of life that existed and could exist, and the potentialities that such a life could release and inspire in the care of others. This is the culmination of Blake's poetics.[40]

Blake argued in the *Songs* that we could make life a continuous experiment, where the true depths of our engagement would reveal, constantly, new ontological relations between all created and creative beings.[41] This potential was being denied and deformed, and thus we see a conversation beginning in *Innocence* and *Experience* between, as the subtitle reads: 'Shewing the Two Contrary States of the Human Soul'.[42] In *Innocence* Blake constructs a mode of relating to a world that he aspires to, a world that is both wishful thinking (the world does not exist, but is something that we should want) but also attainable. It is ideal not in the sense of impossible, but a necessary form of being that is worthy and necessary. Yet while Experience is in many ways the inverted other of Innocence, the latter not only provides a model of life after the dominance of Experience has ended, but shows that Innocence can be enacted and could become a form of resistance on the one hand, and a form of, an example of, a resisting inspiration, on the other.

Blake and Brecht are defined very much by their relation to the aesthetic traditions they inherited, not to mention the political-economic contexts that determined their texts. Yet there was a combined commitment for both to investigate the key contradictions of their age and respond in oppositional ways that could both engage with their historical moments, and articulate an aesthetics of resistance.[43] In this way they have a unique but overlapping strategy

---

[40] The chief texts that will be dealt with here are Makdisi 2003 and Thompson 1995.
[41] While Makdisi will deal with this point extensively, John H. Jones articulates this process using Mikhail Bahktin: 'Blake's creative process, then, can be seen as based on what Bahktin would later call dialogue. In order for a poet's discourse to be inclusive, to be more than a single, subjective viewpoint, the poet must restrain his impulse toward Selfhood and engage the world dialogically' (Jones 1994, pp. 8–9).
[42] Erdman 1998, p. 7.
[43] The origins of this phrase can be traced to Peter Weiss' *Aesthetics of Resistance*. Weiss aims to produce a resistant aesthetic across time, in which different cultural formal movements and strategies (antique, modernist, classical, social realism, etc.) converse with each other. As Inez Hedges notes on the text, it 'provided a sweeping reinterpretation of major elements of the Western cultural canon from the point of view of a hitherto marginalized perspective. To read this novel is to experience a re-education; to be receptive to it is to undergo an intellectual transformation'. Hedges 2006, p. 69. This against-the-grain reading of history is central to the final two Blake and Brecht chapters, and the conclusion of

to stand on the edge of their respective historical conjunctures, between understanding and what one makes of, and how one acts on, this understanding; between engaging with structures of dominance, and locating ways of unlocking them and releasing the powerful hold they have over others.

Whereas Chapter 2 centres on the role of the newness and *Jetztzeit* of Brecht's society, the works dealt with in Chapter 4 are important for his use of history. Yet this is not, as mentioned, history 'wie es eigentlich gewesen ist' or 'how it actually happened'. Rather, Brecht articulates a redemptive 'political hermeneutics'[44] of history that he formed in his discussions with Benjamin in the late 1930s, capturing and using what he finds fruitful to engage productive material for the struggles of his present.[45] This is not a use of history in order to rewrite it for a specific political purpose, or as a means to right historical wrongs. Rather, Brecht's tasks are to provide a voice to those which have been written out of ruling-class models of historiography[46] and to re-make what is known, setting aside historical veracity, of history in the public consciousness. Knowledge of public forms of knowing, what Raymond Williams has termed residual cultures,[47] provides an opportunity for Brecht to connect with his society while making of this something, even if only a starting point, with which to convey an argument about his world.

Chapter 4 begins by examining Brecht's most famous history play, *Mutter Courage und ihre Kinder*. The play presents a mirage of historical accuracy in the firm dates listed throughout the text, the map that was originally used to show Courage's movements across northern Europe, and the backdrop of an historical war. However, the play uses these to evoke the stereotypical image of the peasant because, in popular imagination, Courage clearly signifies forms of exploitation and oppression while also being the terrified object of war and famine.[48] Despite the fact that Courage is not a peasant but a struggling small

---

      this text will explore the potential for a resistive aesthetics with reference to the work of Ernst Bloch. While Weiss's text will not be examined here, it is interesting that in building his aesthetics, he relies on what Fredric Jameson in his foreward to the text refers to as a 'depersonalized collective' which Jameson terms a 'dialectical agon'. See Jameson in Weiss 2005, p. xxiv. The notion of a contest or battle that relies on a judgment is central to much of Brecht's and Blake's later work.

44   Knudsen 2014, p. 167.
45   Although the definitive text on Brecht and Benjamin remains, in my view, Wizisla's, a useful chapter that rethinks on the level of philosophy the relationship of the two is 'Walter Benjamin and Bertolt Brecht Discuss Franz Kafka: Exilic Journeys', in Rokem 2010, pp. 118–40.
46   See Vork 2013.
47   Williams 1977.
48   Jameson 1998.

INTRODUCTION 15

businessperson, the play depicts historical forms of oppression and exploitation to identify the Nazi death drive and to argue that the interchangeability of national and religious identity can muster opposition to resurgent forms and the underlying material bases of fascism, and also the crises of capitalism that make it possible. History is therefore not that which has happened, but continues to happen. The play allows for the audience member to be a producer of alternate meanings and history for the present, a strategy that Brecht further developed in exile.[49]

A similar process is at work in *Der Kaukasische Kreidekreis*, where Brecht uses a moral narrative to engage in the question of land distribution in post-WWII Eastern Europe. By drawing on the biblical story of Solomon, Brecht argues about the right of production over tradition, interestingly by using traditional tropes. In *bricolage* fashion, Brecht uses what is presently available to him, yet he does so to articulate a political project. In using the fable, Brecht performs a redemptive hermeneutic of the form and mixes it with his earlier techniques, particularly regarding engaging the audience.[50]

This political intervention also provides the backdrop behind the writing of *Leben des Galilei* which, as in *Mann ist Mann*, was subject to numerous revisions and incarnations. As in other works, Brecht uses an historical figure or setting to make an argument about the present. Yet here Brecht uses history to argue against the mistakes of others and to distance the audience from these histories.[51] In all three textual analyses, I show how history is used to both distance the audience from their own circumstances and connect the actions on stage to their own experiences. The role of history is absolutely central to Brecht's developing oppositional aesthetics and serves to reinforce the necessity of accessing the ideologies and contradictions of the lived relations he encounters.

In conversation with Chapter 4, Chapter 5 speaks to the role of history in Blake's work by building on the work of E.P. Thompson's classic *Witness Against the Beast: William Blake and the Moral Law*. While this seminal text offers a profoundly incisive way of reading Blake's directly politically engaging work from the 1790s, its focus stops there. My work will connect further with Benjamin. I

---

49 As Raymond Williams notes: 'Deprived of such a public, and having tried and largely failed to produce a drama which could confront Fascism directly, Brecht moved, both in technique and in choice of subject, towards new and deliberate forms of distance' (Williams 1996, p. 90).
50 Fiebach 1999, pp. 207–13.
51 As Michael Sprinker notes while quoting Althusser: 'The confrontation of two entirely distinct temporalities in Bertolazzi's play "is in essentials also the structure the of plays such as *Mother Courage* and (above all) *Galileo*"' (Sprinker 1987, p. 278).

will examine Blake's larger text, the epic *Milton*, showing how this work of historical re-investigation connects the present to the past to illuminate what the former lacks. It presents a manifestly oppositional alternative to the dominant ideologies and structures of his society.

Blake's recovery of history involves a proto-Benjaminian attention to the messianic impulse, except in this case the stakes are higher in that the messianic in Blake's work is the desire for the actual redeeming vision of Christ. It is not enough that the messianic may enter the lived world at any point; rather its impulse offers a mode of historical re-fashioning for cultural producers as well. Given the inspirational logic that Blake derives from Christ, it is hard to avoid not having this structure the form and content of the artworker's material. In other words, Blake's problem is not simply about creating an oppositional ideology of being in the world but also required him to undo the historical injustices that have created it, especially those involved in *Milton*.[52] As history is filled with loss, a resurrection of historical failures (Milton's own feature prominently) is therefore always a fundamental part of Blakean aesthetics. The resurrection is fundamentally political and therefore an object of struggle between the contending classes. Building on Chapter 3's exegetical reading of the *Songs* and the discussion of the central dynamics in Blake's society that motivated the casting of the two as opposites, Chapter 5 argues that the discussion of the time of the now is inextricably intertwined with historical reinvestigation and rediscovery.

Such a gesture necessitates a return to history and locates the radical tradition as a real and openly oppositional alternative. History and its recovery are not, however, a return to before the new evils of capitalism and religious orthodoxy. This would be a nostalgic formulation. Rather, the organisation of the everyday is merely made visible and accessible for the artist through the contrast of history with the contemporary. As Thompson writes, Blake is arguing for 'not a place at all, but a way of breaking out from received wisdom and

---

52   Thomas J.J. Altizier notes the stakes for Blake: 'Blake's most revolutionary vision revolves around an absolute reversal of Milton's Satan, a reversal in which Satan is envisioned as the absolute Lord and Creator ...'. 'That reversal occurs through an absolute death, but that death in crucifixion is apocalypse itself ...'. 'Yes, Blake is a visionary of eternal death, but an eternal death that is an apocalyptic death, and precisely so as the eternal death of Satan. Only that eternal death realizes an absolute compassion or the compassion of Christ, a compassion truly reversing all Satanic judgment and repression, but a compassion in actual apart from that reversal; hence the absolute necessity of Satan, the absolute necessity of Satan for apocalypse itself, and the primacy of Satan in all apocalyptic vision, and the fuller the apocalyptic vision, the fuller the vision of Satan' (Altizer 2009, p. 37).

moralism, and entering new possibilities'.[53] This need not occur only through articulating the moment of the now, even though extra-historical notions of time leap out of the past into new possibilities.

In addition to the attention to Blake's version of history, I will investigate how Blake uses various, broadly defined notions of labour to articulate a politics that – while acknowledging that we are always already determined by a variety of social processes outside of our control – is always attuned to the task of providing a way out of contemporary oppression. Focusing on the metaphors of labour and production in *Milton*, this chapter argues that while his historical situation may not have allowed it, and definitely discouraged it, Blake advanced a redemptive politics of history placed firmly in the time of the now.

While much of this book analyses the comparative aesthetic strategies of Blake and Brecht, the conclusion continues a comparison of the forms of experience that each uses to think through, and beyond, contemporary dynamics. Such an understanding of oppositional aesthetics must stretch back to its principal figures in order to understand its position today. Brought together, Brecht and Blake offer a powerful argument for a contemporary political aesthetics that both seeks to witness and to lay bare the destructive contradictions of capitalism. They do so not by skirting around capitalism's contradictions but rather offering a powerful analysis of the system's heart. Thus, their work is not merely a rejection of the system, but a productive attempt to understand capital's movements, its abilities to create new meanings consistently and produce new avenues of exploitation and production, in order to produce a revolutionary analysis that is useful and able to speak to capitalism's present and historical destructiveness. Capitalism's destructiveness refers to both the material wrecking of forms of life in its drive to commodify the world (a world that resists reification and commodification) but also to the sense in which capitalism has and continues to ideologically re-order and re-imagine the world. As Peter Osborne argues, 'With capitalism came the homogenization of labour-time: the time of abstract labour (money, the universal equivalent), the time of the clock'. And with each new imposition of its logic, capitalism has stretched back into history, creating ways of ordering past worlds. 'Capitalism has "universalised" history, in the sense that it has established systematic relations of social interdependence on a planetary scale (encompassing non-capitalist societies), thereby producing a single global space of temporal co-existence or coevalness, within which actions are quantifiable chronologically in terms of single stand-

53 Thompson 1995, p. 20.

ard of measurement: world standard-time'.[54] Given that this is a once complete and ongoing project – capitalism will always reorder the world anew for its own purposes and needs – criticism of capitalism will always be nascent, taking seriously the social movements that exist and that pose questions of exploitative practices in new and old ways, as both are needed to express a living aesthetic. By mere dint of the fact that a criticism has been used before, it does not necessarily follow that it is without usefulness. This is not a fetishising of the new, but a more analysis of the potentials for opposition.

Although this argument rests on a relatively small corpus of works, given the authors' exhaustive body of textual production, I have provided a closer reading of major texts, rather than survey all of the materials. Following from Benjamin, this book pulls out a narrative from these works, according to which both authors held a commitment to read history against the grain, in order to translate the politics of the now into the contemporary moment. This book's engagement with secondary literature suggests that its central ideas are transferable to each author's other major works.

I have been greatly inspired by two of the most important books written on each author in the past quarter century: Fredric Jameson's *Brecht and Method* and Saree Makdisi's *William Blake and the Impossible History of the 1790s*. Both are single-author focussed, even if they are guided by an awareness of the political and literary climate of the time. Jameson's work, partly if not wholly true to his Lukácsian tradition, intelligently poses the question as to whether there is 'not something itself unBrechtian in the attempt to reinvent and revive some "Brecht for our times"'.[55] I have attempted something similar, presenting a version of Brecht that I believe to be evocative enough to be brought into conversation with Blake. My reading of Blake is heavily indebted to Makdisi's work. Makdisi's engagement is, perhaps more than any other reader of his, structured around an understanding of the liberating philosophy that guides Blake's work, a philosophy of living and creating in the world that is arguably unmatched in its intensity. This philosophy is driven by purposeful action and is underpinned by a necessity to respond to human need that I will engage with in my reading of the *Songs*. I will carry this forward in my examination of Blake's *Milton*, arguing that while this text was written later in Blake's career than is the main focus of Makdisi's *William Blake and the Impossible History of the 1790s*, many of the core ideas as regards Blakean philosophy are still useful and illuminating.

---

54 Osborne 1995, p. 34.
55 Jameson 1998, p. 5.

INTRODUCTION

Alternatively, while the chosen texts are representative, others would no doubt provide different emphases in the interpretation of Brecht and Blake. Perhaps most glaring here is the omission of an extended engagement with Brecht's significant poetic works, a recent collected version of which numbers over one thousand pages. A larger analysis of their poetry's Romantic and Modernist strategies would require greater interrogation. I have suggested some comparisons in the first Brecht chapter, but avoided a fuller discussion, since this is not the text's main occupation.

Blake's treatment of *Milton* provides a snapshot of the central cast of his characters, in particular the ways in which the characters stand in relation to the other characters in his cosmology. The shifting grounds on which Blake develops his materialist frame, and how the characters of Locke, Urizen and Newton develop, runs counter to the idea of a fundamental opposition of individual characters, which is in turn structured by the idea of the (prosecutorial and condemnatory) judgment. In Blake's worldview, redemption is always a possibility. This is especially interesting when contrasted to Brechtian materialism and its critique of bourgeois morality politics, which first develops in earlier works (especially *Die Kleinbürgerhochzeit*) and shifts to judgement in later works such as *Antigone* or *Die Verurteilung des Lukullus*. The emphasis on judgment in Brecht, in part motivated by a desire to deliver judgment on the wreckage of the Nazi tyranny, should be counterbalanced with Blake's later work, *Jerusalem: The Emanation of the Giant Albion*, with its focus on the ability of flawed actors to be welcomed back into a caring community.

This text tries not to reproduce the problematics of other oppositional criticisms that retreat into those moments when they were in power or in the ascendancy. Rather, I argue that these past works can provide much needed useful direction and succour at a moment when the left needs it most. This book's non-chronological method – alternating chapters between Brecht and Blake – mirrors my argument about history. This procedure is 'constellative' in Benjamin's sense, bringing both Brecht and Blake (as well as Benjamin and Bloch) into a non-linear relationship, in which each is read in the light projected by the other. The connection between different historical moments, and the argument about how these can be brought together for a common liberatory aesthetics, is dialectical in nature. The images of Blake and Brecht here, defined in relation to the Modernist and Romantic historical projects, provide an alternate reading very much against the grain of literary history.[56]

---

56   This focus on a constellative approach is also taken up by Adorno in his 'The Actuality of Philosophy', where he refers 'to the manipulation of conceptual material by philosophy ... I speak purposely of grouping and trial arrangement, of constellation and construction' (Adorno 1977, p. 131).

CHAPTER 2

Brecht and the Now

A Brechtian maxim: "Don't start from the good old things but the bad new ones."[1]

∴

This chapter compares three of Brecht's earlier texts, all written pre-exile from Nazi Germany.[2] In *Mann ist Mann*, *Die Heilige Johanna der Schlachthöfe*, and *Kuhle Wampe: Oder wem gehört die Welt?*, two plays and a film respectively, Brecht was motivated to provide responses to the key, and to varying degrees nascent, political questions facing the socialist left of his day. Rather than advance a propagandistic approach, Brecht sought to navigate these questions with a highly developed (yet itself always developing) formal aesthetic politics. While each of the three texts attempts to deal with a specific problem on its own, taken together the three share a unified and complementary response to the larger issues that confronted Brecht as a committed cultural producer. Each text builds on and follows from the text that precedes it, providing a fuller analysis of Weimar capitalism than any one single work could achieve. Although I am not arguing that these three texts represent a prescribed path on which Brecht moved – that is, that the texts necessarily had to follow the order they did – these three works nevertheless represent a coherent attempt to deal with the myriad political, social and economic problems of his time on a deeper and deeper level. They came to terms with the core problematics of the time period in more integrative, direct and aggressive ways as the works progressed. Following Benjamin, Brecht sought to engage radically with his present to make possible a radically engaged future. In this, Brecht was both the immediate inheritor of the revolutionary struggles of early Weimar and the Russian Revolution and a participant in one of the most politically radical yet culturally productive periods in modernity.

---

1 Benjamin 1998, p. 121.
2 Part of this chapter has been previously published as "The View from Below: Film and Class Representation in Brecht and Loach", *Cinema: Journal of Philosophy and the Moving Image*, 8 (2016): 88–107.

In these texts, Brecht addresses dynamics that capitalism itself creates on both an immediate and largely historical scale, its crises and its political responses. Most important here are the rise of fascism in terms of the social construction of the modern individual/class and the breakdown/reconfiguration of the capitalist order, and the appropriate political action needed to halt it and construct a viable socialist alternative. Later, this book examines Brecht's use of history; here, I explore how Brecht constructs an aesthetic politics of the now. These three texts are deeply complex investigations of the contemporary moment and all three in their own way provide not merely a critique of Brecht's own society but speak to a deep-seated opposition to the current order. For this, it was necessary for Brecht to understand the motives and potentials of what this world could produce. In *Mann ist Mann*, this is the menacing figure of the 'bad collective' and the uses and abuses of its continued reproduction.

It is important not to homogenise this earlier period of Brecht's work. More than almost any other, it was defined by internal conflict and social and political dissonances, owing to a lack of a lasting ruling class hegemony that approached anything like stability. The early years, determined by the particularly disastrous nature of the defeat of the German military in the First World War, were soon to be defined by the successes of the Russian Revolution and the emboldened German communist movement, and the swift period of revolutionary occupation and counter-revolution that it spawned. Weimar's most politically coherent age, known as the *Goldenen Zwaniger* (the Golden Twenties) between 1924 and 1929, was short lived. This period witnessed the consolidation of Stalin's power and the theoretical alignment around a Socialism in One Country policy, and the Stalinisation of the German communist party, the KPD. These years provided only a brief and illusory political and economic stabilisation of the capitalist-liberal order, which was completely ill-prepared to deal with the post-financial crash era following the stock market crashes of September 1929. Following in the wake of that collapse, the period between 1929 and 1933 is a highpoint of Brecht's work, and the three works under investigation in this chapter were either written or re-written during this time, providing Brecht's most coherent critique of Weimar's failing. Despite the incoherent and contradictory nature of this period, taken as a whole, the oppositional cultural production of the Weimar era provides hope for an experimental future defined by neither of the dead ends of capitalism and Stalinism. Following Robert Heynen, 'in the utopian imaginings of the Weimar period ... we can find resources for a culture and politics that challenges a normative liberal democratic perspective in which capitalism disappears from view, but also offers alternatives to the increasingly rigid culture of the Stalinized KPD'.[3]

---

3 Heynen 2015, p. 29.

What Weimar offers, in an uneven way, is the beginning of a period of radical aesthetic creation, guided by and given birth through the dramatic and implausible successes of the Russian Revolution and the defeats, at first partial, of the revolutionary period between 1918–19. It is important in this regard to further highlight the potentialities that existed, and those that could exist in Brecht's work. An overly simplified periodisation that obscures more than it explains has become lamentably commonplace. One recent contribution commenting on Anglo-American Brecht scholarship, while noting that the division was 'necessarily simplified', nevertheless constructs 'a three-part periodization of his mature career'. That this second period, covering the *Lehrstücke*, omits all of the texts under discussion here, is inconvenient. What is more, that this 'occurred simultaneously with Brecht's study of Marxism and his interaction with contemporary German Marxist thinkers'[4] tends to reinforce the idea of Brecht finding Marx, rather than locating him in the much more intricate environments in which he was working, especially including the important legacies of 1917 and 1918–19. Heynen's text again is useful here:

> The KPD was one of a number of parties, organizations, or movements claiming to speak for and mobilise the working class, although of those many, most notably the German Social Democratic Party (*Sozialdemokratische Partei Deutschlands*, or SPD), eschewed a revolutionary politics. These movements mounted a serious challenge to the power of both older and newer elites. Especially during the events of 1918–19, the sense that a revolutionary transformation had become possible was widespread. It was this sense of possibility that animated the work of many of the Weimar critical theorists.[5]

The influence of traditions of progressive cultural expression, made more openly possible by the freedoms of speech attained through the Weimar constitution, allowed (however imperfectly, and still with censorship both formal and practical) for a flourishing of leftist culture.[6] Although Expressionism was to become the more entrenched form of theatre during the first half of Weimar, 'after the Revolution radical agitprop theater groups (for example, mass spectacles, speech choruses of workers' organizations, Piscator's Proletarian

---

4 Thorsteinsson 2017, p. 61.
5 Heynen 2015, p. 7.
6 Stuart Jeffries makes the case that this 'tentative democratic flowering was readily crushed in part, to get dialectical for a moment, by the very structure of its foundation' (Jeffries 2016, p. 161).

Theater, and Red Revues) mushroomed ...', argues Ronnie Bai.[7] Indeed, it was Erwin Piscator who, with Brecht, developed the notion of Epic Theatre that was to become so synonymous with Brecht's practice. Yet, as Bai continues, the fact that the relationship combined both political engagement and the ways in which that engagement could be translated into culture means that while 'Piscator may have provided Brecht with a working example of Marxist political theater that aimed to instruct and induce change in a politically turbulent age, their relationship centers more importantly around the idea of epic drama as an innovation of the modern German theater'.[8]

In this chapter I will investigate the key problematic in each of three important late Weimar texts. For *Mann ist Mann*, I will focus on the formation of what Brecht terms the 'bad collective' and its relation to forming (as well as deforming and then re-forming) a new individuality and new class formations in Weimar capitalism. I will then focus on *Die Heilige Johanna*, a play which deals with the new formation of the working class (and the ability of the capitalist system, at a time of considerable economic and social crisis, to integrate and control those whom it exploits) and its relation to the disastrous financial system. Finally, the chapter will end with a discussion of Brecht's first major film (as ever, in collaboration with others), *Kuhle Wampe*, to show how oppositional groups must respond to this financial system that oppresses them and also how, given that this new system is a class system, they must respond as a class. In light of these earlier works, Brecht responds in ways that subvert the system he analyses, unravelling and working through its logics.

1   *Mann ist Mann*: The Right Question and the Precision of Time

Despite the fact that Benjamin wrote the words that open this chapter as late as 1931, they apply equally well before Brecht's oft-cited transformation into a full-fledged Marxist thinker, however overblown this transformation is made out to be.[9] I believe there is a constant effort in Brecht, from the point of the first productions of *Mann ist Mann* onwards, to involve himself wholeheartedly

---

7 Bai 1998, p. 391.
8 Bai 1998, p. 394.
9 This is a serious problem in Brecht scholarship. Efforts have been made to locate the specific point in Brecht's political development when his political outlook became Marxist. The fault in this investigation seems to be the excessive preoccupation with a specific point in time when Brecht read Marx. Rather, I would like to shift focus from this to a more com-

in an exhaustive, and at times exhausting, experiment of the present. This begins with an understanding of the contemporary moment, but the process of experimentation involves a far more thoroughgoing appreciation of, and playing with, the often under-theorised impulses that are necessary to maintain the contemporary order. This exercise, this practice, is not one which ends at any one point in Brecht's life's but rather continues until the end of his work.[10]

Evidence of this preoccupation with the contemporary moment is perhaps no more clearly present than in the full title of *Mann ist Mann*. In its entirety it reads *Die Verwandlung des Packers Galy Gay in den Militärbaracken von Kilkoa im Jahre neunzehnhundertfünfundzwanzig*.[11] The full script version, including the exact date of 1925, denotes the intentional laying down of a marker of time. This suggests precision in a specific moment in time above all else. The inexact qualifier 'Packer' – which shares the exact spelling and inexact meaning of the English equivalent – stands in contrast with such an explicit moment. The term Packer is translated as 'Dockarbeiter' or, in English, 'Stevedore' or 'Docker'. This is a specific interpretation, losing the broad generality that the term Packer entails, and such a translation provides an opportunity for the audience member/reader to fully comprehend the social codes and locations involved in the popular imagination of such a profession. The sense of specificity in the space and time of continual change – that is, who one is, for whom one is, and where one stands in relation to others – will become the central dialectical relation in Brecht's play. The important production in Darmstadt in 1926 makes manifest the clarity that was demanded, in order

---

plex view of the process, a view which sees Marxism not as a formal endpoint that one arrives at, but rather a process which helps to make sense of society. Brecht himself seemed to share in this outlook, as noted when he states that 'When I read Marx I understood more deeply my own work ... this man Marx was the only spectator for my plays I'd ever come across' (Brecht 1978a, pp. 24–5). This remark suggests Brecht was, at the very least, already posing questions that Marx's work can inspire and help understand. Also, Brecht's comment that he had not yet found spectators for his plays is substantiated by how Brecht's *Mann ist Mann*, along with other early works, were often dismissed as a 'satirical polemic against bourgeois value systems' (See Ostmeier 2000, p. 275).

10   Fredric Jameson has very usefully referred to a 'Brechtian doctrine of activity' which is similar to what I am describing here. It is particularly apt given its Luxemburgist connotations, something to which Brecht himself would have been very sympathetic (See Jameson 1998, p. 4).

11   The English translation of the subtitle reads *The transformation of the packer Galy Gay in the military Cantonment of Kilkoa during the year nineteen hundred and twenty five*.

... to show the play's underlying sense by making the surface meaning as clear as possible. In other words, no implications, hidden meanings, ambiguities, half-light; but facts, brilliant illumination, light into every corner, absence of feeling, no humour with tears to fall back on. The theatre as craft rather than art, no private issues – these should emerge only secondarily, as self-evident.[12]

An almost documentary-like effect is achieved, representing the beginnings of an early distancing effect that Brecht had learned from, and worked on together with, Piscator. The latter had in the early 1920s harnessed this approach in order to 'break down boundaries between art and political life, making the theatre continuous with communist rallies and forging his audience members into a political collective'.[13] During this time Brecht began working on an unfinished play, *Der Untergang des Egoisten Johann Fatzer* (*The Downfall of the Egoist Johann Fatzer*) and in this text Brecht 'outlines his idea of the document as an artifact or even a fake that would become "authentic" only by provoking conflicting commentaries'.[14] Brecht was developing the notion of an incomplete theatre, in that the production required the intervention of the audience's agency to 'complete' the piece.[15]

Indeed, there are many instances throughout Brecht's works where the predominance and overt highlighting of the exact intervention, particularly regarding specific dates, is apparent. *Mann ist Mann*, which Brecht admitted he had rewritten no less than ten times,[16] provides a fruitful starting point as

---

12   Patterson 1981, p. 160.
13   Arjomand 2016, pp. 50–1.
14   Wilke 1999, p. 122.
15   Wilke continues: 'In the context of *Fatzer* the document is reflected as a theatrical potential, vacillating between true or false, real or fictitious. Its meaning depends on the audience, which is obliged to enact and discuss it. Thus, Brecht favors the idea of a theatre where the spectators would be able to take part in the making of documents, embodying thereby a revolution of the theatrical process itself' (Wilke 1999, p. 122). Rather than be an intimidating space, what is sought after is the audience's inclusion, not through 'austere distancing' but through a liberatory, even enjoyable connection to the producer of art. Kimberly Jannarone describes this usefully: 'The theatre, in this light, can intellectually empower the audience; here, the audience assumes, in the artist's mind, the identity of a collective, a group of individuals encouraged, through the configuration of the new theatrical event, to be active, thinking, physically free, engaged, and debating artistic, social, or political issues' (Jannarone 2009, p. 197).
16   'I feel myself I must still, must always, learn. From what I learned from the audience that saw it, I rewrote *Mann ist Mann* ten times, and presented it at different times and in different ways – for example, in Darmstadt in 1926, at the Berlin Volksbühne in 1927, at the Berlin

the history of this play and its various productions mirrors the history of the development of Brecht's Marxist aesthetic praxis.[17]

As has been the case in many other non-materialist interpretations of avowedly materialist texts, critics have (either willingly or unwillingly, consciously or unconsciously) attempted to extract the class politics from Brecht's early work and to reinforce the image of the playwright as essentially an operator in formal matters. For example:

> Since all things in nature change, it may be assumed that man is also changeable and capable of being changed, capable even of changing himself. ... The issue, as Brecht sees it, is much more pragmatic; it is a matter of sizing up situations in terms of flux, of tracing the course of events by which change manifests itself, and then of gauging the possibilities (including those in human nature itself) for alteration. In short, the problem of change, measured by its effects, becomes the problem of method – of selecting the proper means for controlling the direction of change in order to bring about the results one desires.[18]

Federal Theatre in 1929. We worked with different means and in different strata of society. These experiments were theatrical performances meant not so much for the spectator as for those who were engaged in the performance. It was, so to speak, art for the producer, not art for the consumer' (Brecht, 1993, p. 943).

17   What is interesting in this regard is that Brecht encouraged others to make concrete interventions with the play as well. As Brecht wrote in 1936 in regards to an interest from London in re-staging the play in Nazi Germany, 'Die Parabel *Mann ist Mann* kann ohne grosse Mühe konkretisiert werden. Die Verwandlung des Kleinbürgers Galy gay in eine "menschliche Kampfmaschine" kann statt in Indien in Deutschland spielen. Die Sammlung der Armee zu kilkoa kann in den Parteitag der NSDAP zu Nurnberg verwandelt werden'. [The parable *Mann ist Mann* can be concretised without much effort. The transformation of the petty bourgeois Galy Gay into a "human fighting machine" can take place in Germany instead of India. The gathering of the army at Kilkoa can be transformed into the party congress of the NSDAP at Nurnberg]. (Brecht 1988e, p. 51).

18   Shaw 1970, pp. 146–7. This analysis of the play is also (albeit more adroitly and complexly) offered by Jan Knopf in his 'Die Austauschbarkeit Individualität' section on *Mann ist Mann*. See Knopf 2002, p. 156. A further criticism of the type of position held by Shaw is advanced by Fredric Jameson when discussing Manipulation theory. Important to note in the following is the move away from abstraction. Jameson notes that 'Manipulation theory implies a psychology, but this is all very well and good: Brecht taught us that under the right circumstances you could remake anybody over into anything you liked (*Mann ist Mann*), only he insisted on the situation and the raw materials fully as much or more than on the techniques' (Jameson 1979, pp. 140–1).

From this passage, seasoned with an oddly Aristotelian flavour given Brecht's pronounced aversion to this in his own statements on Epic Theatre, one could be misled into thinking that the lead character of the play, Galy Gay, is the classical universal figure, existing at any time and in any place. Change here is a concern not at the level of content, of a specific type of determined historical change, but is instead an abstracted one, a change in methodology. However, the play offers several ways in which this abstracted reading is bucked by the motivations and, importantly, pressures of change in the text and its production. Not least significant in this regard is the role of Widow Leocadia Begbick, a key character and the play's only female character. It is interesting to note here that Begbick is the only character who operates under their own rules and volitions, as much as that is possible given the military settings. Whereas all the male characters in, as a common English translation of the title goes, *A Man's a Man*, are representative of the inability to shape their own lives, Begbick, as Margaret Setje-Eilers notes, 'remains paradoxically stable in each version'. The character 'resists manipulation and influences others for her purposes'.[19] In this way, the form of change or remodelling of humanity that the play offers is specifically gendered, and our notions of agency and mobility are constantly being confronted by changing notions of life in a world dominated by gender norms.[20]

The play is further brought down to earth when we learn what sets Galy Gay out on the path to becoming re-functioned: a concrete pursuit of material goods, specifically a fish for the family's dinner. This basic impetus to the action in the play has more or less been lost in critical engagement with the work. The specificity of the position not only of worker but also the task of buying food is central in assessing the role of the lead character. The materiality of the act, and the importance of that materiality in determining or limiting dir-

---

19   Setje-Eilers 2008, p. 97. Indeed, Setje-Eilers will link the peculiar position of Begbick's power in the text to growing achievements for feminists during the Weimar period as an explanation for her strength in the play. The larger frame for this development should be traced back to the fundamental shifts in gender roles from 1918 onwards. As Kathleen Canning writes, 'The First World War, the revolution of 1918, and the subsequent realignment of military and civilian society in Germany brought about a profound transformation of women's experiences of citizenship and ship, of family and sexuality, as well as a rapid disordering of the discursive domain of gender' (Canning 2006, p. 85).

20   Adding to this, before Galy Gay leaves, his wife assures him that she will not leave the kitchen so as to avoid any potential harm coming to her. Yet as we learn, it is Galy Gay, not his wife, who is in danger. Here the gendered version of the title – it is not Mensch ist Mensch or a Person's a Person – suggests that a danger for men is the particular way they fall prey to a militarised identity reformation.

ection in the unravelling of the play, is key. In this regard it is useful to recall one of Brecht's most famous aphorisms, 'Erst kommt das Fressen, dann die Morale [First comes eating, then morals]'. It is first in the basic act of reproducing himself and surviving that Galy Gay will be subject to his transformation. In this regard, his class position is also vital in analysing his unenviable, but explainable, shift in persona. It is a simple motivation, yet one that determines his action and that of those around him.

While this may resemble a straightforward fulfilment of the oft vulgarised and highly static base/superstructure metaphor – whereby the economy determines all aspects of politics and human emotions – one should be cautious about such an interpretation. I am dealing with something more important in the Brechtian aesthetic than the foregrounding of materiality, although this is fundamental to Brecht's aesthetics. It is the foregrounding of precision which will propel Brecht to experiment in order to meet this level of exactitude that is his focus. Precision here is the fullest understanding of a moment in time that necessitates a full-blown process of continual reinvestigation of the bare grounds on which Brecht as a cultural producer stands, but also of the ground upon which we all stand. The process itself, due to its historical specificities, will never allow for a moment of stasis. The aesthetic which Brecht seeks to shape will be necessarily in flux. At a later stage in Brecht's cultural production, when a fuller and deeper understanding of Marxism forces him to rethink his political trajectory (most obvious here is the rewriting of the play *Die Dreigroschenoper* into novel form), he will revisit his earlier work in order to make the texts more prescient for contemporary interventions. Yet what will stick with Brecht will be this always-already moment of precision or accuracy at a temporal and spatial point when, paradoxically, it is at its most elusive, i.e., *in medias res*.

Due to this positioning, the task of the aesthetic producer must therefore be quick but at the same time open to specific political developments and revisions. For this reason, the *Mann ist Mann* document (i.e. the physical text) is the least relevant for a Brechtian aesthetic. It is this new form of aesthetic response that Walter Benjamin argued was so difficult for professional theatre reviewers to get their collective heads around. Thus, the first productions of the play bear the mark of a working-class movement that had been under the threat of imperialism and militarism, and would soon be confronted with their uglier sibling, Nazism. The question for Brecht is: how could such a situation arise? What would make the victory of such a 'movement' possible and realisable? While it would be dangerous to state that Nazism was *a fait accompli* as early as 1923 or even 1926, Brecht was clearly grappling with the implications of the potential for such a movement, and these implications were later made the guiding principle of the play. Brecht writes:

I turned to the comedy *Man Equals Man* with particular apprehension. Here again I had a socially negative hero who was by no means unsympathetically treated. The play's theme is the false, bad collective (the 'gang') and its powers of attraction, the same collectivity which Hitler and his backers were even then in the process of recruiting by an exploitation of the petty-bourgeoisie's vague longing for the historically timely, genuinely social collectivity of the workers. Before me were two versions, the one performed at the Berlin Volksbühne in 1928 and the other at the Berlin Staatstheater in 1931. I decided to restore the earlier version, where Galy Gay captures the mountain fortress of Sir El-Djower. In 1931 I had allowed the play to end with the great dismantling operation, having been unable to see any way of giving a negative character to the hero's growth within the collectivity. I decided to leave that growth undescribed.[21]

Brecht began writing the earliest version of the play shortly after the First World War in 1919, and the impulse for creating a passive character who is co-opted and transformed into a 'menschliche Kampfsmachine' [human fighting machine][22] is not difficult, at least in hindsight, to ascertain.[23] Yet the first production of the play came only in 1926 when a new 'dangerous affair' was rearing its head, something of which Brecht himself was aware. Yet most interesting in the quote above is the notion of 'schlechte Kollektiv', or the bad collective. This has interests that run counter to those of the working class, but it could also transform these people who, as Galy Gay, 'can't say no'. In this sense Brecht's

---

[21] This translation can be found in Robinson 2008, p. 245. The original German reads as follows: 'An die Lektüre des Lustspiels *Mann ist Mann* machte ich mich mit besonderen Befürchtungen. Auch hier hatte ich wieder einen sozial negativen Helden, der nicht ohne Sympathie behandelt war. Das Problem des Stückes ist das falsche, schlechte Kollektiv (*der Bande*) und seine Verführungskraft, jenes Kollektiv, das in diesen Jahren Hitler und seine Geldgeber rekrutieren, das unbestimmte Verlagen der Kleinbürger nach dem geschichtlich reifen, echten sozialen Kollektiv der Arbeiter ausbeutend. Es lagen zwei Fassungen vor, die in 1928 in der Berliner Volksbühne und die 1931 am Berliner Staatstheater gespielte. Wiederherzustellen, fand ich, war die erste Fassung, in der Galy Gay die Bergfestung Sir el Dchowr erobert. Ich hatte 1931 das Stück nach dem grossen Montageakt enden lassen, da ich keine Möglichkeit sah, dem Wachsum des helden im Kollektiv einen negativen Charakter zu verleihen. So hatte ich lieber auf die Beschreibung des Wachtums verzichtet'. See Brecht 1988d, pp. 244–5.

[22] The reference to the 'menschliche Kampfmaschine' is the description given to Galy Gay at the end of the play (but before the elephant calf). See Brecht 1988a, p. 157.

[23] It is also important to note, as Kate Elswit argues, that the reassembly of the character Galy Gay is similar to the way in which many 'disfigured' WWI veterans were rebuilt with prosthetics after the war. See Elswit 2008, pp. 389–410.

play is a valuable heuristic model and parable, which from its very beginning allows itself to act out the spoken and silent moments in which the potentials of the future, but more importantly of the present, are made known.[24] It is for this reason – that the present is always with us but never fully understood nor understandable – that Brecht relies on many levels of experimentation and revision. One cannot know the ground upon which one stands, and so chances need to be taken in order to arrive at an unknown answer.

This was something that Walter Benjamin understood very well. He was, of course, a very significant analyst of the play in its early 1930s iterations and was unequivocal in his positive reading of the play. However, Benjamin's view of these versions emphasises understanding the key contradictions and 'newness' of the piece. In his 'What is Epic Theatre?', Benjamin argued for the importance of that understanding and presentation in *Mann ist Mann*. He writes:

> The plays of a Toller or a Lampel do not take this detour [via Epic Theatre]; exactly like the works of German pseudo-classicism, they "award primacy to the idea, and all the time make the spectator desire a specific aim, creating, as it were, an ever-increasing demand for the supply". Such writers attack the conditions in which we live from the outside; Brecht lets the conditions speak for themselves, so that they confront each other dialectically. Their various elements are played off logically against one another. The docker Galy Gay in Brecht's A Man's a Man is like an empty stage on which the contradictions of our society are acted out.[25]

Benjamin's reading of *Mann ist Mann* is written in the context of an analysis of Epic Theatre as a whole, and his reading is inevitable, as the central tenets of this aesthetic approach are articulated thoroughly in the play.[26] The key contribution of Brecht is an attempt to do what others do not: to attack the conditions in which we live from the inside in order – to some degree – to supply a means of resistance. This approach to cultural production asks us to think differently our connection to the 'real'. As Terry Eagleton writes, 'Brecht's practice is not to

---

24   I am using the notion of the unspoken or silence as that expressed by Pierre Macherey which attempts to get at what a work 'refuses to say' or 'what a work cannot say' (Macherey 1978, p. 87).
25   Benjamin 1998, p. 8.
26   What is interesting to note here is that while professional critics attacked Brecht, they also sought to make it difficult for his supporters to be heard in defending the merits of his play. This included Benjamin himself, whose piece 'What is Epic Theatre?' was blocked from being published by, among others, no less a figure than Siegfried Kracauer. See Wizisla 2009, p. 114.

dispel the miasma of "false consciousness" so that we may "fix" the object as it really is; it is to persuade us into living a new discursive and practical relation to the real. "Rationality" for Brecht is thus indissociable from scepticism, experiment, refusal and subversion'.[27] The idea of not attempting to fix the object in a moment in time is vital in understanding how the Brechtian aesthetic seeks, not to capture an essentialist image of capitalism, but to understand it as a dialectical image. The refusal to which Eagleton refers represents what is at stake in the play. Galy Gay is introduced to us at the very outset as a man 'who can't say no', and for this he must work through the imperatives that capitalism and colonialism place upon him, not by chance or exception but rather by the fullest set of determinations, impulses and rules. The inability to say no is what makes the structural contradictions absorb Galy Gay so definitively, rendering him vulnerable to the unique demands and general rules of the dominant societal impulses. Benjamin again: 'And so it happens that the wise proletarian Galy Gay, the man who keeps himself to himself, agrees to join the berserk ranks of the British colonial army, thereby consenting to the denial of his own wisdom'.[28] In stressing the class position of the lead character, Benjamin employs and grounds his argument with a distinct notion of contemporaneity. The contemporary moment manifests itself in the relationship between the audience and the cultural producer's own process of politicisation. This itself is made possible only through a combination of the analysis/interpretation of the contemporary moment and the form of theatre put forward by Brecht.[29] Astrid Oesmann has commented on the centrality of the question of positionality in her 2005 book *Staging History: Brecht's Social Concepts of Ideology*. She writes: 'This vision of social existence informs Brecht's changing political vision and becomes a formative element in his teaching plays, in which every question is negotiated in a strictly defined space. This renders political problems as questions of social positioning: "Wo stehst du und wie stehst du zu uns?" (Where do you stand and how do you stand toward us?)'.[30] The question of where one stands in relation to the other, both in terms of an individual to a social group,

---

27 Eagleton 1994, p. 85.
28 Benjamin 1998, p. 9.
29 'Brecht's theatre, Benjamin now argued in "What is Epic Theatre? (1)," changed the function of theatre from entertainment to knowledge, whereby the political thesis-play was superseded. This change exploded at a stroke the 'functional relationship between stage and public, text and performance, direction and actor' (Wizisla 2009, p. 112).
30 Oesmann 2005, p. 95. An important note to make here is that there is a growing refusal or partial rejection in recent Brechtian scholarship which argues, as I do here, that rather than provide a periodisation of Brecht – the experimental Brecht, Brecht in exile, etc. – or even to try and locate the precise moment when Brecht has reached Marxism, Brecht's

or one social group to another, is fundamental to Epic Theatre. How the question of this relation gets posed likewise gets at the heart of Brecht's politics and aesthetics.

Brecht's interest here is to design an ongoing project that will most clearly illuminate the current historical moment in which he operates. This project is larger than any one moment and becomes a philosophy of agency. As Brecht noted on this play: 'It does not make the hero the victim of an inevitable fate, nor does it wish to make the spectator the victim, so to speak, of a hypnotic experience in the theatre. In fact, it has a purpose of "teaching" the spectator a certain quite practical attitude; we have to make it possible for him to take a critical attitude while he is in the theatre (as opposed to a subjective attitude of becoming completely "entangled" in what is going on)'.[31] Behind this is an entire aesthetic philosophy trained towards agency, whereby we attempt to delve as deeply as possible into our social situation and, from that position, articulate a politics from which we can make visible to a larger audience the current state we find ourselves in. Brecht's cultural project (because it suggests it is larger than a project for theatre) creates formal techniques designed to show how individuals and collectives are socially/economically structured. How they act (or, as is more common in Brecht, fail to act) is not pre-determined and is decisive for social outcomes.[32] This theatre of the now (or, alternatively, a political aesthetics of the now) must be continually updated (as societies change so must oppositional movements) and be open to experimentation and the intricate materiality of the current historical moment.

The foregrounding of materiality in *Mann ist Mann* and the development of Epic Theatre are deeply intertwined.[33] Lost in 'an abstracted Brecht' is a

---

works are full of continuities and are better judged as a unity of central ideas and unfolding practices.

31   Brecht 1988c, p. 941.
32   On the question of Galy Gay's own repeated transformations, Eugene Lunn notes that this is evidence that 'it would be anachronistic to see him as alienated from himself in these roles: his "self" is in each of the transformations'. The point here is that there is great potential in such a transformation: 'total changeability encourages the hope that things can be very different. The issue for Brecht was not any inevitable psychic depersonalization in the modern, collectivist age – a common traditionalist reading of the theory of alienation – but the question of how technology is used and to whose advantage' (Lunn 1974, p. 27).
33   Brecht would remark that his first full Epic Theatre text is in fact *Mann ist Mann*. 'Ja, diese Theorie vom epischen Drama ist allerdings von uns. Wir haben auch versucht, einige epische Dramen herzustellen. Ich habe *Mann ist Mann*, Bronnen hat den *Ostpolzug* und die Fleisser hat ihre Ingolstädter Dramen in epischer Technik verfasst. [Yes, the theory of Epic Theatre is ours. We also tried to produce some Epic Dramas. I had *Mann ist*

fuller understanding of the piece and the greater political impetus of the play. Through the character Begbick, the play offers the reader a midway summary of what Brecht would like the audience to take from the piece. The last four lines of her 'Zwischenspruch' read as follows:

> Herr Bertolt Brecht hopes you'll see the ground on which you stand
> Slither between your toes like shifting sand
> So that the case of Galy Gay the porter makes you aware
> Life on this earth is a hazardous affair.[34]

These four lines offer two possible avenues for reading Brecht's work. The first two lines seem to match the reading of the play focused only on an abstracting changing of humanity. 'The ground on which you stand / Slither between your toes like shifting sand',[35] is akin to the unrelenting change that is so much the part and parcel of human existence. The last two lines, however, point towards something decidedly less abstract. 'So that the case of the porter Galy Gay will make you aware / Life on this earth is a dangerous affair'. These last two lines bring us down from the abstract to the specific, which is a necessary movement for Brecht. They bring us into the realm of history, one's precise historical moment and the stakes involved for its main actors. This is the chief point of the bad collective, and there is simply no other option but to confront it. Confrontation means not merely to militate against it, but to examine how this entity seeks to multiply itself, how it manipulates contemporary experience and reintegrates forms of past experience, and wards off other alternatives in order to meet its own needs. Not only must the bad collective reproduce itself, it must consume anything that suggests another form of being in the world can exist.

If we take Brecht's use of 'hazardous' seriously here, the abstracted reading of the play reads as inadequate. By shifting discussion from the malleability of humans to the specific historical conditions of the play's production, we are obliged to take into consideration Brecht's interventionist strategy. In this regard, the vaguely unspecific nature of Galy Gay (he is an empty vessel, besides the markers mentioned earlier) poses a difficult question for Marxist analysis:

Mann, Bronnen had *Ostpolzug*, and Fleisser composed her Ingolstadt dramas using Epic techniques]. Brecht 1988b, p. 273.

34 Brecht 2000b, p. 38.
35 This dialectic relationship is reflected in the staging of the actors. As Olga Taxidou notes in her analysis of Mei Lan-fang, a Chinese actor who influenced Brecht at an early stage: 'In the Brechtian world this dialectic is never fully resolved and points towards an endless "changeability" as the actor's body denotes "this way of changing"' (Taxidou 2007, p. 142).

how does capitalism not merely reproduce workers for its own purposes, but then reproduce differently on disparate trajectories? Brecht's play is not an abstract interpretation of the general re-formation of humans but rather of the potential for the capitalist class to make workers into killing machines. This is the bad collective making true on Brecht's promise that life is dangerous.[36]

The worker's position, however, needs to be highlighted here. As opposed to earlier forms of relatively fixed identities based on one's work, the modern worker in capital's logic must re-imagine themselves and the way in which they fit into the market. In this sense Galy Gay's transformation is mirrored by capitalism's drives, crises and needs. This is a structured 'reassembling', wherein one aimed to be 'the right man in the right place, "*der rechte Mann am rechten Platz*" (Benjamin's own adaptation of a Taylorist catchphrase)'. This restructuring bears considerable similarities to the problems of 're-functioning' for theatrical and cinematic production, as both Brigid Doherty and Lucia Ruprecht note throughout in their useful essays.[37] While the refunctioning need not have the same underlying purpose, given that the nature of capital is to refashion completely class structure, the oppositional cultural forces must respond. In this way, this response is fundamentally linked with Brecht's ability and desire to make an intervention. It is what makes Brecht's theatre so fundamentally political, even in the earlier, 'non-Marxist', phase. The reactions against this political rethinking of the theatre were found in Brecht's own time, as seen in the critical reaction to the 1931 production (but not, if we believe Benjamin, the audiences), as the critics were either unable and/or unwilling to locate the real importance of the play, as they sought to maintain cultural production's safe distance from the now. Benjamin articulates this in his analysis of *Mann ist Mann*: 'For the difficulties encountered by epic theatre in achieving recognition are, after all, nothing other than an expression of its closeness to real life, while theory languishes in the Babylonian exile of a praxis which has nothing to do with the way we live'.[38] Benjamin's emphasis on the 'closeness to real life' embodies more than a politics of intervention, it must be noted. Yet without

---

36 Marc Silberman sees this in more purely economic class terms. He writes: 'Galy Gay in Man Equals Man is the most extreme example of this class mobility. He has no individual personality but conforms to the changing circumstances around him because he simply cannot say no' (Marc Silberman 2012, p. 178).

37 Doherty 2000, pp. 442–81. Lucia Ruprecht further argues that the use of Gestus in the play is also evident in shaping and being shaped by 'the gestural aesthetic of silent film', and Brecht was involved in using video in his many productions of the play (Ruprecht 2010, p. 271).

38 Benjamin 1998, p. 3.

a definite location/theatre/stadium wherein the form of intervention is taken into account, the potential of this closeness will remain unresolved.

The fulfilling of this potential is of course no simple business. Suffice it to say, however, that the intervention, in order to be meaningful, requires a deep understanding of the situation one is in. To this end, as times changed, Brecht relied heavily on a sustained interrogation and re-examination of his work. This constant re-examination further belies a theory and practice of production that undermines the notion of a work of art being a totality in itself and develops a prescriptive practice. Terry Eagleton very usefully notes that Brecht offers a 'suggestive model for the notion of the literary text as practice rather than object'.[39] The emphasis on the notion of ongoing process in a creative piece as opposed to a reified, static text may seem, in today's conjuncture at least, a less-than-dramatic statement. In Brecht's own time the situation could not have been more different, especially so for such an influential cultural producer of the left. While visiting Brecht in exile in Denmark, Benjamin notes Brecht's reaction to the growing influence of Stalinist literary policy. Dogmatic socialist realists, Brecht contends,

> ... are, to put it bluntly, enemies of production. Production makes them uncomfortable. You never know where you are with production; production is the unforeseeable. You never know what's going to come out. And they themselves don't want to produce. Every one of their criticisms contains a threat.[40]

There exists a deep connection between Brecht's aesthetic politics of the now and the notion of production that he uses in the above passage. While this use of production is influenced by his visits to the Soviet Union in the 1930s,[41] Brecht was developing this concept earlier, as evidenced by his work with *Mann ist Mann*. Important in this regard is how production is coterminous with a specific cultural labour/work process, which demands of the producer a continual self-reflexivity.[42] Yet the production was not univocal – that is, it was not one of

---

39   Eagleton 1979, p. 66.
40   Brecht in Benjamin 1998, p. 118.
41   It is important to note Brecht's politics aesthetics were influenced by Sergei Tretjakov, who as Eugene Lunn notes, also 'was developing ... an aesthetics of "production" from which Brecht would learn in formulating his own Marxist cultural theories in the 1930s' (Lunn 1982, p. 102). Brecht was mutually admired by Tretjakov, and the two had been planning a production of *Die Heilige Johanna* in the Soviet Union, although that production never was produced. See Pike 1985, p. 200.
42   As Lunn notes specifically on *Mann ist Mann* 'Brecht's theatre became an experimental

the producers directed towards the audience. In order for production to be successful it must also make the most of the productive capacities of the audience involved. In this way the audience produces itself and part of its own history. This process rejects the idea of the naturalistic passive audience. In the field of language studies this passive process is reminiscent of Valentin Volosinov's notion of *uniaccentuality* – a process which extinguishes the way in which signs are struggled over by all social actors. This stands opposed to Brecht's theatre, which acknowledges the agency of the audience. This would be similar to Volosinov's corresponding concept of the *multiaccentual* sign – 'a sign that maintains its vitality and dynamism and the capacity for further development'[43] and is directed towards a multi-vocal response. In this way production for Brecht centres on showing how audiences might actively produce themselves and their history (Brecht noted that a particular audience also included the actors involved in this performance). History, while structured, cannot be known in advance, since history itself is always open-ended.

Brecht was clearly not averse to experimentation and continually rethinking his work. In fact, as aforementioned, *Mann ist Mann* went through at least ten rewrites, and he continually revised the work in order to be able address the current conjuncture as directly as possible. Suggestively, Brecht also considered renaming the subtitle for the play to match the year it was presented – for example, the transformation of the packer Galy Gay in the military barracks of Kilkoa in the year 1925 (or 1926 or 1930 depending on the year of the performance). This reworking was not an empty gesture. Besides the continual rewriting, Brecht showed the play to audiences of different social classes in an effort to understand as deeply as possible the structures of contemporary society and the place for his contribution in relation to them, which manifested also in questioning the appropriate form of intervention into the social order. In order to reach a wider audience, Brecht produced a radio version of the play, broadcast in 1927. What's more, on the basis of this work Brecht was moved to

---

self-reflexive workshop in which humans and social reality were shown to be constructions capable of being "reassembled" (ummontiert)' (Lunn 1982, p. 103). While I disagree slightly with Lunn's chronology, I am sympathetic to the importance he places on production. He continues: 'Soon after working out the rudiments of a new theatre, Brecht began to develop (after 1928) a conception of "production aesthetics", which he formed with a Marxism filtered through constructivist lenses: e.g., he viewed art as an aspect of material labour; as a construction based on the formal principle of technological modes of production, such as montage; and as an activity which was tied to new mechanical media, such as film and radio' (1982, p. 103).

43   See Volosinov 1996, p. 23.

change the form of the play from a *Lustspiel* or comedy,[44] to what Benjamin refers to as a parable.[45] This is especially interesting as the switch speaks to Brecht's changing response to the rise of fascism, the threat of which was obviously much clearer in 1930. Where the need was more urgent, Brecht opted for the more direct method of a *Lehrstuck* or didactic learning piece, in order to structure his intervention.

Despite the many revisions, what Brecht took seriously throughout the whole project was the development of the 'new man' (sic). Rather than assuming an audience, a fault he analysed in the modern theatre of the time, Brecht attempted to work through the dominant logics of his capitalist modernity in order to engage with an audience which would question and mobilise around these developments. In awe of the modern sports spectator, Brecht sought to realise a cultural space where the audience's reaction was to question what they were seeing rather than be simple consumers and passive in reception. Brecht's cultural politics of production acknowledged the *multiaccentuality* involved in his theatrical practice.

In 1931, at around the same time that Brecht was putting on the production of *Mann ist Mann* that so influenced Benjamin, Brecht was heavily involved in the production of the film *Kuhle Wampe, Wem gehört die Welt?*. In this film we see an alternative to the bad collective as it is depicted in *Mann ist Mann*. This is also an intervention beyond abstraction. *Mann ist Mann* calls for practical consideration based upon the needs and limits of a contemporary moment. Drawn to its conclusion, as Bert Cardullo argues, it necessitates a response to the system. He notes: 'A change for the worse, or no change at all in already bad conditions, as in *Mann ist Mann*, can only lead ultimately to further deterioration in the relations among men. Unless, that is, *a man* takes action'.[46] Because Brecht seeks to hammer the current situation on the head, the response to any

---

44 Brecht would come back to the comic form in other circumstances, especially in his exile plays. There he began to use comedy as distancing effects, linked with the almost incomprehensible devastation of the post war-era. This is a politicised comedy, as Marc Silberman notes: 'Brecht's experiments sought to develop a kind of thinking that can understand the process of historical change and the changeability of human behavior. Naturally, he understood human behavior to be historically contingent, neither universal nor anthropologically based. Because the comic depends on the incongruous, the paradoxical, and the absurd in behavior and situations, it generates that distance so crucial to Brecht's aesthetic strategies: opening up a space for historical cognition while rendering visible the contradictions in society that make the status quo impossible. This is comedy in the service of disillusionment' (Marc Silberman 2012, p. 185).
45 Doherty 2000, p. 448.
46 Cardullo 1984, p. 263.

historical moment must be an accurate one. There is no way in which theoretical or analytical looseness can be allowed to slip into the precise task of meeting the historical conjuncture with a political aesthetic. All political debates concerning progressive change are subject to the determination, or framing, of a political historical moment. Even the supposed logic of the societal structure should be examined ruthlessly. In this regard we have the issues that are key subjects in this chapter – exactitude and generality, precision and flexibility, recourse to specific events and the simultaneous evocation of broad struggle, a Marxist aesthetic science and the making of the problems of the individual worker into the problem of every worker.

All of this makes the notes of Walter Benjamin on *Mann ist Mann* very important, given that he would have seen the production in its various opening stages, as well as in 1931. Benjamin was in this regard Brecht's greatest reader, and his ability to carefully parse out Brecht's work is hard to overstate. The work during this period was marked by a crucial experimentation meant to deal with the intense challenges that were presented to the working-class movement of the time. And *Mann ist Mann* is a play that is specifically attuned to begin a project that could understand and respond to these challenges.

2　The Knowing *Johanna*

> Because I praised the useful, and that
> Was held in my times to be coarse
> Because I fought against religion
> Because I fought against oppression or
> For another reason[47]

As with *Mann ist Mann*, there has been an approach to interpreting Brecht's work which attempts to abstract it from the intense materiality in which it is based. By rejecting such an approach, I am not suggesting the impossibility of locating or positing a philosophy of Brecht, nor am I disputing the presence of a Brechtian method, a topic presented mostly clearly in Jameson's excellent offering. Rather, I am arguing that to isolate Brecht from the political nature of his project and to remove the connections to his own time, place, and strategic imperatives (to be useful, for instance) is to obfuscate and misunderstand both the nature and potential of his work.[48] While the opposite approach has been

---

47　Brecht 2019, p. 571.
48　In opposition to this argument, and while I would take issue with the heavy handed nature

largely confined to non-materialist theories and criticisms, another version of this has been advanced by professed materialist theorists.

This vein of criticism has sought to view the play (and others at the time) as a distilled explication of the workings of capitalism and, because the explication was insufficient, Brecht failed (usefully or not) in its chief pursuit. In part, such explanations have been sourced from Brecht's biography. The narrative runs that during the period of 1926 to 1929, Brecht began to study Marxism with the noted theorist Karl Korsch, author of the renowned *Marxism and Philosophy*, and that through these studies Brecht became a Marxist.[49] That Korsch had a profound effect on Brecht's formulation and conception of Marxist economics should not be in dispute. The problem appears when the suggestion becomes that through his work with Korsch, Brecht on the one hand 'found Marxism' and that, as a result, he decided that it was necessary to teach Marxian economics on stage.[50] As Jameson sums up this interpretation, the play 'has so often been taken as Brecht's most comprehensive initiation into Marxian analysis', particularly as it often is singled out as the high point of leftist cultural critique.[51] This has also been the main fault line of the piece. An alternative approach, put forward by Marc Silberman, is that 'What appealed to him about

---

 of the claim, there is something very important to defend in Patty Lee Parmalee's argument regarding the important milestone of this text: '*St. Joan of the Stockyards*, the first major play since *A Man's a Man*, is in every sense the culmination of Brecht's early work' (Parmalee 1981, p. 244).

49 This well-rehearsed argument is put forward in various ways. Mark Clark puts it forward here when discussing the idea that Brecht 'found Marxism'. 'In the early 1930s Brecht not only reinterpreted his earlier plays through a Marxist lens, but also wrote a series of *Lehrstücke* or didactic plays, which were meant to be models of political commitment for children' (Clark 2006, p. 132).

50 Another vital moment in Brecht's life seems to have been witnessing first-hand a worker's demonstration, although there is little attention paid to this. As a group of Communists protested a ban on public meetings, Brecht witnessed the violence meted out by the police response while at the apartment of his friend Fritz Sternberg. Sternberg writes: 'As far as we could make out, these people were not armed. The police fired repeatedly. We thought at first that they were firing warning-shots. Then we saw several of the demonstrators falling, and later being carried away on stretchers. At that time, as far as I remember, there were more than twenty dead among the demonstrators in Berlin. When Brecht heard the shots and saw that people were being hit, he went whiter in the face than I had ever seen him before in my life. I believe it was not least this experience which drove him ever more strongly towards the Communists'. See Sternberg in Wizisla 2009, pp. 5–6. Also worthy of note is the fact that the police chief at the time, Karl Zoergiebel, was a Social Democrat. This would have given Brecht another reason to shift his support more firmly towards the more clearly oppositional Communists.

51 Jameson 1998, p. 148.

Marxism was neither the theory of political economy nor the history of the proletariat but rather its power as a cognitive method that understands social conditions as processes and pursues their contradictions'.[52] Astrid Oesmann's otherwise excellent *Staging History* has advanced this line of argument, arguing that when read in such a way, the play necessarily loses the specificity that was such a fundamental aspect of *Mann ist Mann*. She writes: 'His plays grow hazy, however, when he seeks to present the workings of capitalism outside of social interaction by staging the working of capital itself. Brecht's claim that it is incomprehensible how, exactly, processes are not presentable on stage in *Die Heilige Johanna der Schlachthöfe* (*Saint Joan of the Stockyards*), the trading of money and meat is mentioned, but it never becomes part of the performance'.[53] The odd formulation here states that when we abstract Brecht's work into a space where he merely seeks to represent capitalism (a typically 'unuseful' Brechtian project) Brecht fails to understand class struggle (or 'social interaction', as Oesmann somewhat ambiguously puts it). Yet Oesmann is not alone here. *Die Heilige Johanna* is also seen thus by Jameson. He writes: 'But in the great representations of capitalism – particularly in the two fundamental Brechtian works *St Joan* and the *Three-Penny Novel* – these last are reduced to Dickensian misery, lumpen status (Peachum's beggars) or desperate objects of charity. It is as though in Brecht's works that radically different temporality of peasant life had absorbed the actantial position of the "proletariat", the position of the oppressed and exploited in capitalism, of the dominant class'.[54] Here the problem is restated but the belief is the same, and that is that *Die Heilige Johanna* fails in its task to represent capitalism effectively.

I do not wish to suggest that the play is not fundamentally concerned with trying to come to terms with the larger capitalist economic system. On the contrary, essential to the play's structure is Joan's movement throughout different socio-economic settings, from an initial point of naiveté as to the intentions of the capitalist class, through the delightfully horrible character of Mauler, the play's chief capitalist, to a Marxian understanding of the role of profit in Mauler's life, and how this creates her own misery.[55] As with the progress of Galy Gay before, the point to stress here is the *social* aspect of Joan's journey

---

52 Marc Silberman 2012, p. 174.
53 Oesmann 2005, p. 108.
54 Jameson 1998, p. 151.
55 Karl-Heinz Schoeps notes that the issue of Die Heilige Johanna's naiveté is central to not only this text, but also continues in much of Brecht's work. 'The fact that Brecht used a Saint Joan figure [a naïve figure] in three of his plays (Saint Joan of the Stockyards, The Visions of Simone Machard, and The Trial of Joan of Arc at Rouen 1431) highlights the particular importance he attached to this character' (See Schoeps 1989, p. 196). While I

and then, for the latter, the lesson it contains for her ultimate rejection of the capitalist system.[56] In this way it 'is a play about how ideology is used to obscure reality. Simultaneously, its effect on the audience is to teach them how to see through the ideology to the reality ...'[57] This may be over-stating the analysis, but there is a clear attempt to distinguish between capitalism's outer and inner layers as they are expressed in social understanding. For Joan, nothing could be a more concrete instantiation of capitalism than the bourgeoisie's profiting off of the working poor. The emphasis on the concreteness of this socio-economic relation is exactly the problem for Brecht: how to construct a theatre that recognises this relation and responds by promoting the primacy of establishing what he called a 'critical attitude'.[58]

The development of such a viewpoint begins with the title of the play and its often problematic English translation. The German title is *Die Heilige Johanna der Schlachthöfe*.[59] This has most commonly been translated as *St. Joan of the Stockyards*. A less common translation, although one truer to Brecht's purposes, is *St. Joan of the Slaughterhouses*.[60] A stockyard is literally a storage

---

disagree with Schoeps's negation of Epic Theatre's centrality to Brecht's work, his argument about the centrality of the naïve in Brecht is useful.

56   Interesting in this regard is a recent essay on the play by noted Brazilian poet Roberto Schwarz. In the essay Schwarz continues along the same lines of Jameson and Oesmann in claiming that the representability of capitalism is the key issue throughout. Schwarz further argues that the capitalist system has fundamentally changed in the way it represents itself and thus the play loses an important currency. He writes 'Today, the picture has changed. Economic determinism has switched sides and functions as an explicit ideology of the dominant classes, a justification for social inequality' (Schwarz 2009, pp. 85–105). While Schwarz further criticises the suitability of a 'revolutionary exit' as a contemporary option that the play offers – a position I would agree with – his dilution of the play's representation of capitalism is something that I dispute.

57   Parmalee 1981, p. 246.

58   On this point Brecht is quite explicit. He writes, 'In fact, it has a purpose, the "teaching" of the spectator a certain quite practical attitude; we have to make it possible for him to take a critical attitude while he is in the theatre (as opposed to a subjective attitude of becoming completely "entangled" in what is going on). Some of my plays in this type of dramaturgy are *St. Joan of the Stockyards*, *Mann ist Mann*, and *Round Heads and Pointed Heads*'. See Brecht 1988c, p. 941.

59   It is important to note that the play that Brecht found so hard to produce over the years has been subject to a renewed interest, at least in Germany (other production figures are unavailable), with more productions of the play in the 1990s or 2000s than in all other decades combined. Knopf 2002, p. 286. For information on the problems that Brecht encountered in putting on the play see Bahr 1971, pp. 211–31.

60   Interestingly, as Brecht develops his aesthetic further, there is also a strong shift in the focus of his work to places of production and the question of how gender is used to represent labour. As Laureen Nussbaum notes, 'All through his previous work Brecht had

point, a building or set of buildings normally adjacent to the slaughterhouse. A slaughterhouse requires no mediation. It is about the deed of killing, of premeditated and systematic carnage for the sake of producing food and its sale. The slaughterhouse is the more exact location for Brecht, as it is killing, its product, *and* the reasons for killing which are important and undergird the play's structure.

In this regard, seeing as the play revolves around the slaughterhouses, meat acts as a structuring metaphor.[61] On the most basic level, flesh is the stuff upon which fortunes sink or soar. The key economic downturn is in part a product of Mauler's playing with the stock market, and the way in which he makes the value of meat abstract. This abstractness of meat is and can only be partial, however, as Mauler's toying with the price of meat is in fact his toying with human life itself.[62]

As a metaphor, meat embodies and personifies the human. This happens in a few ways. Firstly, workers are meat in that they are, like the cattle which they are supposed to kill, the commercial good that is routinely bought and sold. They are manipulated so as to disregard or negate feelings of solidarity or independent thought and promoted to become passive creatures worried only about their next meal. As such they are similar to the beasts they look over and ultimately slaughter. Brecht, when referring to workers eating, uses the German word *fressen* to describe their eating, a word which translates to a specific form of animalistic eating or devouring. They will eat anything that will satiate their hunger.

---

mainly identified bourgeois society with male predominance. Now, working for change, he developed new, self-reliant, and politically conscious roles for proletarian women'. *Die Heilige Johanna* and Anni from *Kuhle Wampe* are clear examples of this shift. Nussbaum 1985, p. 228.

61 The depiction of the butcher as *Urkapitalist* was previously shown in Pabst's *Die freudlose Gasse*. The dancer and cabaretist Valeska Gert had worked on the film, and subsequently on Brecht's *Die Dreigroschenoper*. See Kolb 2009, for a discussion on this connection and Gert's influence more generally. The film also puts the lie to the idea of the gullible, helpless 'young girls', and features an act of revenge against the callous butcher. For more on the connection between Brecht and the role of sex work and Brecht's filmic work, see Smith 2010.

62 In this case, however, Mauler as capitalist seems to know and understand what the price of meat is. Brecht will also use to great comedic and didactic effect the capitalist who has no idea what his products are. See for instance the 'Song of Supply and Demand', in which the character Trader sings 'What is a man actually, Do I know what a man is? / God knows what a man is! / I don't know what a man is / I only know his price!' See Brecht 1992, pp. 95–6.

In one bizarre case – but only bizarre when one does not understand the system – a man literally becomes meat. Luckerniddle, a worker in the slaughterhouse, falls into the 'bacon maker' and is processed into canned meat. The brutality of the situation is compounded when his wife comes to enquire about his whereabouts. She is advised to drop any case she may have for the price of twenty lunches. As she has not eaten in two days, she accepts the offer. Yet while meat is literally a matter of life and death for workers, it knows only one referent for the capitalist. The lead capitalist, Mauler, when he has a bad spell on the market, consoles himself by having a steak prepared for him. Almost as soon as the meat touches his lips, Mauler is returned to good humour. Here meat acts as an elixir for the ruling classes. Its substance and its abstracted value bring only them pleasure.

By using meat as a structuring metaphor, Brecht makes clear that what may be abstract to one is the most concrete for another. While Luckerniddle's widow is made the offer of food in exchange for forgetting, Joan watches in the wings. Playing the intermediary witness, she is able to spot the connections between the abstract workings of the financial system and the bare processes of workers being chewed up, not of their own volition but by compulsion, by and for the system. Darko Suvin expresses this point succinctly in his *To Brecht and Beyond*. He notes: '… the Marxist political economics undoubtedly present in *Saint Joan* (the labour theory of value, and the crisis theory) happens in the flesh and blood of the workers and packers, Mauler and Joan. Political economics determining the existential destiny of all strata of society represent here a first, basic exchange-system or code'.[63] The rejection of the body, of abstracting the body from its material conditions, will thus be Joan's final position. She has understood the fundamental barbarity of the system and its lived class oppression. In her final lines, Joan rails against her former position and beliefs and calls out for a violent end to the system of religion (as a former 'Black Straw Hats' worker [equivalent to the Salvation Army] she notes its particular importance) and its complicity in reproducing capitalism. She exclaims:

> And those preachers who tell the people they can rise in spirit
> Even if their bodies are stuck in the mud, they too should have their
>   heads

---

63   Suvin 1984, p. 148.

Bashed against the sidewalk. The truth is that
Where force rules only force can help and
In the human world only humans can help.[64]

While there is little doubt that this is the position Brecht would wish his audience to be won over to, he realises that such a simple transference is not possible and would only provide a partial answer. The point of the audience's discovery is not what is presented but what is missing. To locate this, we must see the reaction of the cast to Joan's radical statement. For the first time in the play, the cast sings out in unison, attempting to drown out Joan's final words before she dies. The Cast sings out:

> Shower the rich with Thy treasure! Hosanna!
> And virtue and leisure! Hosanna!
> Pile high the rich man's plate! Hosanna!
> Give him the city and state! Hosanna!
> Give to the winner in full measure![65]

Over these 'declamations' are broadcast disastrous headlines from Brecht's time, including: 'EIGHT MILLION UNEMPLOYED IN THE USA!' 'BRAZIL DUMPS A WHOLE YEAR'S COFFEE CROP INTO THE OCEAN!' 'EVERY BANK AND STOCK EXCHANGE IN GERMANY CLOSED BY GOVERNMENT ORDERS' 'POLICE BATTLE UNEMPLOYED OUTSIDE HENRY FORD'S DETROIT FACTORY'.[66] The point here is to explicitly state the point that knowing is not enough. While individual knowing is highly recommended (we are clearly better for knowing), there is little doubt that individual realisation amid chaos is not enough. One must be able to understand a situation for what it is and then use that to alter the system in which one is living. This is what Brecht himself did with his own studies of Marxist economics. As *Mann ist Mann* was a warning of the bad collective, *Die Heilige Johanna* argues that mere comprehension must be met with effective practice.

When the disastrous news over the loudspeakers has sunk in, there is an exchange of vituperative exclamations, wherein the competing groups gather on stage seeking to place the blame for the crisis on each other. 'The middlemen are to blame for the high price of meat!' 'The grain profiteers are to blame

---

64   Brecht 1991, p. 108.
65   Ibid.
66   Brecht 1991, pp. 108–9.

for the high price of livestock!' 'It's all the fault of the railroads with their freight rates!'[67] The material and pressing nature of the situation will require an extra-individual response that the individual alone cannot advance, no matter how knowledgeable about capitalism she becomes. This response is an organised knowing. A knowing which seeks to change, as Joan notes, in 'the human world where only humans can help'.[68] This is the response that will be offered in *Kuhle Wampe*.

While *Mann ist Mann* was an endeavour which set Brecht off on a course towards a fuller Epic Theatre, *Die Heilige Johanna* was an expression of his further understanding of his society, but also his place within that society as a politically committed cultural producer. As he himself notes:

> Simply to comprehend the new areas of subject-matter imposes a new dramatic and theatrical form. Can we speak of money in the form of iambics? 'The Mark, first quoted yesterday at 50 dollars, now beyond 100, soon may rise, etc.' – how about? Petroleum resists the five-act form; today's catastrophes do not progress in a straight line but in cyclical crises; the 'heroes' change with the different phases, are interchangeable, etc.; the graph of people's actions is complicated by abortive actions; fate is no longer a single coherent power; rather there are fields of force which can be seen radiating in opposite directions; the power groups themselves comprise movements not only against one another but within themselves ...[69]

It is interesting to note that the play that Brecht was working on when he wrote the above theoretical piece was *Die Heilige Johanna*, as it suggests further evidence that Epic Theatre was taking a step away from simply modern sociality to a specifically capitalist structured and dialectical form. Epic Theatre at this stage is falling even further from the sky of the abstract and plummets to earth. On this note, the emphasis on religion in the play is especially noteworthy. When

---

67 Brecht 1991, p. 109.
68 Julie Stone Peters's article is very useful in noting that despite the obvious different political attitudes of George Bernard Shaw (the author of *Saint Joan*, a piece first produced in the early 1920s examining the trial of Joan of Arc) and Brecht, there are similarities between the two uses of the Joan of Arc trope. She notes that 'each nonetheless offered a critique of the international sphere order that saw past its subterfuges to the possibilities beyond' (Peters 2005, p. 374). What is more interesting for our purposes, however, is the way in which the article focuses on how the 'taken-for-granted' world that Joan initially inhabits is part of 'wordless oppression does not equal peace' (2005, p. 367).
69 Brecht 1978a, p. 30.

it lands, it finds a scenario far more akin to Benjamin's analysis of Paul Klee's celebrated *Angelus Novus*.[70] I will explore the meaning of the painting and its importance for Brecht's theatre of history at the end of the next chapter. Of importance now is that, as with the painting itself, what is emphasised is not the single solitary moment of discovery but the larger repetitive disaster beneath it. In such a setting, we find St. Joan, caught adrift in the winds of catastrophe wherein, by witnessing the horrors beneath, she rejects all that she sees from above. Yet in this way Brecht also eschews a crude didacticism and recognises that the potential for such events to recur is significant. Yet recognising that such events can continue simultaneously allows for us to acknowledge that the moment where we apply the brake on endless disaster is also available only if we work *through* the contemporary moment. The moment of historical recognition – this has happened and it could happen to us – allows for a moment of change only if we grasp the historical structure of our moment. This is particularly characteristic of Brecht's aesthetics of the now.

In his lengthy mapping out of the logics and dynamics of *Die Heilige Johanna*, Suvin details the highly stratified positions that exist in the work. These positions stretch from the 'New York friends' and Mauler at the 'Empyrean' and 'Sardonic Heavens' levels respectively, down to 'Cold Hell' occupied by the 'Strike Leaders, Workers, Ranchers and Cattle'. In Suvin's arrangement, Joan is not at the bottom (even though we are clear that Joan does not have much money) but in 'Limbo' along with 'Newsmen' and 'Black Straw Hats'.[71] In this setting, St. Joan belongs to the intermediary professional class that includes intellectuals and those whose overall social position the intellectual occupies, yet her position is very much an unsettled matter. She can reside comfortably in the position of what Brecht would later call the 'Tuis',[72] or she could align herself with the workers. Her position is in Limbo, in both the state between the heavenly state of the Black Straw Hats and the earthly reality of the workers *and* the state of the undecided intellectual. While workers and Mauler are defined and locked in to their social positions, St. Joan is free (or freer) to choose her position. Yet

---

70 Such a connection should not seem a stretch. Brecht and Benjamin were great collaborators, and it is useful to note that Brecht also was helped in the writing of the text of Saint Joan by Benjamin himself. A collaborator of Brecht's, Margarete Steffin, 'often brought variants of the text or plot to Benjamin; the experience of working together on the text, as in the case of the *Saint Joan* play, or the crime novel, aroused hope of a useful response' (Wizisla 2009, p. 147).

71 Suvin 1984, p. 135.

72 The term Tuis originates from the German word for intellectuals, Intellektuellen, which Brecht often reformatted to 'Tellekt-uell-in' to refer to those who understand the real cause of social problems yet seek to divert attention to other, less directly political factors. Mar-

it is this position which will be Joan's downfall, as she stands in for a classic petit-bourgeois intellectual. The person who foregrounds the 'rational' mind yet dismisses the complexities of the ideology of the conjuncture must fail.[73] We learn from her failure. As Suvin notes: 'The only attempts at communication and pressure going from below upward come from Joan and the strike leaders (Communists). The ideological failure of the former and the pragmatic failure of the latter are complementary; the reasons for that complementarity are not explained in the universe *Saint Joan*, and would have to be inferred from the larger context of Brecht's opus'.[74] While the last point here is somewhat contestable, the important aspect to note is the ideological failure of the intellectual. This was understood by Benjamin, at the time increasingly involved in Brecht's work.[75] A few years after *Die Heilige Johanna* was written, Benjamin presented his views on the subject in his important foundational text, 'The Author as Producer'. The last few lines of the text read:

> The mind, the spirit that makes itself heard in the name of fascism must disappear. The mind which only believes in its own magic strength will disappear. For the revolutionary struggle is not fought between capitalism and mind. It is fought between capitalism and the proletariat.[76]

Benjamin echoes quite neatly the *plumpes Denken* (crude thought) of Brecht. And this, as we learn, is *St. Joan*'s central error. This is not a merely subjective error (one of pure agency) but rather a question of her only realising her agency too late, such that no blame is attached to her. Indeed, we may sympathise with her, and most definitely are meant to, but we also must learn that she did not succeed and examine why. In the same way, we are to learn from the transformation of Galy Gay as a portent from the present. We are not to come to this realisation, a stance of knowing, alone. The play rejects the mere presentation of the abstract functioning of capitalism, and thus an attempt to 'represent capitalism'. Rather, it focuses on capitalism's wreckages and how not to respond to them: St. Joan, for all her labours, dies. The point is to produce

---

tin Jay in his discussion of the Frankfurt School, formally known as the Institute for Social Research: 'To Brecht, the Institut consisted of "Tui-intellectuals", who prostituted themselves for American foundation support' (Jay 1996, pp. 201–2).

73   Suvin 1984, p. 151.
74   Suvin 1984, p. 150.
75   For a much fuller examination, which highlights just how fully Brecht and Benjamin were involved in each other's work, and also displays how each was seen as co-creating the other's work, see Wizisla 2009.
76   Benjamin 1998, p. 103.

a committed intellectual project that has a class politics as its engine. On this level, the rejection of the social position of the 'petit-bourgeois intellectual', and the worldview that is associated with it, as well as what could replace it, are the key issues for Brecht. This is the task in *Kuhle Wampe*.

3   *Kuhle Wampe* and the Good Answer

It is interesting to note that given Brecht's numerous misgivings with the cinematic production of *Die Dreigroschenoper* – *Dreigroschenfilm* – misgivings which went as far as initiating a lawsuit to stop its airing as well as the writing of a novel to counter both the play and film, it is that work, and not his ideologically and aesthetically coherent and preferred *Kuhle Wampe: Oder wem gehört die Welt?* (*Kuhle Wampe: Or who owns the World*), that has received the larger amount of scholarly attention and public interest. This is especially ironic given the film's ideological achievement in developing and furthering Brechtian practice beyond the theatre.[77] While *Kuhle Wampe* carries forward Brecht's move from abstract to the real refunctioning ('umfunctionierung') of individuality in capitalist society, here we witness the collective response. Whereas in the previous two texts we learn from the mistakes of those on stage (we will see this also very clearly in the analysis of *Mutter Courage*), here this message is brought forward specifically through a recognition of the power of organised oppositional activity as the logical reaction to capitalism.

If the chief problem in *Mann ist Mann* was the relation of the bad collective and the individual in capitalist society, and if *Die Heilige Johanna* articulates the worker's understanding of the functioning of that society and the way economic functions are made known in the life of the worker, *Kuhle Wampe* provides the organised left's answer. On this collective point, it is important to be careful not to approach Brecht in the way that much of Brecht studies have approached his *oeuvre*: as a solitary artistic producer, singularly responsible for all work that was published under his name. Brecht's practice, one of the constants throughout his career from very early on, depended upon a strong staff of mostly women whose involvement helped to define what we now refer to as 'Brechtian'. While some literature has sought to correct this clear omission, others – particularly the work of John Fuegi – have sought to construct a version of Brecht as a fraudulent confiscator of other's labour, and a worn and

---

77   For an analysis of the influence of Brecht's problems with the *Dreigroschenfilm*, see Giles 1997.

shabby carbon copy of the capitalist class's appropriation that he so ruthlessly criticised. Rather than look for meagre sustenance in this well-tilled field, it is useful to remind ourselves that 'Collaborative work arouses scandal',[78] as Fredric Jameson provocatively writes in *Brecht and Method*. The scandal originates when discussions of social and cultural production take place not on the work's own terms but instead under the rubric of a market logic of the 'private property of the signature'. This then elides the primacy of the work of the many in place of 'personal and of individual ownership'.[79] A social process is attributed to a single social actor, rather than social production becoming a chief way through which meaning is produced and distributed. The attempt to transpose this sociality onto an individual character naturally obscures the processes at work, and also the ways in which those processes make possible an alternative way of seeing the world and putting this on stage or on film. In this alternative way of seeing, one set free from the constraints of authorial logic or the primacy of property rule, the singular is born anew. As Jameson argues, in this context 'individuality is not effaced but completed by collectivity'.[80]

The emphasis on collectivity involves two forms of collaborative work. The first was the heavy reliance on the activity of the audience. This primarily acknowledged the place of structured experience that the audience brought into the cultural space, and how Brecht sought to refunction this through the audience's participation. It is through this refunctioning that Brecht locates the entry point for emancipatory theatre. Jacques Rancière has noted that emancipation begins in the 'blurring of the boundary between those who act and those who look; between individuals and members of the collective body'.[81] Brecht responded to the one-way system of distribution in capitalist culture (and definitely anti-collaborative culture) by theorising its refunctionalisation, arguing for instance about radio that it 'should step out of the supply business and organise its listeners as suppliers'.

Beginning with his collaborations with Elisabeth Hauptmann in 1925, the abstracted experimental nature of Brecht's work rapidly dissipates and, from then on, the primacy of the social experience is paramount. This is the second form of collaborative work, although it grows out of the understanding of the first. In order to be most within the social, individual cultural producers must relinquish the idea of the individual artist and give themselves over to, or work towards, an aesthetics of experimentation and ushering in of new experience.

---

78 Jameson 1998, p. 14.
79 Ibid.
80 Jameson 1998, p. 15.
81 Rancière 2011, p. 19.

As Esther Leslie describes Brecht's position, 'Artistic production must have the character of a model able to introduce other producers to production, by placing an "improved apparatus" at the disposal of authors and audience, bringing audiences into contact with the production process, turning readers or spectators into collaborators'.[82] The collaborative form practised by Brecht defines his process and is ideologically intertwined with, and produces, the displayed work. This collaborative form of work is, if anything, what defines the Brechtian filmic project most clearly, as it is dependent on both drawing in and working with other cultural producers. From the director Slatan Dudow's original idea, to the work of novelist of Ernst Ottwalt in crafting the narrative, the collaborationist project that *Kuhle Wampe* became was 'the only example of his practical work that came close to realizing the idea of deindividualizing (aesthetic) production in the cinema'.[83] As such, while the film was the product of many hands, what ties it to works such as *Mann ist Mann*, *Die Heilige Johanna* and others is that the film, more than any other example of his work in the medium, represented an 'opportunity for Brecht to test his Epic Theatre principles in the film medium, which he thought used the most advanced artistic means of representation and therefore promised the greatest political impact'.[84] As the most clearly collaborative of his late-Weimar works, it becomes, as Nenad Jovanovic notes, 'paradigmatic in being the sole Brecht film that embodies his aesthetic, production, and in political principles as presented in such writings as "The Threepenny Lawsuit" and the various articulations of epic/dialectic theatre theory'.[85] The emphasis on collaboration also required using oppositional technical forms that experimental left cultural producers were developing, including montage, not merely as a formal aspect or technical frame but 'as a structuring dramaturgical principle, applied at the respective levels of its three parts and the scenes these consist of. The parts are relatively independent from one another, each one centering on a separate issue ...'[86] In large measure the use of montage was borrowed from Soviet cinema, which 'revealed an experimental energy parallel to his own explorations in the Epic Theatre'.[87] This borrowing also represented a rescue act, in that it sought to maintain the 'continued revolutionary potential of the filmic medium in the

---

82 Leslie 2000, p. 96.
83 Silberman 2008, p. 316.
84 Silberman 2008, p. 317.
85 Jovanovic 2017, pp. 61–62.
86 Jovanovic 2017, p. 58.
87 Silberman 2009, p. 317.

wake of Soviet socialist realism'.[88] Brecht's left response is not to deal abstractly with the theoretical worker but rather to meet the worker where not only 'he' is, but – and this is vitally important for the gender politics of the film – where 'she' is as well. Thus, while I have argued that in *Die Heilige Johanna* we witnessed, not an attempt to represent capitalism, but the way in which capital feeds off workers, in the same way *Kuhle Wampe* is not about concretising the extraction of surplus value (although this may have merit for a Marxist cultural producer) but rather showing how the lived relations of working people are slowly destroyed and systematically ground down. In this regard, we have a necessary examination of class, wherein issues of choice, marriage, employment and unemployment all intermingle and intersect with each other. The collaborative form of artistic production was highly adaptive at articulating this new reality (especially through the use of montage) as it opened ways not only for these seemingly disparate social realities to be connected, but 'through this kind of participatory production ... new proletarian subjectivities could be engineered'.[89] These new subjectivities were social in nature and provided for individual realities to be reframed through a social constructive lens.

While individuality in the film is refracted through the lens of the social, the individual must first of all be seen, at least partly.[90] For Brecht, the theory of classes lacked an understanding of the viewpoint of the individual and their relation to the social. As he was to state of 'Me-Ti' in his 1930s theoretical text *Book of Changes* (published in English only in 2016 under the title *Me-Ti: Book of Interventions in the Flow of Things*), 'Me-ti found few enough indications in

---

88 Alter 2004, p. 79. This essay investigates the music and sound of the film, and Alter concludes that it '*is* certain that Eisler, Brecht, and Dudow were at the time collaborating on a theory of dialectic music for film', although she concludes that 'it was indeed Brecht who developed *the theory* of music as a self-standing element' (2004, p. 84).
89 Heynen 2015, p. 512.
90 This is valid at the level of the social world but also at an aesthetic level. Angelos Koutsourakis argues that in Brecht's filmic strategy, he understood that 'cinema challenges the understanding of art as a reflectionist process, and the medium's political efficiency is grounded in its ability to engage with the material reality, so as to point to structures that are not necessarily comprehended even by the filmmaker. The prerequisite for the radical employment of the medium is that the story is an epiphenomenon. What matters most is the ability to use the technological apparatus so as to engage with the social reality and point to social mechanisms beyond the narrative world' (Koutsourakis 2015, p. 252). Koutsourakis examines the connections between Brecht and Benjamin's famous essay 'The Work of Art in the Age of Mechanical Reproduction'. For more on the influence that the one had on the other, see Silberman 1987, pp. 448–60.

the writings of the classics about the behaviour of individuals. Most often they spoke of classes or of other large groups of people'.[91]

While the latter sections of the film provide a stunning depiction of the depths of alternative organisations active in Weimar Berlin, the first of the three acts of the film provides a dynamic exercise in the relation of the individual to the social and the abstract to the concrete. In the opening scenes of the film the frantic spinning of wheels dominates the screen. Workers speed on bicycles from factory to factory in the hopes of finding a day's work. At this stage we see only a group of workers, and a blur of disappointment and despair as they are told again and again that there is no work available. Here the workers are without names, and while the locations may have been known to Berlin audiences, no attention is paid to establishing the meaning of the buildings beyond the fact that the occupants have no need for workers. Seen from capital's perspective, they are a mass of unproductive labour, even though they are all literally 'on their bikes'. Soon we will learn the effects of this abstract unemployment. Particularly through the story of Franz, the son of the Bönike family, we see how unemployment makes itself felt on individual workers, while Brecht also displays how this problem is anything but reducible to an individual's own decision-making. This conception is unified in another Marxist view of the relational significance of the individual, particularly as regards aesthetic representation. Neil Larsen, drawing heavily from Lukács's *Theory of the Novel*, argues that individuality is framed as a category that often shields from view the function of the character. As Larsen writes, 'The modern, private "isolated" individual is, evidently, an abstraction in itself, a monad experientially "incommensurable" with other monads – but one that by that very fact becomes abstractly interchangeable with them ...'.[92] Brecht complicates and plays with this abstracted yet also lived version of individuality in order to extract political meaning. Although the young son's mother and father seem intent on personalising his unemployment, his communist sister defends him against the complex causes that exist outside of the individual's door. Hers is a social perspective, and one representative of a generation of young workers who see no hope that capitalism can rescue itself and provide anything like lasting employment, no matter how thrifty or self-denying one is.[93]

---

91   Brecht in Adorno et al. 1998, p. 36.
92   Larsen 2001, p. 180.
93   This sentiment will be succinctly expressed in Brecht's *Die Mutter* as follows 'über das Fleisch das die in der kuche fällt, wär nicht in küche entschieden' translated into English as: 'The meat not there in your kitchen / won't get there, if you stay in your kitchen!' (Brecht 1965, p. 39). This translation seems to arrive at only part of the point, however. There is also

In his narrowing in on the Bönike family, however, Brecht is wary of creating a predominantly emotive response to the material via an emotional identification with Franz. He does not desire for us to have pity for the young character but rather to examine what is going wrong in these scenes and approach the situation on that basis. In order to achieve this, Brecht utilises distancing techniques to break the audience from the habit of emotional identification. One way of accomplishing this, as Bruce Murray notes, was to introduce each act in such a way as to '... interrupt the narrative flow and encourage the audience's intellectual engagement. They do so by commenting ironically on the unfolding, by foreshadowing what will transpire and, in every case, by minimizing the potential for building suspense'.[94] This negation of suspense-building is particularly effective and acts as a barrier to the acceptance of official responses to Franz's death. The police officer's statement of 'unknown' as the cause of Franz's suicide marks the judgment as complicit in the act. Again we are confronted with an interesting connection of individual and social here, for without recourse to the social we cannot interpret the real life decisions of the individual.[95]

In both the depiction of anguish in the present world and hope for the new, the individual and individuality are crushed. Indeed, it is this leading marker of bourgeois morality that marks out Brecht's early work and that continues in *Kuhle Wampe*. The notion of the lone individual protagonist battling for his family is defeated before we are introduced to young Franz. We see only him and others gathering around together waiting in the very early morning, as the mass of unemployed clamour for newspaper listings of what work is to be had for that day. The pursuit of those jobs with the 'suicidal panic'[96] of the spinning of bicycle wheels will come to fruition with the actual suicide of the young man. The depiction of the suicide, and the reporting officer's response to it, are yet another demonstration of the failure of the notion of the bourgeois individual in both a formal and then political sense. The integration of the social and the

---

the suggestion in this sentiment that the reasons for there not being enough food are not because you are not thrifty enough.

94   Murray 1990, p. 222.
95   The suicide itself, coming as it does in the first third of the film, 'practically defies all German screen traditions', states Siegfried Kracauer. It was placed at this point in the narrative in spite of repeated requests to shift the scene towards the end, 'so as to re-establish the natural order of things ... And disavows psychological retrogression' (that is, the making of a social act into an individual one) (Kracauer 1966, p. 246). This shift would have also 'prevented spectators from interacting with it as they had grown accustomed to interacting with mainstream films' (Murray 1990, p. 224).
96   Jameson 1998, p. 150.

individual here marks a deep connection in the specific moment of the now – we are now in the moment of the crisis of the dissolution of the individual – and this is, as mentioned above, a tactic to maintain the viewer's recognition of this connection in mind.

Before he jumps out of his parent's window, Franz is careful and considerate in his actions. He slowly evaluates his actions, and he even takes off his watch so that its value will not be lost to his family. *Pace* the central metaphor of Kassovitz's powerful *La Haine*, where a man also jumps from a tall building, young Bönike does not delude himself that 'so far so good'. And as in the French film, we are witness to both an individual and social moment bound up together. For him, the matter is tragically announced in the spinning away of his time. Before he jumps, however, he pauses to gaze into the camera. As Franz Birgel notes: 'The suicide is presented as purely mechanical rather than an impulsive act, which, as the censor in "Kleiner Beitrag zum Realismus" asserts, the viewer does not even want to prevent in the absence of 'artistic, human, warm-hearted representation'.[97] This 'purely mechanical' act marks a significant challenge to traditional aesthetics. Theodore Rippey notes that this is the film's

> ... first breach of the cinematic fourth wall. The turn is virtually his only action in the entire apartment sequence; his expression conveys his powerlessness and visually poses the question: 'What other options do I have?' He now views suicide as the only viable release from oppression. In a bow to the family's economic plight, young Bönike leaves his watch on the windowsill before leaping to his death. Dudov[sic] (the film's director) adds emphasis with an extreme close-up of the watch two shots after the jump.[98]

Once the viewer has seen this depiction of the state of things, the question will eventually become that of the response to such horrific predictability.

Often lost in analysis of the film is probably its most deliberate statement about (or presentation of) politics and aesthetics.[99] I refer here to the play within a play put on by the *Rote Sprachchor*, and the particular role of art in

---

97   Brigel 2009, p. 51.
98   Rippey 2007, p. 7.
99   While they may too easily accept the transition from a 'pre-Marxist' to a Marxist Brecht, Jeff Kinkle and Alberto Toscano note how the precise historical fact of the destruction of perfectly good coffee to raise the price of it, a fact that is mentioned in *Die Heilige Johanna*, '... led Brecht to Marx, and to the dramatization of the link between class position, social knowledge, and aesthetic form evident in the coffee scene from Kuhle Wampe' (See Kinkle and Toscano 2011, p. 48). Also useful in this regard is Nenad Jovanovic's discussion of Pet-

changing social scenarios. Throughout the film we are witness to tales of homelessness not as an abstract category or ontology but as a process, or social event. A person or group is not simply homeless as a state of being through some fault of their own; rather the process by which this has come about consistently acts as a frame for the film. Its offshoots, such as suicide, expressing the right to choice,[100] not to mention the broader role of sexism in the society, a punishing judicial system, and a raft of destructive emotions, are not backdrops but the subject matter itself. The role of art is necessarily to assess these states of affairs and then respond. This is the distinctly social nature of Brecht's formal practice.

In this regard, Franz's unstated question as to 'what other options do I have' is an important one, as it also poses the political aspect of the cultural producer's position through a formal method. On formal invention in the film, Katie Trumpener notes that: 'Brecht's writings around his 1932 film script for *Kuhle Wampe* suggest how non-traditional and dialectical uses of film syntax (the establishment of a counterpointal relationship between image and music, for instance) can be used to unsettle the spectator and to create a critical space for (political) reflection ...'.[101] That is, the political aspect is not, and in this moment cannot be, separate from the formal strategy. The moment is one of a social-political aesthetics that seeks to liberate both in a propagandistic sense – challenging the dominant views – as well as interrogating the dominant modes of viewing. This involves confronting the problems of production and collaboration in communist film.

Kuhle Wampe is an interesting case in point, as its success (particularly in comparison to other filmic projects during the Weimar period) highlight the extent to which artistic influences outside of Brecht's control would limit his ability to work through his innovative formal contributions. Brecht learned the value of this during production of his *Dreigroschenfilm*; among other problems,

---

tifer 1977, pp. 49–63. This article occludes the relation of political aesthetics that Brecht et al. advance in the film. See Jovanovic 2017, pp. 53–4.

100   While often overlooked, female sexuality and a woman's right to choose are important aspects of the film, and, as Kerstin Barndt notes, it is the character Anni's 'sexual independence, though, that ultimately determines the heroine's fate and brings the drama of abortion into play' (Barndt 2008, p. 82). It is Brecht's task in the film to show how Anni's positionality is defined by her social setting. This politics of situatedness is contrasted with the ephemeral notion of young lovers.

101   The formulation 'unsettle the spectator' needs further thought: this quote is useful as it clearly articulates that Brecht began to articulate a formal strategy aligned with his political purpose. This key point often gets lost in discussions of Brecht's political aesthetics. See Trumpener 1990, p. 300.

he lost control of the script to the writer Béla Balázs. As Bruce Murray notes, without this control, 'most of Brecht's alienation effects either disappeared or were aestheticized'. The director, G.W. Pabst, made Balázs's script the basis of his film, which 'attracted filmgoers interested foremost in entertainment, and Bertolt Brecht was deeply disappointed'.[102]

Kuhle Wampe was a different experience. Rather than feeling that the project was no longer under his direct control, Brecht showed a great deal of willingness to collaborate fully, but also to learn how this collaborative experience could shape his political aesthetics. The growth of the Communist Party in the latter part of the 1920s and early 1930s witnessed a new period of leftist social struggle and the formation of organisations, in part through funding from the Soviet Union, designed to provide avenues for international artistic cooperation. The principal organisation was the *Arbeiterhilfe*, which was able to fund a wide variety of cultural groups. For instance, 'the *Arbeiterhilfe's* agitprop theatre troupes created a vital public space for the celebration of international solidarity which created a new and innovative way of spreading the *Arbeiterhilfe's* counter-cultural message'.[103] The *Arbeiterhilfe's* film company, *Prometheus*, was responsible for producing Brecht et al.'s *Kuhle Wampe*. Because of this source of funding, and due to its funds being limited, Brecht 'decided to accept Dudow's proposal for enlisting the help of the Communist-led Fichte Sport Club ... The interaction between Dudow, Brecht, and the Fichte Sport Club characterized the film's production'.[104] Brecht examined the problems of making political film under capitalism, particularly when that art threatens the material basis of its production. He notes in a short piece entitled 'Film without Commercial Value' that 'A Communist film no longer has commercial value because Communism is no longer a threat for the bourgeois public. It no longer arouses interest'. Thus, 'Artistically valuable films are commercially damaging because they ruin the public's taste by improving it. They are themselves, however, not commercial'.[105] This lack of commercial appeal would have severely hampered Brecht's efforts had it not been for the intervention of an oppositional media infrastructure which could present new aesthetic subjectivities, or ones that involved bridging different political-aesthetic strategies

---

102   Murray 1990, p. 164.
103   Braskén 2015, p. 177.
104   Murray 1990, p. 218.
105   Brecht 2000a, p. 207. As an aside, it is hard to imagine any more trenchant criticism of film production than the Brechtian-inspired *Contempt* by Jean-Luc Godard, featuring a brilliant performance by the German film-director, Fritz Lang, a fellow cultural producer who produced his masterpiece, *M*, with Nero Films.

based on working-class lives. Making the working-class collectives partners in this process brings about what Christoph Schaub terms a 'labor movement modernism' which 'appropriates and articulates modernist aesthetics to imagine urban modernity from the standpoint of proletarian collectives'.[106] The integration of the working-class producers in this process helped redirect the subject matter to more immediate working-class concerns.

While Jameson may be correct in stating that, in Brecht's oeuvre, it is 'not the worker's work that is representable but their poverty',[107] this is hardly a shortcoming. The oppression of rent and how to respond to it are equally valid 'representables' in understanding the complex of pressures brought to bear on the working class. This raw material of lived relations is taken up in the play within the play. The play's latter section, which offers the expression of organised opposition, frames itself as the socialist cultural response to the capitalist crisis. Whereas in *Die Mutter* a worker responds to the owner's demands for firings and reduced wages due to financial crisis as 'Capitalism is sick and you're the doctor', there is little effective organised response, as *Die Mutter* is a learning play based on defeat (as are *Die Heilige Johanna* and arguably *Mann ist Mann*).[108] The offering in *Kuhle Wampe* is much more overtly combative and positive. If we learn through sport to win, we also learn through protest aesthetics to aim to win, and respond to the concerns of people immediately. The positioning of the unsuccessful jobseekers bicycling through the city, scraping by against the motorcycle racers driving forward to win, not so much in competition with others but pushing each other on, starkly illustrates the power of workers working with or against each other. This is not, one should clarify, a template for oppositional aesthetics. Rather, this is how a particular form of aesthetics responds in this situation (particularly one that is protest-oriented). What is important and worthy of generalisation is the emphasis on beginning from the concerns of the contemporary problem and then finding ways of addressing it by encouraging collective activity. In this instance, the film's depiction of the Bönikes's eviction is mirrored in the content of the Agit-Prop group. Brecht's aesthetics are responsive: they must be focussed on addressing and shaping actual lived social situations. The importance that Brecht gives to

---

106 Schaub 2018, p. 318.
107 Jameson 1998, p. 150.
108 *Die Mutter* was also produced prior to *Kuhle Wampe* and was, like *Die Heilige Johanna* before it, perhaps less concerned with producing a directly oppositional project given the proximity to the strongest showings of the NSDAP electorally and on the ground as 1933 approached.

the troupe 'Das Rote Sprachrohr' ('The Red Megaphone') in the film suggests a larger proposal for action and strategy. Here is one 'critic's' take on the film:

> Yes, you will be astonished that I reproach your depiction for not being sufficiently *human*. You have not depicted a person but, well, let's admit it, a type. Your unemployed worker is not a real individual, not a real flesh-and-blood person, distinct from every other person, with his particular worries, particular joys and finally his particular fate. He is drawn very superficially. As artists you must forgive me for the strong expression that *we learn too little about him*, but the consequences are of a *political* nature and force me to object to the film's release.[109]

The critic was the censor who blocked earlier releases of the film.[110] This is particularly relevant given that Brecht, upon hearing this appraisal, had the 'unpleasant impression of being caught red-handed' and went further to commend the censor by stating that 'he had penetrated far deeper into the essence of our artistic intentions than our most supportive critics'.[111] What this censor had understood was the attempts at redefinition of the individual in capitalist society, although clearly the censor objects to this for the reasons stated above. What Brecht constructs is a cinematic form whereby the individual is, as evidenced in *Mann ist Mann*, capable of reconstruction. The reconstruction is the gap filled by the narrative arc created by the suicide at the beginning of the film. Whereas the speeding of the wheels locates workers in a race against each other (and at the expense of each other), the collective marching through the streets on the way to the festivities presents the opportunity to highlight what Eugene Lunn terms the 'positive potentials of the depersonalised, urban, machine age'.[112] That is, by working through the constructs that capitalism provides, we are able to produce something that may liberate itself.

---

109 Brecht 2000a, p. 208.
110 One should note that besides the obstacle of getting the film through the censors, the film was affected by the very depression it sought to examine on film. Brecht and Dudow had to find another film company to finance the completion of the project as the Prometheus Company dealt with liquidation proceedings. *Kuhle Wampe* was, despite the best efforts of the authorities to keep the film from being seen, relatively successful. After a promising first week, the film was prolonged and opened in 15 separate cinemas. This was followed by showings in London, Amsterdam and Paris. See for further Kepley Jr. 1983, pp. 7–23.
111 Brecht 2000a, pp. 208–9.
112 Lunn 1982, p. 103. As Katherine Roper notes, *Kuhle Wampe* was unique (alongside Piel

In his excellent essay 'A Brechtian Aesthetics', Dana Polan argues that the production of an over-formalised Brecht has lost sight of or obscured the importance of Brecht's political aesthetics. Brecht himself, notes Polan, insisted that all art contained a distancing or alienating feature to it. Yet there is nothing 'socially distancing' about this.[113] Whereas audiences may have become used to these alienating forms of making strange, many artists themselves have shied away from conscious distancing towards intuitive abstraction. In order to meet the historical moment, Polan notes, we must replace the process which 'keeps literary production in the realm of accident and signals a refusal to situate such production within the actual workings of history'. For this we must adopt a 'scientific attitude'.[114] The emphasis on the 'actual workings of history' cannot be underestimated in Brecht, as it implies a supple ability to address and act as redress in the *now*. However, the 'scientific attitude' need not privilege an anti-communal or anti-social experience. In fact, the living out of this attitude is made clear only in the moment where a plurality is involved. Unfortunately, very little has been written on the play within a play aspect of *Kuhle Wampe*, though the political aesthetics of the now are nowhere clearer than here.

Just preceding the play there is a round of socialist games that highlights the ideals of comradeship, learning through sport to win, and the larger metaphor that to 'win' socialism is key. It is not enough to respond to injustice, however; one must create an oppositional project aimed at overthrowing the world that makes injustice possible. At this point the purpose of the play seems to be a lesson in responding to the social problems repeatedly addressed throughout the film. The actors illustrate the particularities of their position in the play (for instance, that they are active in the working-class district of Wedding, Berlin) and make clear their role in the daily activities of the lives of those facing eviction. The purpose of their action is to support those being made homeless by late Weimar capitalism. In this way their practice is necessarily defined by the positions of their allies in their particular historical moment and location. This adeptness requires a collective experience that liberates the construct of the singular bourgeois artist from their individuality, placing them in the position of collective cultural producer. As noted by Birgel below, such a political aesthetic project was itself attempted in *Kuhle Wampe*:

Jutzi's *Mutter Krausens Fahrt ins Glück*) in that it was the only film to 'refer to revolutionary transformation of institutions and the Communist movement that would carry it out' (Roper 1998, p. 90).
113   Polan 1985, p. 92.
114   Polan 1985, p. 93.

Working with over 4,000 participants, including the members of the leftist Fichte Sports Club, the agit-prop group *Das Rote Sprachrohr* (The Red Megaphone), and several choruses, Brecht wanted the production to be a learning experience for all involved. As in his *Lehrstücke* from this period, the collaborative process was just as important, if not more so, than the final product. In addition, the audience was to be a co-producer of the film. By disrupting the illusion of reality through his well-known alienation technique, Brecht wanted the viewers to become active participants who reflect on what was happening on the screen and relate it to their own lives.[115]

The collective nature of the production and its nimble nature, able to respond in a meaningful way to the lives of workers in a moment of great need (eviction), necessitates a move away from a firm formal structure (so often the cause of misunderstandings of Brecht). This understanding situates Brecht's political aesthetics as a process, requiring the move towards experimentation that, for instance, one can witness so dramatically in the many productions and reproductions of *Mann ist Mann*.[116] As Dana Polan explains, 'Brecht's interest in experimentation, his strictures against any too rigidly constructed theory of political art, are so many attempts to minimize predictability and keep art open to the changing demands of history'.[117]

4 Concluding Brecht to 1933

In Benjamin, Brecht finds not only a collaborator on many texts, including *Die Heilige Johanna* (although of these Brecht had more than most),[118] but rather

---

[115] Birgel 2009, p. 49. Brecht's admiration for groups such as *Das Rote Sprachchor* was in part due to their ability to put forward arguments to workers directly. Yet Brecht also was keen to show, as in the tram scene at the end of the film, 'the value of proletarian common sense, in which young workers successfully debated older bourgeois passengers about the need to change the world' (Bodek 1997, p. 146).

[116] On the idea of change in Brecht, Marc Silberman convincingly notes that 'Brecht's entire oeuvre, his very mode of thought, derives from the conviction that society can and must be changed' (Silberman 1993, p. 8). Silberman's article provides a very useful riposte to postmodern appropriations of Brecht while also noting the current power of Brecht's work where this work has not been as of yet been institutionalised.

[117] Polan 1985, p. 5.

[118] That said, it would be hard to overestimate Benjamin's contribution to Brecht's work during their friendship. One example of this deep connection is the fact that the two had been involved in an open journal project, the purpose of which was to 'account for itself

someone – at least from the period – whose understanding and perceptions of Brecht's work, even if they did not always agree, was unrivalled for his age. While Brecht notes in 1927 that his first spectator was Karl Marx, the argument could be made that in Walter Benjamin he had found his second.[119] In fact, Brecht himself would admit to as much. Wizisla notes:

> Benjamin was Brecht's first systematic critic with a claim to theory, and he was the first to identify Brecht's originality and his role in contemporary writing. According to Hannah Arendt, Brecht knew that in Benjamin he had encountered 'the most important critic of the time'. This was confirmed by a note by Adorno, certainly in this case an incorruptible source, and certainly free from suspicion of having represented the relationship between Benjamin and Brecht as closer than it was: 'Story that BB, when I saw him again for the first time since 1932, in exile in the autumn of 1941, spoke of WB as his best critic'.[120]

What concerned both was to develop a method and a system of practice that would rethink how a political aesthetics could be uniquely attuned to its age, an 'expression of its closeness to real life', that sought to understand and change the world in which it operated.

What Benjamin recognises as powerful in Brecht is the necessity of working through the logic of the system. It is vital to understand and experiment in order to respond to that system at a particular moment, let its contradictions

---

in regard to positions and challenges which uniquely – in current circumstances – permit it an active, interventionist role, with tangible consequences, as opposed to its usual ineffectual arbitrariness' (Wizisla 2009, p. 66). For more on this exciting project, which unfortunately never saw publication, and the way in which this was key in the development of the aesthetics and politics of the day, see Wizisla 2009, pp. 66–97. Of course, this was not a one-way street, and Brecht's influence can be seen clearly in key Benjamin works such as the Arcades Projects, 'The Author as Producer', 'The Work of Art in the Age of Its Mechanical Reproduction', and 'Theses on History'. 'Brecht's work, as Guenter Hartung has observed, was for Benjamin the unexpected phenomenon of a great modern non-auratic art, and in the German language to boot – to the extent that even the powerful effect on Benjamin of surrealist texts paled by comparison'. Hartung in Wizisla 2009, p. 103.

119 Fascinatingly, before he committed suicide Benjamin had intended to send a copy of the essay to Brecht, envisaging Brecht as 'one of the first readers of the theses' (2009, p. 173). In this he was correct. As Brecht wrote of the essay in his journal: 'In short, the little treatise is clear and presents complex issues simply (despite its metaphors and its Judaisms), and it is frightening to think how few people there are who are prepared even at least to misunderstand such a piece'. Brecht in Wizisla 2009, p. 173.

120 Wizisla 2009, p. 151.

loose so that they can play out on stage, and situate the audience so that they will be able to critically engage the piece with which they have been presented. A chief part of this project is not to abstract the key tensions and struggles but rather to embody them as much as possible. Thus the problem is not, as Jameson may argue, that Brecht is unable to represent capitalism in its totality. This, I have argued here, is not Brecht's chief pursuit, although it is one that has been attributed to him. Rather, Brecht is focussed on depicting how capitalism figures in remaking itself and a working class (as in *Mann ist Mann*), on the necessity of learning how the capitalist system manipulates and produces a system of complex ideological obfuscations (in relation to things that need not be obfuscated, as is seen in *Die Heilige Johanna*) and ultimately on the way in which art and culture can respond to the perpetual crises and daily horrors that are part and parcel of capitalism (*Kuhle Wampe*). In Chapter 4 I will continue to show this influence at work, with a focus on retrieving history for the purposes of making arguments for the present.

CHAPTER 3

Blake, Opposition, and the Now

The following two chapters on William Blake (Chapters 3 and 5) argue that, as with Brecht, there are two distinct moments in Blake's work. The circumstances for their interventions are comparable, marked by major historical defeats: the cause for Brecht's shift occurs with the rise of Nazi power, exiling him from his political and artistic connections, whereas for Blake we see a generation's hopes and desires expressed by the French Revolution destroyed by its failures.[1] The earlier periods of each writer are structured by explorations of their own moment of capitalism and by a working through of its specific contradictions. This exploration involves examining how to be as close to that moment as possible – a process dedicated to understanding that historical moment's impulses most deeply – while producing an oppositional aesthetic that speaks of and to that moment. This moment is representative but not exclusive to the ideological division of the city and country (although both are sites of capitalist exploitation), the growing body of urban poor (particularly young children), and the distortions of religion and care that act to cover these abuses. Yet just as we see the connections in producing this aesthetic – what I have termed, following Benjamin, a political aesthetics of the now – so too do we see a moment of historical re-examination as a means to think through an otherwise historically unfavourable period for militant working-class activity more generally and progressive cultural producers in particular.

Just as *Mann ist Mann*'s Galy Gay is a character who begins his quest in response to a need (to find food), likewise in the 'Introduction' to *The Songs of Innocence* we meet the poet responding to a need. A religious vision (a child upon a cloud) entreats Blake to pipe and sing and ultimately to write down his lyrics 'that all may read'.[2] This poem, like many of the poems in *Innocence*, is a thoughtful moment of introspection, seemingly very personal in nature, so that the desire to spread the word is especially notable. The poem bears many marks

---

1 Erdman notes that Blake's work at the time and in response is 'alive with the sense of a new and revolutionary break with the past and a great hopeful movement of the people' (Erdman 1969, p. 130). Once the Revolution had collapsed, however, the figure of Orc, a harbinger of rebellious spirit, is described by Erdman as 'the Napoleonic serpent' (1969, p. 375). See also Christensen 2000, and for a more nuanced approach, considering Blake's hesitation to violence, see Manquis 1989, pp. 365–95.
2 Blake 1988, p. 7.

of a perceived simplicity in Blake. The intended audience for the poetry, which is meant to be written so that 'Every child may joy to hear', hints further at the naive purpose of the poem. But what comprises this Innocence and, perhaps more relevantly, from what and where does it originate? What in the make-up of this cycle defines Innocence, and likewise, is there something that points us towards its definition through its absence?

Innocence is a conscious space of rejection against the dominating oppressive and exploitative world of capitalism. These poems offer a conception of Innocence that is constituted by an absence of, or retreat from and rejection of, the dominance of exploitation and oppression: this Innocence embodies a conscious rejection of this dominance. It is important to clarify that there is one popular usage in which Innocence more broadly suggests a state of ignorance; to be innocent is to not know. Blakean Innocence, it cannot be stressed enough, is neither indicative of, nor a signal of, ignorance, nor does it constitute a worldview wilfully unknowing of the horrors of the world that exist around it.[3] Indeed, Innocence stands specifically against ignorance and obfuscation, especially in regards to the dominant ideology's desire to manipulate that which is radical and (radically) pleasurable about life in Blake's world (care for another, love of God, sexuality, etc.), and so to make of it a cover for their own misery-making domination. That is, Innocence is a block on or a refusal against its own possible inversion and perversion.

Innocence involves carving out a space where the rules of oppression and exploitation do not, and cannot, apply. In part, Innocence in Blake relies on a retrieval of the past, whereas for Brecht the move into history is a form of accessing the disastrousness of the present. In contrast, the past exists for Blake not merely in the sense of a particular historical conjuncture but rather as a state of being that is at once originary and historically determined. The absence (or negation) of an exploitative worldview in *Songs of Innocence* does narrow the options available as to what can comprise Innocence: it is not simply a universal, always existing category reliant on an essentialist notion of itself.[4] Innocence is both responsive to and determined by its own structures. In Blake's cosmology there is a conceit in which he combines the absolute and the contemporary and presents it merely as the absolute. Yet in Blake's formulation, Innocence is determined by this other of exploitation and oppres-

---

[3] Robert Rix, in contrast to my argument, states that in the poem 'Chimney Sweeper' Innocence 'becomes ignorance blinding [children] to the way they are socially exploited' (Rix 2007, p. 111). I take issue with this argument below using Thompson and Makdisi, although Michael Löwy and Robert Sayre's work also suggests concurrence with my position.

[4] See Makdisi 1998. Also important in this regard is Siskin 1988, pp. 3–13; Welch 2010.

sion, even as he maintains a clear position that determination does not equal being solely comprised of exploitative and oppressive ways of being. Following Raymond Williams's intervention in *Marxism and Literature*, determination is better translated as limitation, a closer translation of Marx's concept of *bestimmen*.[5] In this sense, Innocence is limited to what can be rejected by the dominant society. Innocence involves a (concealed) knowing rejection of the world of Experience.

Yet Innocence is only half of the equation. The other half exists in the realm of Experience and what it connotes for Blake. Experience is that moment of proof or recognition in Blake that the realm of the actually existing world is one that must be acknowledged and, ideally, oppositionally engaged. That is, Innocence as an oppositional ideology cannot create everything in its image, and likewise cannot opt out of the world of Experience. The process of Innocence is necessary for maintaining an allegiance to something that is good in the abstract, but also very much lived in a deeply practical sense. Experience is equally necessary for the development of a way of understanding how Blakean Innocence is inverted and mobilised by the dominant classes and oppressive actors and institutions. The processes involved in Innocence's survival are always in danger of being co-opted and used in ways in which the ruling ideologies benefit, as 'organized Innocence *springs out* of Experience'.[6] Blake is aware of this and seeks to carve out a space of freedom that repels dominant attempts to reframe Innocence for its own purposes. This is the central dilemma of the *Songs of Innocence and Experience*, and it shows how deeply Blake's poetry is concerned with understanding and operating in his moment.

This may read like an unfaithful reading of Blake, an attempt to smuggle his complex world into an almost explicitly dialectical Marxist one. This suspicion is understandable, albeit misguided. Nor is this the first time that such a misunderstanding has occurred, as I will show later. I am not stating that all in Blake is 'proto-typical' of Marxism (as if such a thing were possible). On the contrary, Blake's process, while ultimately liberatory, is specifically driven through its own moment.

1   **Blake and Romanticism**

Michael Löwy and Robert Sayre's analysis of the central tenets of Romanticism informs this text considerably. Löwy formulates his central arguments in two

---

5   Williams 1977, p. 84.
6   Erdman 1969, p. 118.

pieces: his 1987 essay 'The Romantic and the Marxist Critique of Modern Civilization' and then later again in his book-length text with Robert Sayre. The key failing in critical writings on the Romantics, argue the two in the latter work, is that most examinations have sought to justify a particular theory of Romanticism with examples drawn from a select group of writers, painters, poets etc., at the expense/omission of other figures who do not fit in a particular schema. As a result, such attempts 'no doubt designate significant features that are present in the work of many Romantic writers, but they fail to deliver the essence of the phenomenon'.[7] Löwy argues that it is necessary to examine Romanticism as a way of seeing the world that stretched beyond a particular group or subset of cultural producers and encompasses the movement as a whole. My focus on Blake is informed mainly by the experience of English Romantics, and many of the commentators I refer to are likewise focused on this terrain. However, it is important to highlight that the Romantics across Europe were united in their vision against what they term the 'Quantification of Life'. As Löwy argued in his 1987 essay, 'The central feature of industrial (bourgeois) civilization that Romanticism criticizes is not the exploitation of the workers or social inequality – although these may also be denounced, particularly by leftist Romantics – it is the quantification of life, i.e. the total domination of (quantitative) exchange-value, of the cold calculation of price and profit, and of the laws of the market, over the whole social fabric'.[8] What Löwy's framework makes clear is that the Romantics were met with a rapidly advancing capitalist system which sought to lay waste to all it encountered, letting nothing slip either out of its sphere of domination or its systemic logic. Despite the Romantics' myriad political and aesthetic responses to capitalism, they were fundamentally concerned with the quantification of all aspects of the social, cultural and political economic realities of their age.

Even among more general appreciations of Romanticism, contemporary scholarship has been fully willing to accept that the Romantics were sharply political and often politically active. Aidan Day's *Romanticism* leaves us in no doubt of the connections between politics and literary production of the time, as does Carmen Casaliggi and Porscha Fermanis's *Romanticism: A Literary and Cultural History* in relation to the rise of human rights discourse. Even a mainstream author such as William Vaughan has argued as much in the admittedly clichéd notion that they were 'courageously facing the realities of their age'.[9]

---

7   Löwy and Sayre 2001, p. 4.
8   Löwy 1987, p. 892.
9   Vaughan 1978, p. 9. A less bombastic offering by Raymond Williams achieves the same goal: 'Than the poets from Blake and Wordsworth to Shelley and Keats there have been few gen-

Often described as hopelessly lost in an age that was most definitely no longer theirs – a description with some validity – the Romantics sought to engage with their society by way of a significant rejection of 'modernity'. Yet this opposition was the basis for energising their own times. This rejection of capitalist modernity is highly important for Romanticism in general,[10] but also for Blake in particular.

Part and parcel of the quantification of the world was a disenchantment of ideas that capital deemed antithetical to its own purposes, a point that Marx and Engels, inheritors of the Romantic rebellion, also advanced. Löwy and Sayre quote a particularly telling passage from *The Communist Manifesto* in which the two argued that the effect of the rise of capitalist modernity involved the extinguishing of the non-quantifiable energies of previous systems. They note, 'Marx observed that "the most heavenly ecstasies of religious fervor, of chivalrous enthusiasm, of philistine sentimentalism" of the past had been submerged by the bourgeoisie, "drowned ... in the icy water of egotistical calculation"'.[11] The reaction of the Romantic project, largely defined, was the activation of a resistance meant to reverse this process. As Löwy and Sayre note, 'Romanticism may be viewed as being to a large extent a reaction on the part of "chivalrous enthusiasm" against the "icy water" of rational calculation and against the Entzauberung der Welt – leading to an often desperate attempt to reenchant the world'.[12] The idea that Blake's work represents a reaction to the 'icy water of rational calculation' should incite little argument. However, to describe this rejection of the 'Entzauberung der Welt [disenchantment of the world]' as a 'desperate attempt to reenchant the world' cannot be said as easily of Blake. Blake surely expresses desperation when one considers the fervency with which he rejects his own society. Yet the desperation can often result in a desire merely to reconstruct the past in largely uncritical ways. Rather than a thinking through of the issue at hand, there is lurching back in search of a form of society which is nonetheless deeply implicated in the same abhorrent power relations as the current one. In such a regression, reconstruction of the idealised older order frequently leads to a glorification of and desire for a re-imposition of facets of feudalism, without

---

      erations of creative writers more deeply interested and more involved in study and criticism of the society of their day' (Williams 1983, p. 30). The chapter 'The Romantic Artist', remains a useful analysis and has a refreshing boldness of language. See also Day 2012 and Casaliggi and Fermanis 2016.

10   A general but worthy study in this regard is Lussier and Matsunaga 2008.
11   Löwy and Sayre 2001, p. 29.
12   Löwy and Sayre 2001, p. 30.

critically acknowledging the real oppressive and exploitative nature of that system, merely in an attempt to rid oneself of the present's undesirable circumstances.[13] Blake stands contrary to this desperation in that his rejection of life's quantification is of a more thoroughgoing and comprehensive sort than was the case with most of his fellow Romantics. He seeks to reenergise his society by working through the logic of capitalist modernity and by arguing for justice for those who are oppressed and expropriated. Thus, I agree with Löwy's statement that 'The essential characteristic of Romantic anti-capitalism is a thorough critique of modern industrial (bourgeois) civilization (including the process of production and work) in the name of certain pre-capitalist social and cultural values ...'.[14] However, at the same time, the political impulses of Blake were to re-energise the present and also to occupy it, thereby saving the present from those who sought to monopolise it. This does not involve opting out fully, but rather working through the system's logics and monopolising discourse. Blake takes the contemporary at its face value and makes known that which it occludes or leaves aside. Blake's particular form of oppositional aesthetics necessarily revolves around a dialectical analysis of his modernity, which requires an understanding of its key impulses and drives while simultaneously examining how these require the liberatory spirits to be extinguished and disempowered. This is very far from a naïve re-enchanting of the world. Blake's *Songs of Innocence and Experience* represent an attempt to dialectically dissect society from a dissenting position. These poems argue against the nascent and established ideologies and experienced worlds of modernity by working through its contradictions and omissions.

Unlike Brecht, Blake did not have the fully formed concept of capitalism available to him, nor any systematic or likewise formulated critique of the system upon which he could draw. However, this should not preclude the descriptor 'anti-capitalist' being applied to his work. Charges of anachronism miss the point that Blake's work is not closed to the future. To not have the ability to understand the system in its totality should not invalidate his anti–

---

13 What is particularly important here is the work of Raymond Williams in his major work *The Country and the City*. In that work Williams investigates the way in which the glory days of so-called 'organic' communities are often an attempt to re-impose paternalist forms of oppression onto the present. In this regard, the emphasis of the country manor poems is a background glance at the supposed halcyon days of a peaceable community, which was in fact built on the foundations of one of the largest-scale examples of expropriation in Europe, the Enclosures Act. See Williams 1985.

14 Löwy 1987, p. 891.

capitalism, especially when one considers the extent to which his work foresaw areas of capitalist domination that would become the focus of contemporary scholarship almost two centuries after his death.[15]

2   Expect Poison, Demand Movement

Nothing kills the revolutionary, redemptive, inspiration of God for Blake more than the destruction of its power in the name of those who purport to carry it forward. Conversely, nothing is more prized in Blake than the achievement of that inspiration through the mediation of the mind and enjoyment of the body.[16] In this mediation of the living, working human, the revolutionary impact of Blake's work is most pronounced. In this relationship, the stress on movement in partial dialectical opposition to stillness is vital.[17] Being inside the flow of creativity and experiment as the fulfilment of human activity very much

---

[15]   One case of note, as Joel Kovel argues, is surveillance studies. As he argues in his analysis of Blake's *Milton*, 'There is an entire economy of accusation in the regime of Satanic Mills, watching, nagging, hemming in the mass, extracting power for the aggrandizement of the state. War is its matrix. And the system prepares for war in all its Mills, bringing the Satanic arts of surveillance to bear on the workers in advanced, monopoly capital, where productivity is the mode, and a century-old process of controlling and invading the bodies of workers are the norm: "quality control" is the fine structure of domination, the quiet, everyday humiliation of the worker, the control that does not speak its own name' (Kovel 2010, p. 14).

[16]   One post-modern interpretation of the body in Blake seems to argue that it is impossible for such a connection as the one I suggested above to exist. Erin M. Gross notes that 'The body in Blake's work points to the inability of comprehension to catch up to the lived experience that the body makes possible' (Gross 2010, p. 414). I don't see a necessary disjunction between the thought and action of the body. In fact, in Blake's cosmology, the two can never fully be disassociated from the other. This is not to deny Nicholas Williams's claim that 'If Blake is a poet willing to acknowledge the difficulty of being born, then he is also one who seems to acknowledge the difficulty of seeing and knowing oneself in motion' (Williams 2009, p. 491). Difficulty is one matter, inability is another. The latter invites a discussion of the problems of materiality and becoming, the former invites none.

[17]   In *Innocence* even Blake's own work is implicated in the aversion to permanence. As Edward Said has noted, '… the opening poem of Blake's *Songs of Innocence* represents the poet as using a reed – "a rural pen" – to write his happy songs for the joy of every child. His paper is the water which is stained as he "writes": but one's inclination is to associate innocence in the poem with impossibility of a permanent inscription in the water. The one line of the poem that suggests a troubling of innocence is "And I stain'd the water clear." Nevertheless, the ambiguously placed adjective "clear" offsets the threat in "stain'd", so that one can read the line to mean either "I stained the water until it became clear" or

defines Blake's approach, and its opposite is the product of Blake's greatest fears. This fundamental duality is expressed in the following passage from the 'Excerpt to the Marriage of Heaven and Hell'. Blake writes:

> The fox provides for himself, but God provides for the lion.
> Think in the morning. Act in the noon. Eat in the evening. Sleep in the night.
> He who has suffer'd you to impose on him, knows you.
> As the plow follows words, so God rewards prayers.
> The tygers of wrath are wiser than the horses of instruction.
> Expect poison from the standing water.
> You never know what is enough unless you know what is more than enough.[18]

There is a deeply connected sentiment expressed in these last two lines and one that offers help in finding an origin to the stream of his thought. While Blake will rely at times on a circular logic, wherein the end goal is merely a beginning again of the same process, he does not see all attempts at making or producing as equal. Indeed, what terrifies Blake, and this is the poisonous source of the standing water, is those attempts to rule out the conditions of productive activity. The poison exists when production cannot. It is better thus to go too far than to not go far enough.[19] There are forces, particularly authoritarian religious, commodifying and sexist, which excel in producing standing

---

"my pen stained the clear water": in both cases the conclusion is that because he writes on water, which even if momentarily stained would not retain the imprint, the poet composes happy (and clear) songs' (Said 1975, pp. 203–4).

[18] Blake 1988, p. 37. There is a tendency to read the lines above as the culmination of a particular line of abstracting thought: as in the criticism of the early Brecht, one abstracts from the poetry by treating it as a *mere* philosophy on the role of reading and interpretation, emphasising the importance of doing rather than thinking. Yet such an approach neglects the important line 'As the plow follows words, so God rewards prayers'. What Blake seems to be hinting at here is not a choice of words over actions, but rather words that are inspired by actions. This requires a deeper understanding of the moment of action, of labour in its own instance and its movement that will invoke inspiration. This version of Blake requires a more complex analysis than the clichéd version of the poet with his head trained only towards the sky (particularly of a Blake only obsessed with angels and spirits in the trees). Yet works which have attempted to stress the importance of this relation of the material and the philosophical in Brecht have often left out the role of the structured society that Blake was interested in countering.

[19] Blake's notion of radicalism thus finds comfort in excess, which would have distanced him further from other forms of radicalism of his time. As Makdisi notes, 'Radicalism in

waters of thought. Blake is deeply distrustful of these. He is acutely wary of the colonisation of the one extreme of Innocence, of potential, of pleasurable lived experiences, by the other, in particular those elements in Experience that seek to make Innocence a commodifiable, useable entity to reinforce their own power and clamp down on innocent desire and need.

The trepidation that builds around such extreme caution is borne out of an acknowledgment of the destructive powers of capitalism. The lack of movement is a symbol of organised inertia causing a virtual death, as one is not aware of one's life's potential. The constriction of movement both destroys life-making potential while benefiting those who profit from such a constriction. To paraphrase Rosa Luxemburg, in a metaphor that Blake would like, one cannot notice one's chains if one doesn't move. These energies, while constricted, are never fully extinguished and their potential sets up a moment of tension between the state of things, understood as the totality of human experience and action and the possibility of what could be different. Saree Makdisi has nicely articulated this point in his *William Blake and the Impossible History of the 1790s*. He writes: 'The question, in other words, is whether life is to be the instrumental and reified life of the organized organism ... or, on the contrary, the joyous life of the "prolific", indefinite open, reaching out toward an infinitely prolific number of re-makings, re-connections, re-imaginations – life as pure potential, life as constituent, rather than constituted power'.[20] For Blake this constituted power makes itself known in all aspects of life; in work, in freedom to and from work, in all of life's spoken and, importantly, unspoken activities. In this way, Blake's poetics have also led to attempts to break down the totality of his 'prolific, indefinite open, reaching out' thought into a reified space which imposes 'an interpretive frame' that limits the reader's creative appreciation of his work.[21] This process abstracts away, as we saw with Brecht's *Mann ist Mann*, the complexity and openness of Blakean materiality. This is an important distinction between Blake and fellow Romantics William Wordsworth and Samuel Taylor Coleridge. There is in the latter two a keen sense of withdrawal from these determining and limiting forces that Raymond Williams highlights in Coleridge's conception of poetic imagination. Williams notes that: '... on the act of creation; as Wordsworth described it so often, or as Coleridge put it, from the disturbance within the apparent calm ... It is not now the will that is to

---

the 1790s, at least in its hegemonic formulation, must be understood as a project to locate and articulate a middle-class sensibility as against the unruly excesses of both higher and lower orders' (Makdisi 2006a, p. 22).

20   Makdisi 2003, p. 266.
21   Makdisi 2015, p. 2.

transform nature; it is the lonely creative imagination; the man (sic) driven back from the cold world and in his own natural perception and language seeking to find and recreate man'.[22] What defines the movement involved above is less hope and inspiration, and more individual escape. In contrast, Blake's reliance on escape is a means to find inspiration, but one that relies on labour to translate into action. The past operates so as to open new possibilities, those unattainable to the 'lonely creative', seemingly divorced from the impurity of the labouring classes. In Blake's construction, often his concept of the imagination (as mentioned more generally within the Romantic tradition) is offered as one which would lead us away from the material and into the realm of pure ideas. Yet there exists another option that seeks to reject that dualism and put forth another possibility: 'For Blake's concept of the imagination unifies body and mind, thought and action, material and immaterial, not in the sense that it mediates between them, but in the sense that it marks the deployment of pure creative ontological power on both a mental and material plane. It is, in other words, the experience of a materialist ontology'.[23] This experience of a materialist ontology attempts to be all-encompassing. Not in the teleological or predictive sense, or even inclusive of all that it produces, but rather in the way in which Innocence implicitly and explicitly celebrates a non-repressive, creative world which is necessarily open-ended. In contrast very much to our own times, the notion of imagination is part of lived reality. Innocence, its production in the everyday, and specifically Blake's production of it, are at one and the same time unique instances of productive life. Imagination is almost coterminous with productivity in this regard. As Makdisi notes, 'Imagination here is the process by which such images of truth are produced: it is the process by which lived, experienced reality is brought into being. The freedom to imagine is the power to create the world ...'.[24]

Blake's emphasis on productivity, his desire to make imagination a lived way of being, provides a reminder also of his connection to God: not as a God of rules and prescriptions, but of good, nurturing life that reproduces itself through the nature of God in our lives. Here, 'power is human rather than divine' in that 'such divine power is here recognized as inherently human'.[25] And yet, as Axel Staehler notes: 'Divine revelation is not a singular occurrence in the past but happens time and again anew, and occurs individually for every

---

22   See Williams 1985, p. 132.
23   Makdisi 2003, p. 266.
24   Makdisi 2003, p. 267.
25   Ibid.

human being'.[26] This unique process of reproduction of innocent life through the imagination is put forward in the poems 'Laughing Song', 'A Cradle Song', and 'The Divine Image'. What we see in these is a progression of nature's connections in (pro-)creation, creation, and maintenance, and a philosophical examination of the natural inclination that is reflected ultimately in God's own vision of the innocent life.

The first six lines of the 'Laughing Song', much as the title would have us believe, centre on how everything in innocent life seems bent on pleasure. They read as follows:

> When the green woods laugh, with the voice of joy
> And the dimpling stream runs laughing by,
> When the air does laugh with our merry wit,
> And the green hill laughs with the noise of it
> When the meadows laugh with lively green
> And the grasshopper laughs in the merry scene[27]

'The green woods', 'the dimpling stream', 'the air', 'the green hill', 'the meadows', and 'the grasshopper' all laugh, either of their own accord or through interaction with the human 'merry wit'.[28] The natural world follows our human lead, and this is reciprocated in the poem as the last six lines are human-centric. Nature is not merely given over to us, but conjoins with the way that humanity conceives of the pleasure-making processes of life. This is not to anthropomorphise the woods, stream, air or hill but to make them a part of the same process. Humanity's life-giving force is mirrored: as nature offers up delights, so too are we then delighted by it. The similarities do not stop here. Nature comes alive with its connection to humanity and reaches a fuller fruition by its extension through the prism of human imagination, often as a metaphor for both human production and reproduction. The poem offers 'a profound unity, a sense of commonality and unruptured mutuality linking us all joyously together'.[29] In order to extend this unruptured mutuality, Blake employs subtle sexual imagery to further bind the two.

The 'sweet round mouths' of 'Mary and Susan and Emily' is a physically pleasurable utterance, as is the fact that they sing 'Ha, ha he!' At the very least, there is a sense of double entendre here. This reading is given more credibility

---

26   Staehler 2008, p. 105.
27   Blake 1988, p. 11.
28   Ibid.
29   Makdisi 2015, p. 73.

when we read that 'our table with cherries and nuts is spread'. The final entreaty to 'Come live, and be merry, and join with me, To sing the sweet chorus of Ha, ha, he!'[30] is an equation of sexual pleasure and the pleasure of the natural world more generally. They are, if not inseparable, at the very least complementary. The introduction of the pleasure and joys of the natural world with their connection to humanity's role in their existence (for instance, 'the painted birds laugh in the shade'), lends a certain degree of conjoined frivolity, and sexual frivolity, herewith.

It would be wrong to equate the physical enjoyment of sex, and in particular the playfulness of this portrayal of sexuality, with procreation, designed with a purpose wherein pleasure is a mere inducement to the larger act. Indeed, we are provided little evidence here that Blake is referring to heteronormative sex, given that the three names mentioned are women's. However, the poem that follows is about the raising of a young child. Love is in this sense extended towards another who cannot appreciate it, especially as regards a unity of multiples (albeit with a maintenance of difference). This involves loving more purely in the sense of a gift. Whereas the joy of nature and sex in 'The Laughing Song' took place during the day, in the evening we find an ode to care and protection of a sleeping child, or perhaps a child struggling to find sleep.[31]

Sleep should offer a moment without hardship, though Blake suggests that all may be not well with the warning that the child should 'Sleep, sleep, happy child, / While o'er thee doth mother weep'.[32] In the midst of this sadness, the child's peace and the parent's care signify the promise of redemption that we

---

30   Blake 1988, p. 11.
31   While not the focus of this text, it should be noted that although Blake is seen as almost synonymous with progressive sexual politics, so much so that Susan Matthews has stated that 'Blake has stood for a prophet of sexual freedom in popular culture in the latter part of the twentieth century', his later writings (not including the *Songs of Innocence and Experience*) have been 'seen as characterized by ambiguity at best, ambivalence, contradiction and even misogyny at worst' (Matthews 2011, p. 1). Likewise, as Jon Mee notes, although Blake will 'return again and again to the theme of sexual freedom' and sexual freedom was 'treated as part and parcel of political liberation', there was nevertheless a 'tendency among the male prophets of women's liberation to limit that liberation to the sexual sphere' (Mee 1992, pp. 144–5). For a considerable grounding of Blake's contradictory feminisms during the 1790s see Bruder 1997, pp. 90–132. As with sexuality more generally, Blake was far more open to including, in at times very non-regressive ways, issues of gay and lesbian sexualities. His notion of homosexuality in many ways bore the marks of his time, yet it is not sufficient simply to state that he reproduced them. An exhaustive view is provided in Hobson 2000 and also Bruder and Connolly 2010.
32   Blake 1988, p. 12.

find in the reliance on others, but also in the innocent world's offering of unity in compassion and love. Humanity is not alone in this as, like Innocence, it is cast in a cosmological frame. In the mother's weeping, for instance, we find the sympathetic nature of God. 'Sweet babe, once like thee / Thy Maker lay, and wept for me'.[33] Nor is the connection between the mother and child, and mother and God, the end of it. There is a third connector: 'Infant smiles are his own smiles; Heaven and earth to peace beguiles'.[34] The correlation of the infant to the heavenly is a further instantiation of the deeper sense of unity that exists in Innocence. At every level of compassion we see how another becomes represented: 'Sweet babe, in thy face / Holy image I can trace'.[35]

It is useful to contrast the focus on care that Blake is at pains to unravel – and which has sunk so deeply into his philosophy – with Wordsworth's 'The Prelude', in particular the encounter between the poet and a discharged soldier. The soldier, worse for wear but seemingly healthy, is in need. During a period of mutual yet distant discussion, the poet leads the soldier to a house where the owner or tenant will take care of him. The poet admonishes the soldier to take better care of himself and the soldier replies: 'My trust is in the God of Heaven, And in the eye of him who passes me'. The reader is left with a sense of support having been offered and received, but in a principally formalistic manner. The soldier's pain provides a backdrop to the poem, and the potential for a sincere connection between the travellers is unfulfilled. As Nancy Yousef writes, 'Sympathetic identification is not achieved, the other's immediate need is nonetheless recognized and met, but both as affective and ethical experience, the encounter is just that: a pause before each passes the other by, a moment of intimacy without consequence'.[36] Blake acknowledges that being free of an oppression that exists everywhere in the tragedy of Experience is at once seemingly an impossibility yet, paradoxically, also the only present antidote for an exploitative world, which seeks to colonise all in and out of its path. Care is the way through to the other side, and therefore Innocence should not be read merely as an exasperated critique of the current order. Blake was mindful of the ways in which there were only a few moments that opened up a possibility incompatible with the tyranny of a totalising capitalist world. All language and activity (not just biblical) is not merely fused with meaning but rather is immersed in the *struggle* over meaning. If exploitation acts in such a way as to almost bar opposition to it, then an aspect of resistance to this involves main-

---

33   Blake 1988, p. 12.
34   Ibid.
35   Ibid.
36   Yousef 2013, p. 88.

taining something that is universally good, and to a very large extent, 'pure'. In Blakean terms, this purity is not uniform but rooted in difference and acceptance.

In the poem 'The Little Black Boy' there is a clear demonstration of the pitfalls associated with the notion of purity. The poem, *prima facie*, suggests offensive racial over/undertones. The opening lines, in particular, stand out as problematic; 'My mother bore me in the southern wild, And I am black, but oh my soul is white!' seems to confirm the racial hierarchies of the time.[37] Whiteness bears the marks of superiority, and likewise there is an equation of whiteness and 'civilized' Englishness. Whiteness also bears the mark of blessings, while blackness stands as a marker for deprivation and lack, as the last line of the first stanza notes, 'But I am black, as if bereaved of light'.[38] Read in relation to the rest of the poem, the meanings here shift considerably. At this stage of the poem we are hearing from the black boy himself, but he is in conversation with his mother, a teacher, who challenges this thought. As Elizabeth A. Bohls notes, 'The child's African mother teaches him a lesson about God, nature and human bodies, a lesson that questions in significant ways what we come to recognize as the imposed colonial mentality of the first stanza'.[39] The lesson involves equating racial attitudes to 'a cloud, and like a shady grove' which obscure from the light of God. This importantly involves our collective 'learn[ing] to bear the beams of love'.[40] The lesson is to jettison the binds of racism and racial authority and, in the second last stanza, the child arrives at a state which contradicts the problematic formulation referenced above. As Blake states, 'When I from black and he from white cloud free, / And round the tent of God like lambs we joy'.[41] Whiteness and Blackness as racial categories of superiority and inferiority obscure us from understanding our indivisible humanity. Interestingly, and in opposition to standard colonial narratives of the time of the learned white and instructed brown learner, in the final stanza it is the black child that takes on the role of his mother in teaching the young white boy how to bear the light of God's love.[42] It is important to note the significance in such a rebuke to ruling

---

37 Blake 1988, p. 9.
38 Ibid.
39 Bohls 2013, p. 63.
40 Blake 1988, p. 9.
41 Ibid.
42 It should be noted that in two persuasive readings of the poem, Makdisi's *William Blake* and Bohls's *Romantic Literature*, much discussion is given over to the physical representation of the black child in Blake's attendant visual to the poem. While this discussion is vital and lends more ambiguity to the reading of the poem (what are we to make of the fact that in one image the child is brown, while in another he is pink?), my main argu-

racial orthodoxy, an orthodoxy that could advocate for freedom through critical reason, and yet suggests the vast majority – the 'mob' especially – were incapable of reaching such heights and could therefore be occluded from political discussions, while 'the dominant radicals would repeatedly point to the Orient as the prime example'[43] of why the tent of the cognoscenti should be small. Makdisi goes further, by arguing that 'Blake was basically the *only* major poet of the late eighteenth and early nineteenth centuries who categorically refused to dabble in recognizably Orientalist themes or motifs'.[44] This was not merely the case in poetry, as there is evidence of these themes occupying Mary Shelley's *Frankenstein; or, The Modern Prometheus*. Anne K. Mellor makes the point that in this text, the reconstruction of a racially hybrid partner for the Creature displays Victor Frankenstein's Orientalism, by way of his assuredness that, as she writes, it 'can only be a degenerate monster'. This stands in contrast to Shelley's description of a racial 'amalgamation' which 'might represent a positive evolution of the human species'.[45] This motif was at the very least occupying Romantic thinkers, yet Blake's poetics stand as an exception to the dominance of racial and imperial norms among them.

In 'The Little Black Boy' humanity is reflective of God's most benevolent state. Despite Blake's protestations against the standing water, there exists a form of stasis in God's purity. Stasis, rather than a block on human creativity and the making possible, acts as a form of protection against the world of Experience in which racial categories are necessary to maintain the system. Yet this version of stasis involves a state of being that is simultaneously a state of becoming. In order for this benevolence to become a reality, we must arrive at a time '… when our souls have learn'd the heat to bear'.[46] That is, in order for God to have purpose, God must be made living in the everyday both in exemplary moments of Innocence but also by maintaining innocent life in trying circumstances.

What is striking in 'The Divine Image' is that Blake suggests how God's action in the world manifests itself, but also suggests that the gesture goes further by portraying humanity as reflective of and constituting the Divine. The clearest evidence presented in defence of the natural goodness that Blake displays is in fact part of *Innocence*. Note the duplication in the following:

---

ment – that the poem offers up the notion that difference and unity are not opposites and need not be reducible in their entirety to racial hierarchies – is still tenable. See Makdisi 2003, p. 165 and Bohls 2013, pp. 64–6.
43 Makdisi 2003, p. 207.
44 Makdisi 2003, p. 209.
45 Mellor 2003, p. 192.
46 Blake 1988, p. 9.

> For Mercy, Pity, Peace, and Love,
> Is God our father dear:
> And Mercy Pity Peace and Love,
> Is Man his child and care.[47]

This is a poem not merely of relation but of equivalence. The mirroring of the two lines provides a clear sense of the reproduction of God in humanity. Yet while the first two lines lend themselves to a description of God's nature, the following two are a description of action, especially when one considers the relational nature of humanity and the natural world in 'A Laughing Song', 'A Cradle Song', and also 'The Little Black Boy'. While God is, in the terms referred to earlier, a pure being of goodness in nature,[48] the trinity of man (as humanity), child, and care are the products of nature in action and in this way inseparable. Christopher Z. Hobson argues similarly that 'Exactly the distinction between human and transcendent Jesus …. is one that Blake has denied since his early works, such as 'The Divine Image''.[49] This connected existence to the Divine is interdependent on its own reproduction. This reproduction necessitates the nature of God made alive, and this is 'Mercy Pity Peace and Love'. The grammar here is particularly telling, as the use of semicolon is literally meant to join the independent clauses.[50] Blake may at times be very creative with grammar and often eschews its norms, but this particular instance seems, given the content here, to be a symbolic formal strategy. This formal aspect is further found in the poem's title, 'The Divine Image'. The poem continues,

> For Mercy has a human heart
> Pity, a human face:
> And Love, the human form divine,
> And Peace, the human dress.[51]

Blake carefully devotes a line to each aspect of humanity's reflection of God made real. In the image, in the moment before it can be spoiled, he maintains

---

47   Blake 1988, p. 12.
48   David Erdman argues the three poems under examination here do not have the satiric bent that others in *Innocence* do. He notes: 'Their social purpose is larger – to construct one of the foundation of an imaginatively organized and truly happy prosperity' (Erdman 1969, pp. 126–7).
49   Hobson 1999, p. 224.
50   On Blake's intentional use of syntax and grammar in *Songs of Innocence* see Chandlers 2006, pp. 112–13.
51   Blake 1988, pp. 12–13.

the belief in cleanliness, in the state of Innocence. What we see here is the beginning of the end of a trinity of a composition of life, founded on an alternative notion of humanity than that offered by the dominant forces and their structures of feeling.

While admitting the advancement of a religious politics of Innocence, it would be a mischaracterisation of Blake to suggest that he looks merely to negate an oppressive politics by his oppositional way of viewing and being in the world. Blake does not offer a mere rejection of the corollary but offers what Thompson terms a 'contrary state'. The distinction is relevant as it illustrates both the necessity of responding to the current moment in Blake and a refusal to accept its dominant features as the only way out. In an earlier model for the poem 'Divine Image', we see an example of this mirroring:

> Cruelty has a Human Heart
> And Jealousy a Human Face
> Terror, the Human Form Divine
> And Secrecy, the Human Dress
> The Human Dress, is forged Iron
> The Human Form, a Fiery Forge.
> The Human Face, a Furnace seal'd
> The Human Heart, its hungry Gorge.[52]

Terror and Love equally stand on opposite poles of the Human Form in this framing. This is likewise the case with Pity and Jealousy, Cruelty and Mercy, etc. The fact that Blake rejected this mirror opposition is telling. The opposite of Innocence is not Experience. Experience, as I will argue, involves a conscious knowing of what you and others desire in the world, and which forces exist to deform and purposefully empty out the content of Blake's productive and active-minded politics. What we should draw from this is that Blake rejects the straight negation of The Divine Image. The trinity is also a representation of unity, and one which attempts to shield us from the penetration of the world depicted in Experience.

While the more common deployment of God, especially those depictions characterised in *Songs of Experience*, works towards an abstraction of human relations, the use of God here produces the opposite effect. The title, 'Divine Image', potentially reflects the source of the human malady, but again one must note that the source of the error is the image of God as a static entity which

---

52   Thompson 1995, p. 204.

must be obeyed, and not God as a process to be discussed and struggled over. In Blake's alternative reading, God produces an ever-greater materiality and becomes a practised thing, even if the dominant practice's object is to remove the idea that God is something that can exist differently to different people. This materiality is caught in an interesting circle, as the more it is grounded in the totality of social relations, the more it attempts to make impossible its own undoing and, in that, change.[53] Here we have again the principle which objects to 'Standing Water'. Nature itself depends on movement, on the overcoming of itself and transference into something else. Thus, an attempt to fix any particular moment of the godly into a series of set rituals is anathema to Blake.[54] It is for this reason that Innocence has an impulse that is its own, devoid of Experience's determining influence. Yet for this reason, Innocence involves the necessity of continual active creation in life as it is constantly lived, and that Innocence must reckon with, and define itself in relation to, *Experience*. And here again is where the connection with Brecht, in the creation of an aesthetic politics of the now, is so vital. For Brecht, the contemporary moment defines the nature of an aesthetic response. It defines what its categories of reference are, but also involves the duty to explore that moment. The general theory of opposition is a *sine qua non* of oppositional political aesthetics, but it must be continually lived and shaped to its own time.

A significant part of Blake's particular constellation is formed with another quite radical tradition.[55] Blake was by no means alone in framing a way of

---

53 Martin Bidney has metaphorically contrasted Blake's natural philosophy with the German Romantic J.W. Goethe in an adept passage: 'Blake and Goethe share a Heraclitean awareness of the omnipresence of change … Blake presents Becoming as a Heraclitean fire; Goethe as a Heraclitean river' (Bidney 1988, p. 76).

54 As Jeremy Tambling suggests in regards to the first half of the poem 'The Garden of Love', but I think this can be applied more broadly to those positive evocations of nature in Blake, 'The 'garden of love', the activity of playing on the green and the 'sweet flowers' exist in a continuum' (Tambling 2005, p. 8). While *Experience* will end this continuum, that it exists in Blake's philosophy is vital.

55 With Brecht, the key frame of reference was a capitalist order that was impacting on the formation of new, easily malleable individuals who would reject their own interests by, among other things, embracing the influence of the 'bad collective'. There is less of an emphasis in Blake on the creation of an oppositional bloc (although there is ample evidence that he was active in creating oppositional movements of his day, most notably through his opposition to slavery, as represented by his work with Richard Steadman). There is nevertheless in his work an attempt to put forward an alternate oppositional thought that would reject the dominant structure of life. The question for Blake in this regard is: what makes the 'standing water stand'? For the *Song of Innocence and Experience*, the concentration of power and the forms of abuse that come with that power is perhaps the best place to begin.

seeing or imagining a world of thought that sought to disentangle itself from dominant ideologies. The tradition that he channels is antinomianism, and its centrality to Blake's work should not be underestimated.[56] Thompson defines this tradition as follows: 'Antinomianism, indeed, is not a place at all, but a way of breaking out from received wisdom and moralism, and entering upon new possibilities'.[57] Blake's own inheritance of the politics of antinomianism, if we follow Thompson,[58] produces a specifically oppositional politics for his own time. While the features of antinomianism will change according to the specific historical time in which they are found,[59] for Blake they are linked to issues of poverty and social justice. It is a feature of this tradition of radical religious thought,[60] as with Blake's conception of Innocence, that God must be made real in lived relations. The greater belief in what God represents and entails is more important than a stricture of observance. As Thompson notes, 'Faith must always take priority to form'.[61] God's form is only a semblance, an

---

56   In contrast to other commentators, Thompson is at pains to make clear that this tradition does not merely influence Blake's work but rather notes 'its structural centrality' (Thompson 1995, p. 20). It is useful to point out, as Michael Ferber does, that through this tradition Blake shared many of the same beliefs and viewpoints as Gerard Winstanley, the radical Digger of the century preceding Blake's, and Ferber goes so far as to state that Blake is Winstanley's political heir. See Ferber 1985. Thompson also briefly notes this influence, particularly when he refers to Winstanley's depiction of 'the God of magistrates, property-owners and the Church [as] "the God Devil"' (Thompson 1995, p. 22). While the political impulse of Winstanley's position would find favour in Blake, the focus on love and imagination would've shaped him as well. See Winstanley 1986, pp. 317–32.
57   Thompson 1995, p. 20.
58   While Thompson's work on Blake's antinomianism is largely its first major treatment, there are some texts that take issue with it, specifically on the exact type of Blake's inheritance of antinomianism. See Davies and Worrall 2012, pp. 30–47. While there may be some validity to such a re-appreciation of the specific strains and trajectories in Blake's work, and while there has been some disagreement of the origins of Thompson's configuration of Blake's inheritance of the antinomian tradition, it should suffice to note, as Jon Mee has done, that 'The point is that antinomianism and millenarianism of varying degrees of extremism remained available in the popular culture of the eighteenth century. If this is accepted, Blake seems less the mystic who reproduced beliefs that had generally disappeared than someone whose radicalism was the product of a dialogue with the complex nexus of popular enthusiasm' (Mee 1994, p. 43).
59   As A.L. Morton has suggestively noted, 'Blake was the greatest English Antinomian, but also the last' (Morton 1966, p. 36).
60   While there is some disagreement on the actual form of antinomianism that Blake allied himself with, Jon Mee writes that: 'Practical antinomianism, on the other hand, involved a conviction of a finished state of salvation in the here and now which led to an active rejection of the authority of the law, sometimes to the point of rejoicing in sinfulness as an occasion for the outpouring of God's grace' (Mee 1992, p. 58).
61   Thompson 1995, p. 9.

outline of an image. It offers a hint towards a particular instantiation, but this is as much as it can offer. As Makdisi notes, '… the antinomian tradition with which Blake engaged locates in its faith in the eternal and the infinite – that is, in God – a concept of particularity that cannot be reduced to a single, definite, and reified – and hence quantifiable, measurable, and interchangeable – form, even though it is "infinitely various"'.[62] The most explicit statement of this form is that Innocence is a love that should be directed towards another, as one would love God. Acceptance of everyone is necessary as God is in everyone. Life is a continuous radical gesture of becoming and developing a connection with one's social world. Innocence thus involves an enacted purity of position.

Innocence is something irreducible that also negates any attempts to deny itself according to religious affiliation. As the final stanza of the 'Divine Image' runs:

> And all must love the human form,
> In heathen, turk, or jew.
> Where Mercy, Love & Pity dwell,
> There God is dwelling too[63]

Innocence here implies an 'immanent understanding of God [that] does not impose unity at the expense of difference'.[64] This immanence of God, 'A God constituted from below rather than existing independently of us from on high',[65] fills every aspect of life, and only when life is fulfilled in this way can we reach the stage of love.

The form of this godly intervention is only possible through human interaction, yet its pulse can often seem faint. While Blake scholarship has at times supported an unhelpful dichotomy of city as place of dirt and decadence and country as place of refuge and hope, such a binary is consistently bucked by Blake himself. He makes clear that the countryside, or the natural world as such, is no simple refuge. There is hope there but the actual living situation is much different, especially as the dominant systems begin to apply their systemic logic, subjecting it to market rule. Indeed, as quoted in George Orwell's 'Such, Such Were the Joys',[66] the conservative representation of the countryside that occludes the laborious reality of rural production and the exploitation which

---

62   Makdisi 2003, p. 323.
63   Blake 1988, p. 13.
64   Makdisi 2015, p. 69.
65   Makdisi 2015, p. 52.
66   See Orwell 1994, p. 147.

sustains it also seeks to present a vision of the pure countryside as the antithesis to the corrupt city. Blake's passage, which Orwell marshals in his essay, reads as follows:

> Such such were the joys.
> When we all girls & boys,
> In our youth-time were seen
> On the Ecchoing Green.[67]

As in Orwell's essay, these lines are intended as a rebuke to those who would idealise nature. Indeed, one need only keep reading to see that this joyous scene is, crucially, no longer to be found:

> Like birds in their nest,
> Are ready for rest,
> And sport no more seen,
> On the darkening Green.[68]

While there is a strong argument to make that Blake dismisses an ideal past of pleasure in nature, it is another thing entirely to suggest that Blake is claiming that the joys of the natural world are gone.[69] Blake is not advancing a nostalgic politics here, but rather attempting, as he is doing across the whole of the *Songs of Innocence*, to show how those who are outwardly different can still be or act in mutually supportive ways. The speaker of 'Such, such were the joys' is Old John, and through the aid of the children, 'Does laugh away care'. And the poem suggests that the children are aware of this beneficence. Just as in nature 'The birds of the bush, / Sing louder around', so too do the youth offer themselves for a greater pleasure 'While our sports shall be seen / On the Ecchoing Green'.[70] The idea of the 'Ecchoing Green' suggests an action in the past, but given this reading's propensity to productivity, it is more accurate that this marks 'the

---

67   Blake 1988, p. 8.
68   Blake 1988, p. 8.
69   Orwell is not alone in this position. Steve Clark follows by arguing that the poem ends with the belief that: 'An idealized past is evoked from which the present narrator is necessarily exiled: "Ecchoing" signifies estrangement rather than proximity, the encroachment of mortality onto the "darkening Green"' (Clark 2007, p. 93). This too-literal reading of the text projects a vision of mortality that a larger reading of *Innocence* tends to negate. There is not only no exile here, the notion of echo seems to, if anything, note maintenance and reverberation as opposed to a definitive stoppage.
70   Blake 1988, p. 8.

convergence of being and becoming, of production and constitution'.[71] In this sense 'echoing' is both the noise being made in a particular moment of time as well as its reverberations felt across time. The metaphor of an echo is useful, however, in that it locates the mark of potential – it has once existed – and will continue to reverberate in another form. The potential of child's play – its inability to be harnessed by rationalist, utilitarian ends – points towards a life outside of Experience.

The 'childlike' simplicity of the poem, and the position given to children as both responders to pain and agents of change, should not be overlooked. Nick Rawlinson argues that 'Indeed, it is the inherent vulnerability of child's play that leads to the need for institutionalized religion, thus exposing the child to exploitation'.[72] While the child's inherent vulnerability makes possible the child's exploitation, it does not produce the need for institutionalised religion. Rather, it is the absence of good care that, in effect, creates a vacuum that exploitation will seek to colonise. In reference to his illuminated works, Blake stated that 'his own work has been particularly well elucidated by children, who "have taken a greater delight in contemplating my Pictures than I have ever hoped"'.[73] This is an example of how Blake's conception of justice is coloured by his analysis of the potential for inspiration in the contemporary moment, and that he cannot disconnect the role of human compassion from this kind of change. Blake shifts the terrain, arguing against the position that regards humanity's emotional world as unthinking (and thus degraded), and locates in thoughtful compassion the power of its own liberation, specifically against those forms which would negate its potential. As Stephen Goldsmith argues:

> Blake stands at the early stage of a modern critical legacy that posits the agency of emotion within and against a world that would subordinate the full capabilities of response and action to instrumental reason. Against the old enlightenment charge that enthusiasm overleaps the space of

---

71   Makdisi 2003, p. 265.
72   See Rawlinson 2003, p. 168. Blake would maintain an interest in childhood vulnerability throughout. Writing on Blake's *Urizen*, George H. Gilpen makes a link between the contrast between *Innocence* and *Experience* in different stages of the Urizenic world. He notes that in later texts, and as I have tried to argue for the *Songs* and Löwy and Sayre do above, 'What Blake does accomplish with fascinating artistry is a clear identification of the errors in the blinkered thinking of unholy priests of Enlightenment science – their stagnant pride, their meaningless abstraction, their spiritual vacuity, and their practical inhumanity' (Gilpen 2004, p. 56).
73   Makdisi 2006b, p. 111.

reflection and is therefore incompatible with the intellectual distance required by modern critical judgment, and against the charge that errant enthusiasm relies instead on experiential immediacy as evidence of its authenticity, this legacy integrates the immediacy of enthusiasm into critical practice, placing charged affect at the vanguard of critique, creativity, and change.[74]

It is illustrative to compare Blake's central inclusion of the 'agency of emotion' with an alternative positing of a duality between the two that occupies Wordsworth's 'Tintern Abbey'. As Orin N.C. Wang argues, '… Wordsworth's poem is structured around a plot of maturation away from youthful sensation to an intellectual and imaginative sobriety'.[75] The emotional world is a source of inspiration and potential for Blake and not an inhibitor of critical practice. Innocence, to extend our reading of Löwy and Sayre above, cannot be positioned (or achieved) without reference to neglect, whether neglect of compassion, human empathy or care, or even of the intellect development that depends on care. They are always inseparable from one another.[76]

The only use of the word 'innocent' in the cycle of poems is in 'Holy Thursday', a poem which more than most in the cycle makes clear the division of young and old, yet emphasises the connection between the two. The last six lines of the poem that establish this, and the state of the godly instantiation, read as follows:

> The hum of multitudes was there but multitudes of lambs
> Thousands of little boys & girls raising their innocent hands
> Now like a mighty wild they raise to heaven the voice of song
> Or like harmonious thunderings the seats of heaven among
> Beneath them sit the aged man wise guardians of the poor
> Then cherish pity, lest you drive an angel from your door[77]

In their infancy, the 'multitude of lambs', innocent, make 'harmonious thunderings' to the heavens. Here the collective is taken care of and the potential of the many (due to their harmony as the 'mighty wild' who 'raise to heaven' their song) is clear. These uproarious descriptions do not seem to harness their

---

74 Goldsmith 2009, p. 446.
75 Wang 2011, p. 177.
76 Thus, the famous line from the Preface of *Milton*, 'I will not cease from mental fight' (Blake 1988, p. 95).
77 Blake 1988, p. 13.

offerings, yet they point again to the connections between young and old, and the immanence of God is offered in the shepherding of the poor and inclusiveness that is a prerequisite of this immanence. The last lines prefigure the state of hardship that resonates through Blake's society, and clearly we are not in a 'pure' setting of the 'Ecchoing Green'. In that scene there is reason to believe Blake is suggesting something that is not the actual order of things, but the order of things as they could and should be. The use of 'lest' is a telling harbinger of the many abuses of power to come in the *Songs of Experience*. This could also be read ironically, as there exists the sense that the echo is the harm of the past that filters through to Blake's poetry. The echo represents both the remembrance of harm done and a desire to move back to a place where harm cannot exist. Immanence in this instance necessarily undercuts the reliance on the socially constructed notion of individuality. The individual is positioned in Blake's world in relation to the social fields that limit and structure their worldview. On this point, Jameson usefully interrogates the individual-centred notion of immanence. He writes, 'What this impossibility of immanence means in practice is that the dialectical reversal must always involve a painful "decentring" of the consciousness of the individual subject, whom it confronts with a determination ...'. Immanence is impossible as history cannot be received through the prism of an individual's experience. Such reception requires the active participation of a group, or, as Jameson continues, a class. There exists no moment 'in which the individual subject would be somehow fully conscious of his or her determination by class ...'. This does not, however, discount the impossibility of immanence to disrupt the tyranny of determination. This requires the unity of an organisation, as Jameson continues. 'But in the Marxian system, only a collective unity – whether that of a particular class, the proletariat, or of its "organ of consciousness", the revolutionary party – can achieve this transparency; the individual subject is always positioned within the social totality ...'.[78] Blake writes at a time before the above is anything like a fully formed idea, but his work suggests a movement in the direction towards the understanding of the social nature of the capitalist class project, while also sensing the need for a communal poetics of resistance.

 Blake was not alone in occupying this in-between space among Romantics. John Clare's 'Helpstone Green', for instance, specifically points to harm done to nature. 'Ye injur'd fields ye once where gay', Clare writes. The injury owes itself to 'The woodmans axe their shade devours / And cuts down every tree'. The destruction of nature ripples throughout, and those in charge 'They no com-

---

[78] Jameson 1994, p. 283.

passion show'.[79] The effect on nature is profound and resonates throughout Clare's society. As John Goodridge notes, 'At the heart of Clare's writing lies an intense sense of the importance and precious fragility of a "community"; most centrally, the community of the village he grew up in'.[80] Despite the time difference between the two poets, (Blake was born thirty-five years before Clare) capitalism was dominant in Blake's time, and its role in dispossessing working people continued apace in Clare's. As Jordy Rosenberg and Chi-ming Yang argue, the process of capitalist destruction for profit was the same, despite the time difference. 'The point that concerns us is this: the history of dispossession is embedded in the ontologies of capitalist spatio-temporality and in the contours of subject-formation at once'.[81] The processes of accumulation that Clare's poetry so stridently makes clear is made of the same stuff that Blake's poetry seeks to pierce through. This is the logic of capitalist accumulation.

There is a balance, an edge, on which things stand. If anything, the deployment of the term 'wise' – so categorically a term of derision in the 'Marriage of Heaven and Hell' – instructs us to beware the potential of abuse or misdirection, and as such wisdom is employed here rhetorically. This deployment of rhetorical questions is employed in the same way as Blake's question in 'On Another's Sorrow';

> Can I see another's woe,
> And not be in sorrow too.
> Can I see another's grief,
> And not seek for kind relief?[82]

At this stage, in the world of Innocence and all that comprises it, the answer is no. Yet Innocence is also lived and is thus a direction, a way of acting, being and becoming in the world, and a response to a need, as we saw at the beginning of the *Songs of Innocence* cycle. As the poem concludes, the last in the cycle, the shift to a world of Experience is prefigured;

> O! he gives to us his joy,
> That our grief he may destroy
> Till our grief is fled & gone
> He doth sit by us and moan.[83]

---

79 Clare 1986, p. 71.
80 Goodridge 2013, p. 190.
81 Rosenberg and Yang 2014, p. 142.
82 Blake 1988, p. 17.
83 Ibid.

As 'He' sits, so did the Mother before in 'A Cradle Song', and they both moan in empathy with the sufferer. Comforting someone in grief is an end in itself. Compassion is pure and necessary. It evokes that moment of connection between those in need and those able to help. This simple, loving logic of Innocence, at home in all manner of peoples and protective of differences, is consistently undone and prohibited in the world of Experience.

3 Innocence's Opposition to Experience

If in the *Songs of Innocence* we witnessed a vision or a worldview that attempted to offer a totalising (read all-encompassing – cosmological) picture of Blake's possibility-making, inspiring world, in the *Songs of Experience* we see that world toppled and replaced by an equally totalising worldview of modern capitalism and its commodifying, monopolising rationality. While Blake is not shy in using repetition of words, images or metaphors throughout his work as a formal strategy (which is sometimes problematic for critics, as the same signifier denotes an entirely different meaning depending on a subtle shift of context), few are as pronounced as the repetition of the 'every' in one of the most notable offerings, 'London', in the *Songs of Experience*. The word is repeated seven times[84] and in each we are left with little ambiguity as to its intent.

> I wander thro' each charter'd street,
> Near where the charter'd Thames does flow.
> And mark in every face I meet
> Marks of weakness, marks of woe.
> In every cry of every Man,
> In every Infants cry of fear,
> In every voice: in every ban,
> The mind-forg'd manacles I hear:
> How the Chimney-sweepers cry

---

[84] While 'charter'd' and 'every' capture attention, given the repetition, the words dirt and dirty should also be noted. As Susan Matthews argues, 'But the flatly unpoetic "dirty" was there for a reason. Dirt is not only a literal feature of Blake's Lambeth but also an image of the corruption of childhood and marriage ...' (Matthews 2009, p. 65). Note, however, the depiction of the process of consistent life-giving force in *Innocence*: 'Significantly, Blake's Sweep in *Innocence* is envisioned as a weaving Caterpillar, a creature regenerated from death' (Milner 2002, p. 293). Pramod K. Nayar has provided a modern take on the poem, suggesting that one of the forms of authority depicted in the poem is the surveillance state. See Nayar 2014, pp. 328–32.

> Every blackning Church appalls,
> And the hapless Soldiers sigh
> Runs in blood down Palace walls
> But most thro' midnight streets I hear
> How the youthful Harlots curse
> Blasts the new-born Infants tear
> And blights with plagues the Marriage hearse.[85]

This is the closest vision of a system that leaves nothing outside the wake of its destructive power. The overwhelming sense of despair in the poem is introduced not merely by the dirt and destruction of London[86] but through its specifically commodified nature, most notably in the repeated use of 'charter'd', a reference to commercial organisations that existed in London connecting the political and economic systems that profited from its management.[87] The system turned streets and rivers into profit-making entities. Blake's London builds 'out of the indirect translation of radical oppositional politics and nonconformist discourse, while attempting to "unbuild" the mainstream manifestations of London's political power'.[88] Yet London reveals, in its supposed specificity, more than the city itself. As Raymond Williams notes, the 'London' of the poem is more than a signifier for the metropolis:

> A dominant part of the life of the nation was reflected but also created within it [London]. As its population grew it went into deficit, not only in food but in the balance of material production; but this was much more than compensated by the fact of its social production: it was producing and reproducing, to a dominant degree, the social reality of the nation as

---

[85] Blake 1988, pp. 26–7. On the subject of marriage and submission, 'What Blake has most in mind is the bringing of a thing into a state of acquiescence or submission to another, the establishment of an unequal relation between two things, indeed a kind of "marriage" in which one partner is, perhaps forcibly, reconciled to the domination of the other' (Prather 2007, p. 509).

[86] It is interesting to note that the original poem had the word Chartered replaced by 'dirty'. See Williams 1985, p. 148.

[87] On this point we can further see how the totalising essence of capitalism is reflected in capital's attempts to disrupt the connection between humans and the natural world. This runs counter to a Blakean stance which argues that in nature and ecology one finds that 'all things are complexly interrelated. Thus, to argue against this inter-relatedness is to be "anti-ecologic", and there is little that is more anti-Blakean than being anti-ecological'. See Hutchings 2002, p. 13. This argument is contended *passim*.

[88] Wolfreys 1998, p. 37.

a whole. It was in this still eighteenth-century sense that Blake, himself a craftsman and a Londoner, saw the capital city.[89]

The capitalist society in which he lived, in a period in which capital represented the dominant form of social relation, was doing all it could to make alternative ontologies risible and impossible. Those who labour in London are not representative of labour universally but are connected with those who labour universally. This labour, importantly, has no specific location, but Blake gives the processes at work a name. As Makdisi notes, 'The London of the *Songs of Innocence and* Experience does not restrict itself – nor should we restrict it – to the city whose name it takes ... it [London] marks the arrival of the much broader processes of modernisation itself'.[90] In this sense, Blake's London existed across much of Europe by this time and was rapidly expanding. Goethe had himself railed against the new coupling of religious dogmatism and the commodifying and destruction of nature. The ironic notes of his *Die Leiden des Jungen Werthers* should not be underplayed. However, consider the viciousness with which Werther fulminates against a vicar and his wife who 'works hard on today's new-fangled moral and critical reformation of Christianity and shrugs off Lavater's rhapsodic effusions' but whose greatest crime is to have cut down walnut trees that bound the community together as a place of relaxation, joy and non-commodified food. That the tree would ultimately be sold off by the vicar and an accomplice 'stood to gain' draws the most ire from Goethe, whose narrator wishes murderous vengeance, before stepping away from the debasing nature of the entire situation.[91] In this and in Blake's formulation, we see that

---

89 Williams 1985, pp. 147–8. Jennifer Davis Michael argues in regards to the poem 'London' that 'The potential danger of pastoral, illustrated in the deadly gardens above [The Garden of Love], is that while it enables us to envision an ideal world, it also enables us to ignore the elements in the world around us that fall short of the ideal'. This misses the point of Blake's criticism of the pastoral, as Blake's philosophy seems to buck the ideal/real formulation, as in Blake everything is in a sense real – even, as Makdisi will argue, the imagination. Michael's slight on materialist criticism, referring to 'London' as 'the poem most favored by Marxist interpreters of Blake' – which, she says, 'is hardly a realistic description' – is informative as to the inattention to materialism in that regard. Raymond Williams also dismisses the notion that Blake maintains a notion of the pastoral (especially as opposed to the city) (See Davis 2006, pp. 67 & 26). In a similar vein, Christopher Tomlins writes: 'The London of Blake's poem was Patrick Colquhoun's London – the London, that is, of the *Police of the Metropolis* (1796), the world's greatest commercial city, the riverine heart of an imperial political economy, inhabited by a laboring population disciplined by the sciences of magistracy' (Tomlins 2009, p. 196).
90 Makdisi 1998, pp. 156–7.
91 See Goethe 1989, p. 94. There is an interesting triangle between Goethe, Johann Kasper

the totalising system produces 'educated' readers for itself, trained carefully in rebutting criticisms of their own oppression, which hinders the possibilities for thinking outside of the system within which they are trapped or manacled. For this reason, Makdisi questions how we begin to approach Blake in the first place, given that we have come through this process ourselves. 'It may be, in other words, that the very way we have learned to read is precisely what prevents us from reading Blake properly'.[92] While this book does not take into account the visual aesthetics of Blake's approach, it is important to highlight that the logics that activate much of Blake's poetic worldview are present in both his paintings and illuminations as much as they are in his poetical works. In Blake's visual constructions, he sought to liberate the activity of his audience in making new meaning in their own reception of his work. As opposed to divining secret truths or unlocking the hidden messages embedded in his artworks, Blake's 'text emerges from the process of reading itself – the kind of reading towards which the illuminated books "rouze" our faculties'.[93] Counterbalance this with Andrew Hemingway's description of the institutional art world of Blake's time, as represented in the figure of Sir Joshua Reynolds, and in the institution of the Royal Academy of the Arts of which he was president. 'Like his friend Burke, Reynolds was a conservative defender of an "entailed inheritance" of received wisdom, who saw an inequitable distribution of economic and cultural capital alike as inescapable. In reality, the Royal Academy contributed to ensure that the "lower orders" had no opportunity to acquire the distinction it marketed by physically excluding them from its exhibitions through an entrance fee introduced expressly for that purpose'.[94] What is striking here is not only the naked class rule in art but the equation of this class rule with the appreciation of art, and the impossibility of art being appreciated by anyone outside of the 'lower orders'. Hemingway notes that Reynolds 'maintained that the norms of taste were fixed in the universal characteristics of human nature', but also regarded the "lower orders" as unfitted by their place in

---

Lavater, and Blake. Born in Switzerland in 1741 and trained as a physiognomist, Lavater became a widely distinguished pastor (his friend for a time, Goethe refers to his dramatic style in the passage quoted above) and published his *Aphorisms of Man*, a text which Blake annotated. But it goes further. After purchasing a copy of the book, and, as Alexander Regier explains, Blake 'signed his name into it, claiming it as his own. After he had finished reading and annotating it, he went back to his own signature and drew a heart around it and Lavater's printed name' (Regier 2018, p. 120).

92 Makdisi 2006b, p. 111.
93 Makdisi 2006b, p. 112.
94 Hemingway 2017, p. 91. For an excellent analysis of the historical and contemporary relationship of art and economics, see Beech 2015.

the social hierarchy to enjoy "intellectual entertainments".[95] The desire to 'fix' norms in universal terms, and to restrict the enjoyment of the art world to the 'higher orders', is a ruling class project in art. In the lengthy passage that follows, note how the activity of the reader / viewer is centred in Makdisi's description of the visual poetics of the illuminated Songs. He writes,

> What we can think of as the gap between different plates (such as *Chimney Sweeper* in *Innocence*, *Chimney Sweeper* in *Experience*) can thus be compared to the gap within the same plate (such as two copies of *The Little Black Boy*), and, in turn, the gap within the same work (like the multiple non-identical copies of *Songs of Innocence and of Experience*). Thus the stable self-containment of a single illuminated book is superseded by the wide virtual network of traces among different plates, different copies, different illuminated books; *virtual* because it is not always necessarily activated, and, even when it is, not always activated in the same way. This is also the case with the many images, phrases, and lines of text that we see repeated and recycled in Blake's work. When we encounter apparently the same line of text, or the same image, in multiple contexts (whether multiple versions of the same plate, or altogether different plates), our reading can expand to draw together these multiple appearances. Determining the meaning of a particular text (whether verbal or visual) involves reading it in an ever-expanding – though not an unlimited – number of contexts.[96]

The levels of indeterminacy require less a singular uncovering of deeper meanings than an attempt to unravel these strategies and dominant discourses of Reynolds, along with the class project that Blake's visual world sought to undercut.

Yet these strategies are largely marginal. Perhaps the most significant determining factor in working through/reading Blake's society against the grain is acknowledging its profoundly totalising quantification. The 'Charter'd streets' and 'charter'd Thames',[97] the urban and natural in London's duality, were im-

---

95   Hemingway 2017, p. 91.
96   Makdisi 2006b, p. 113.
97   David Erdman usefully notes that in 'London' Blake borrows Thomas Paine's notion 'that all charters are purely negative in effect and that city charters, by annulling the rights of the majority, cheat the inhabitants and destroy the town's prosperity ...' (Erdman 1969, p. 277). This further speaks to the universality that Blake aims to represent, a point that Raymond Williams also makes here: 'It is worth stressing this in Blake, since although he

posing other forms of living and surviving, and Blake is at odds with this process. The construction of Blake's aesthetic politics of this time is grounded in this relation to (and ultimate rejection of) his society. As argued above, the *Songs of Innocence*, particularly in the ways that questions of care and love for another are fundamental to his system of thought, act as a bulwark against Experience's devaluing of a good, redeemable life.

As argued earlier, the temporal and spatial co-ordinates of Innocence do not exclude moments of difficulty and sadness or even physical or emotional pain. Innocence is not a secluded space where certain realities of human hardship are magically whisked away. The relevance of Innocence is not in the absence of human suffering or depression, but in the way in which that suffering is responded to, and how the others in the same space are implicated and responsible for the misery. In 'A Cradle Song', the moment of anguish ('While o'er thee doth mother weep') is deemed part of life's cycle on the one hand (parents worrying over their children), and a consequence of capitalism on the other (the poverty that one presumes exists so widely in Experience also exists in the realm of Innocence). The difference is that in the realm of Innocence there is an offer of assistance or guidance and ultimately a sharing in that pain. In the realm of Experience, there is no aid to pain; rather, that pain is portrayed not as an unfortunate by-product of the system but an aspect of its very core functioning. Thus in 'Holy Thursday' Blake notes this bare contradiction in another rhetorical question:

> Is this a holy thing to see,
> In a rich and fruitful land,
> Babes reducd to misery,
> Fed with cold and usurous hand?[98]

The comment that these babes are 'fed with cold and usurous hand' should prick up our ears. There is a deep connection here between the depiction of money and its force in the world. It seems that they are two mains criticisms that Blake is laying out for us. Money's corrupting power makes humanity move away from the notions of pity and mercy that were so prevalent in Innocence. Yet it goes one step further, insofar as there is a long-term plan in place for these children: to spend their entire lives in the service of this misery. The usury to

---
inherits many eighteenth-century pastoral images, in his whole work he transforms them to elements of a general condition. The simplifying contrast between country and city is then decisively transcended' (Williams 1985, p. 149).

98   Blake 1988, p. 19.

which they are subjected will dominate them and make them beholden against their will to the propertied or moneyed classes.

There exists another form of criticism here, and it is specifically the notion of being chartered and its role in the production of London. The practice of being chartered – literally undergoing a formal training in (the most relevant application here) accountancy – is a formal written arrangement with the state. And here is the most delicate yet venomous entangling for Blake, as power is no longer merely moneyed and coercive, but outright controlling. The moment of freedom cannot exist in this realm, but only in its abolition. Blake may dissect the current system's urges, and show how those urges distort humanity's need for care, but the desire and need for the abolition of its control, its stronghold, is profoundly clear in Experience.

In the absence of the 'wise guardians of the poor', who nourishes the poor?[99] It is those whose specific responsibility is to guard against that mistreatment and provide aid through an impoverished period. Yet the means by which capitalism reproduces itself, its innermost ideology, wishes to make care for those at risk seem an impossibility, despite the concessions it might find necessary to make when pushed.[100] Indeed, not only is care not offered, but the most vul-

---

[99] Interestingly, David Fairer has argued that the presence of poor children, and specifically the visual act of giving charity to a handful of poor children, was in fact a more commonplace act, perpetrated by those who wished to instrumentalise the poverty of children. Often the children's presence was designed to stage a moment of 'national unity'. This was a longer tradition present even before Blake's time. Fairer writes that: 'The awkward subsuming of the political into the national had characterized a comparable occasion earlier in the century, the day of Thanksgiving for the Peace of Utrecht on 7 July 1713, another gesture of Tory triumph marked by the presence of the massed London charity children. Figure 4 shows the scene along the Strand when the procession made its way to the service in St Paul's. 3,925 children, newly clothed for the occasion, were arranged in a specially erected stand 620 feet long, consisting of eight rows of seats, and they sang together two hymns, one for the Queen as she passed along to the church, and a second three hours later as she returned. At least that was the plan, but Anne herself was too ill to be present. Nevertheless, between a repeated chorus of nine Allelujahs, the first hymn greeted her as the nursing mother of the kingdom ("Long, long may she remain"), while the second jubilantly celebrated the Tory Peace ("Peace his best gift to Earth's returnd, Long may it here remain; As we too long its Absence mourn'd, Nor sigh'd to Heaven in vain")' (Fairer 2002, p. 541). In this regard it is best to apply David Erdman's reading that the Chimney Sweep 'is saying to the London citizen: you salve your conscience by handing out a few farthings on May Day, but if you really listened to this bitter cry among the snow you and your icy church would be appalled' (Blake 1988, p. 275).

[100] Indeed, even charity – the supposed bridge to care offered by the powerful – is deeply implicated in the current consensus. As Sarah Haggarty notes, 'Charity, even the direct, voluntary charity so lauded in the eighteenth and nineteenth centuries, was in many

nerable are asked to take part in their own subjugation. The last four lines of the 'Chimney Sweeper' are particularly damning.

> And because I am happy, & dance & sing,
> They think they have done me no injury:
> And are gone to praise God & his Priest & King,
> Who make up a heaven of our misery.[101]

Similar to Brecht's own position, a rejection of the current society requires an understanding of its most intimate impulses. Without this acknowledgement of the way the dominant system perverts the possibility of Blakean ultimate redemption, reproduction of its abuses would proceed unhindered. The logic of capital necessitates the maintenance of an ideological worldview that takes in its very own worst excesses and sells them back at the price of honourable, quiet suffering. This does not mean, however, that this twisted logic, nor the effects it produces, are accepted by those who are harmed by capitalism. Quite the opposite, as Shirley Dent and Jason Whitaker note:

> ... the total omission of quotation marks makes the closure of 'The Chimney Sweeper's' narration highly ambiguous and highly charged ... This is not simply the subjective voice of the naïve sweep, who has internalized religious ideology and dutifully murmurs the dogmas of deferred reward. It is a direct plea from the poet for the audience to do their social duty so that they, the sweeps, need not fear their present life.[102]

In this there is a toying 'with the ideal of a childish Utopia, putting the onus on the reader to actively engage in an imaginative act of emancipation, of seeing grim social reality in order to change it, to envision an emancipated world'.[103] As with Brecht, it is no coincidence that Joan is asked to view the degradation of working by Mauler as not merely an unfortunate bi-product of the system, but as necessary to its proper functioning. And as we have seen, *Die Heilige Johanna* ends with a call to action.

---

respects designed to reconcile the "poor" to the inequality of their status – a reconciliation of especial importance during periods of special crisis. Charity might even create that inequality ...' (Haggarty 2009, p. 108).
101 Blake 1988, p. 23.
102 See Dent and Whittaker 2002, p. 102.
103 Ibid.

Blake presents us here with a compelling analysis of oppression, and how it works and is reproduced. Far from dismissing those who are young and have potential, those in power and their attendees take the evidence of hope and bury it with the weight of misery. Whether they even note their part in this process is an open question. The world of Experience provides the appearance of openness and care; it occupies itself wholeheartedly with producing and reproducing misery, while using the gestures of caring as a means to disguise its actual misdeeds.

Education and the rearing of children are important instruments for Blake in depicting the manner of inversion of life's pleasurable pursuits. This inversion required a move against humanity's nature. This nature, in the Blakean sense, as is so frequently displayed throughout *Innocence*, does not merely secure a bridge between humanity and nature as much as it moulds together. All aspects of humanity's lived relations are a discovery (of life and its endless possibilities), and in every discovery we see a partial return of connected action of nature and humanity, so much so that their existence as experiencing beings becomes interchangeable. Their unity becomes a form of resisting the world of Experience in practice. Note for instance the problem that is experienced in 'The Schoolboy':

> But to go to school in a summer morn,
> O! it drives all joy away;
> Under a cruel eye outworn,
> The little ones spend the day,
> In sighing and dismay.[104]

The depiction here is of making education a source of misery rather than exploration, and the 'cruel eye' denotes a lack of humanity. It is a partial entity in a world that, were it to focus on possibility-making, needs to be made whole, as in the description of the little ones. The question of how one subverts the process of manipulation and destruction of natural innocence by education is through Innocence's own logic. To undercut Experience's use – which has been 'outworn' – humanity and nature respond by reframing the issue. The child questions:

> How can the bird that is born for joy,
> Sit in a cage and sing.

---

[104] Blake 1988, p. 31.

How can a child when fears annoy,
But droop his tender wing,
And forget his youthful spring.[105]

The merging of entities, the boy and the bird in the description of the boy's 'tender wing', returns us to our connection both to ourselves and to our nature and the natural world. This simple discovery of the schoolboy, not because of his education but in response to it, will lead to greater realisations of the logic of both Innocence and Experience. If we have not cared for and gathered the 'summer fruits' because the 'buds are nip'd', how 'shall we gather what griefs destroy / Or bless the mellowing year, / When the blasts of winter appear'.[106] If we do not have reserves of pleasure, if we have not taught ourselves how to experience life's pleasures, how can we respond when in times of anguish? The logic here is that there is no other way if, shorn of life's endless horizons, 'the tender plants are stripped'. This is the monopolising nature of capitalism. It creates despair, while also eliminating how one might counter despair's consequences. In contrast, Innocence offers a way of acting and living in the world. It is a means by which life-making thought, that specific brand of philosophy which is so integral to Blake, is the response to those efforts to make life impossible. The enacting of Innocence is the acknowledgement of Experience and offers the hope for its potential undoing.

If Innocence is the kernel of the greatest potential that we could possibility have, Experience at its most deceitful uses the shell of Innocence, promising everything that Innocence hopes to deliver and ultimately destroying that potential. This is a central tension between the two. There is an alternate version of agency here that feeds off of rather than feeds.[107] The infrastructure of Experience, the 'God and his priest and king', are the key drivers of this exploitative system. While for Blake everything in the constellation of Experience is challengeable (and he explicitly sees his project as that which 'rouzes the faculties to act')[108] Innocence reads Experience's intent and function. In the opening stanza of 'The Human Abstract' we see this dynamic at work, both elucidating the problem and suggesting a way out of it. It reads:

---

105   Ibid.
106   Ibid.
107   On the loving connection between God and active love more generally in Blake, Matthew Green notes: 'This accords well with the experience of the believer who discovers the love of Christ, who is let into or out of the secret that he or she has been loved since before time and is therefore enabled to experience love as an active participant, to have her or his love kindled, even if it must always fall short of the mark' (Green 2005, pp. 103–4).
108   Blake in Makdisi 2006b, p. 111.

> Pity would be no more
> If we did not make somebody Poor:
> And Mercy no more could be,
> If all were happy as we;[109]

The central contradiction of this society requires an intervention, and one that acknowledges that there exists a counter-balance to the attempted universalising logic governing 'Ev'ry chartered street'. Blake was by no means alone in acknowledging the imposition and preponderance of this logic, yet what distinguishes him here is that he is aware that he recognises (in Innocence especially) that in the face of this, the mind often turns to sadness, something Blake diagnoses so adroitly when he writes of the importance of care, and of what happens when it is lost. Percy Bysshe Shelley, no stranger to understanding the pain inflicted by capitalism, relies on the power of the mind to think through and move beyond this problem, developing a form of criticism which struggles to find its way out and which results in despondency. In analysing Shelley's 'The Triumph of Life', Leon Chai argues that '… if we see Shelleyan negativity as an assertion of the power of the mind', then this makes it possible 'to abolish what we perceive'. Chai argues this is a form of idealism, and the purpose of '… Shelleyan idealism is that we can only think what we've perceived'.[110] Shelley's idealism divorces itself from the multitude, and because of its absence, his philosophical break will remain in its present state and revert back to a form of ultimate sadness, even if there is immense power unlocked in the mind's ability and capacity to think and articulate new worlds. The movement towards the mind involves a shift away from the underlying causes in the material world's production of pain and immiseration (read Blakean Experience). This was also the case for Coleridge and 'a key aspect of the power of his aesthetic', as John Whale explains:

> The self-sufficing nature of genius and its production is central to both his sense of art and his Christianity. This is the moment at which he can confidently differentiate himself from the competing and, for him, life- and soul-threatening ideology of utility and its attendant methodologies. At the same moment as he guarantees the morality of genius – the conscientious nature of unconscious genius – he has to sever its links with economics and the external manifestations of social progress.[111]

---

109 Blake 1988, p. 27.
110 Chai 2006, p. 19.
111 Whale 2000, p. 176.

The world of Experience, so attuned to paternalistic manipulation, was not only distrustful of a poetics of production as found in Blake, but sought to make the world answerable to a capitalist logic. Esther Leslie provides a useful contrast of Blake and his age in this regard. She writes:

> Blake was born into the 'Age of Johnson'. This was his misfortune. This was an age dominated by blank English instrumentalist empiricism, such as that promoted by the Royal Society which demanded clear language, mathematical plainness. Samuel Johnson (1709–1784) was a lexicographer. He was a waiter serving up words, fixing meanings rather than creating them. In addition, Johnson saw it as his lexicographer's duty to provide moral instruction for the semi-educated. So Johnson's business was weighty, but dull. It was a chore all round, and who would do it but for financial recompense?[112]

Leslie's presentation of Blake as misfortunate is useful in that it helps focus attention away from his supposed views on rationality and places him in relation to his age. In this reading, Leslie brushes the cold, moneyed calculation then dominating the age against a Romantic, for whom the rescue of words and images for the imagination was paramount. As Löwy and Sayre would argue, while levelling a critique of irrationality is a serious charge, it is also seriously misleading. Such a characterisation of one of Romanticism's key problematics only obfuscates further what is central to Blake (and other Romantics besides). The criticisms of rationality that are present in Blake's texts, and most other Romantics, are mobilised against a particular form of mechanical rationalism and rationalist abstraction, very much akin to the Johnsonian paradigm. Mechanical rationalism was associated with those institutions and forms of life which sought to make all life calculable and subject to mathematical or quantifiable logic.[113]

---

112   Leslie 2007.
113   Many of the same criticisms are levelled against rational abstraction. Here, there are two key points. Not simply are Löwy and Sayre referring to abstract rationalist philosophy, but rather to a totalising system of thought and life which seeks to reproduce itself on every available level. They argue, along with Marx, that this system works: first on the level of 'abstract categories: abstract work, abstract exchange value, money'; next, on the level on which 'modern bourgeois civilization ... organizes all economic, social and political life according to the requirements of rationality-with-respect-to-goals' (Weber); and finally the level on which 'rationalization, disenchantment and quantification' are 'embedded in a psychic attitude and form of experience with regard to things and the world' (Mannheim) (Löwy and Sayre 2001, pp. 39–40). This rationalisation led to two

The necessary effect of this logic was that anything not deemed economic – for instance, compassion and empathy – was discarded and dismissed from the liberatory potential that Blake locates in God. As a contrast, note the pains of the struggling mother to find a way for her child to sleep from 'A Cradle Song' ('Sleep, sleep, happy sleep, / While o'er thee doth my mother weep') to those spoken by the child from 'Infant Sorrow':

> My mother groand! my father wept.
> Into the dangerous world I leapt:
> Helpless, naked, piping loud;
> Like a fiend hid in a cloud.
> Struggling in my father's hands:
> Striving against my swadling bands:
> Bound and weary I thought best
> To sulk upon my mother's breast.[114]

As Ian Balfour has noted in his analysis of the 'Introduction' to the *Songs of Innocence and Experience*, in Blake's works writing is an instrument of dissemination and democratisation, producing books 'that all may read'.[115] Yet the object of this democratic dissemination[116] is Divine and Human, and the ultimate gesture is to join oneself with this coupling, since the Divine and the Human joined together are the 'closest to the moment of birth' in Blake, as Tristanne J. Connolly notes.[117] This literally new moment must involve itself with Experience's anguish and anxiety-making while also holding out the moment of Experience's potential undoing. The entreaty to 'Sleep, sleep, happy

---

important consequences, both evident in Blake simultaneously: a turn towards forms of 'concrete thinking' on the one hand, and a 'rehabilitation of nonrational and/or nonrationalizable behaviours' such as 'love as a pure emotion, a spontaneous attraction that cannot be reduced to any calculation and that is in contradiction with all rationalist strategies of marriage, – marriage for money, marriage "for good reasons"' on the other (2001, p. 4).

114   Blake 1988, p. 28.
115   Balfour 2002, p. 144.
116   Writing on the poem *America*, Peter Otto speaks to the emergence and resonance of the new world in Blake's poetry. Note here the emphasis on democracy. 'I am of course not suggesting that this emergent world is incommensurate with the revolutionary rhetoric of modernity. One could argue that Blake here merely reworks the movement from the old to the new, troping it as the passage from a static world, anchored in a transcendental principle, to a democratic world where form is forged by interaction between its parts' (Otto 2010, p. 179).
117   Connolly 2002, p. 125.

sleep' is at once a good on its own. The act of nourishment in seeking to turn towards its mother's breast is a concluding act as it is representative of a joining with others to deal with one's predicament. This poem is neither a representation of gladness and hope against the odds, nor of quiet suffering. Rather, 'thought best' acts as a means that mirrors the method that 'Our grief he may destroy' as Blake's cites in 'On Another's Sorrow'. Faith here does not stand still, but is the immediate engine for rejecting the systematically imposed grief and 'binding with briars my joys and desires' – the briars of Blake's own age. What Blake is demonstrating in this fissure between the worlds of Innocence and Experience is the need for a messianic power articulable in the moment of the now. As Benjamin would famously note, 'Like every generation that preceded us, we have been endowed with a weak messianic power',[118] and Blake's society was no different. Blake's addendum to Benjamin might well be that not only does the past have a claim to this, but so too does the present. And yet Innocence represents more largely the moment of a godly intervention, an action forever in the now, which the world of Experience attempts to forestall. As Benjamin notes, 'The present, which, as a model of Messianic time, comprises the entire history of making in an enormous abridgement, coincides exactly with the stature which the history of mankind [sic] has in the universe'.[119] Experience attempts to starve the present of this conception of time, of the need for intervention, and ultimately to claim ownership of notions of compassion and empathy. Its role is to clamp down on the potential of the present, and make of the past a stick with which to beat the life out of the living.

4   Conclusion: The Future in the Present

On 6 June 1929, in a letter to his friend Gershom Scholem, Benjamin writes that he has struck up a 'close acquaintance with Brecht'. Erdmut Wizisla notes that 'This was the first hint of a friendship which, in the years that followed, many of Benjamin's friends and associates were to find disturbing'.[120] It is surprising, given the extensive and profound intellectual friendship that the two would forge, how often this connection continues to get lost in a critical appraisal of their work. Indeed, as Wizisla's research has demonstrated, even their more famous disagreements on Benjamin's 'Some Reflections on Kafka' and 'The Author as Producer', were less about the central arguments themselves

---

118   Benjamin 1968, p. 254.
119   Benjamin 1968, p. 263.
120   Wizisla 2009, p. 1.

and more about the specific application of them.[121] In the same way here, I have argued that while Brecht and Blake experience their worlds in different ways and express this difference asymmetrically, the works covered in this and the preceding chapter advance a common oppositional political aesthetic that responds to the time of their now.

In part, what ties Brecht and Blake together is not the specific form of opposition espoused, but rather the philosophical implications of their opposition, taken together. For the two, the object was not merely opposition to an ideology. What was fundamentally necessary was that each articulated a response to the specific predicaments of their society, predicated on a unique yet comprehensive understanding of their respective capitalist worlds and then offering, ultimately, a form of aesthetic articulation that responded to those dominant ideologies and offered ways by which one could undo their logic. But the form that this takes in the two differs in considerable and contradictory ways.

There is a strong sense that Brecht seeks to work through the dominant capitalist logics that he lives through more than Blake is able to. I disagree that this is attributable to the nascent status that Makdisi suggests was characteristic of Blake's modernity (the central forms of capitalist relations had long been dominant, a fact that Blake himself suggests in his use of 'every' and 'chartr'd' above).[122] Rather, Blake had not seen the working-class forces coalescing that Brecht had, and of which Brecht made himself an active proponent. This is not to suggest that Blake can be slotted into the position of Marxist *avant la lettre*, as such a framework would do more to confuse than clarify our sense of Blake's position.

Yet Blake's rejection of capitalism works in the same vein as Brecht's Weimar texts. Fundamental to both is a rejection of any privileged location that can provide protection against the exploitative system's dominating logic. Blake is at pains to overturn the idea that there can be a space outside of capitalism's grasp, most readily identified in the countryside, that will provide a rally point or refuge due to its 'nature'. Interestingly, while this division of the urban and rural does not form any significant backdrop for his plays, Brecht's poem 'Of poor B. B.' in the 'Hauspostille' (often translated as the 'Devotions for the Home') is one of his most explicit evocations of the city/country divide. The dialectical nature of Brecht's aesthetics is shown particularly clearly in 'Of poor B. B.'. The poem is riven with contradictions in the way it splices and folds over positive and negative connotations of the city and the country. It con-

---

121   See Wizisla 2009, pp. 144–187.
122   Makdisi 1998, p. 4.

tains multitudes of slippages exposing – both ironically and unironically – the layers of comfort and brutal exposure of urban and country existence. As Ronald Speirs notes, 'All the utterances of the poetic personality "Bertolt Brecht" who speaks in "Of poor B. B." are characterized by contradiction and ambivalence'.[123] Jameson will point out that this characteristic comes to define Brecht's aesthetics. 'For Brecht is modern first and foremost by way of his discontinuities and his deeper fragmentation: from that dispersal, we can proceed on into a certain unity, but only after having passed through it'.[124] Yet in these contradictions Brecht takes us to the other side of the caesura of a nurturing nature and an exploitative urbanity, similar to but different from Blake's setting of the countryside as a location of exploitation. While in Blake the countryside often contains the seed of human compassion and potential, this can be transported into city life via the caring acts of parents and those 'wise guardians' who will offer protection to those in need. And even then, there is a sense that they are a minority, and against the underlying and over-rushing currents of capitalist modernity. In Brecht, the city becomes both a central locus or recognition of capitalism's harsh realities and the place of socialist resistance. While 'Of poor B. B.' may cede partially to arguments regarding an 'historical pessimism' accorded to the large-scale migration to the cities, 'here, for the first time, the cities are seen as a potentially progressive development', as Peter Whitaker notes.[125] He allows no place for the nostalgia of the past and the metaphorical splendour of care tied to the natural world, particularly in Romantic thought,[126] and he sought to see the consistency of exploitation and poor living standards that prevailed in both.

Blake's *Songs of Innocence* engages the present – knowingly – by rejecting it. Whereas Brecht's engagement was to submerge himself as deeply as he could, Blake's response is to acknowledge and refute, specifically recognising

---

123   Speirs 2002, p. 49.
124   Jameson 1998, p. 6.
125   Whitaker 1985, p. 35. What is interesting to note, following David Midgley, is that the shift to an urban setting has made for the possibility of new ways of expression for both the artist and the individual. 'The world of human relations that he depicts has definitely become abstracted and depersonalized, human individuals have become interchangeable and in obvious senses commodified. But at the same time, that abstraction of relations poses a new challenge to poetic expression, a challenge to identify and articulate the precise nature of such abstracted relations and their implications for the lives of the individuals who inhabit the city environment' (Midgley 2002, p. 92).
126   With the notable exception of those Romantic thinkers and writers who knew well the realities of the labour that sustained the countryside. Exemplary examples in poetry include John Clare, Janet Little and Samuel Thomson.

the moment of capital's barbarity, while maintaining the need for a space outside of its dominance. In this way, the moment of Innocence is a celebration of the Brechtian possibilities of experimentation, wherein a space for productiveness and work outside capitalism is present. Yet this does not mean a withdrawal, but rather a complex coming together. Take, for instance, Brecht's notes on the sporting public, and in particular the bold nature of his claims.

> Make no bones about it, we have our eye on those huge stadiums, filled with 15,000 men and women of every variety of class and physiognomy, the fairest and shrewdest audience in the world. There you will find 15,000 persons paying high prices, and working things out on the basis of a sensible weighing of supply and demand. You cannot expect to get fair conduct on a sinking ship. The demoralization of our theatre audiences springs from the fact that neither theatre nor audience has any idea what is supposed to go on there.[127]

Yet the response that Brecht will offer is not a submission to the crowd, but an engagement with it.

> ... no doubt an artist will fall far short of achieving his maximum effectiveness today if he sails with today's wind. It would be quite wrong to judge a play's relevance or lack of relevance by its current effectiveness. Theatres don't work that way. *A theatre which makes no contact with the public is a nonsense*. Our theatre is accordingly a nonsense. (Italics in original)[128]

Brecht's damning emphasis reiterated the need for connection to the lived experience of the audience, but also that this did not mean succumbing to the ephemeral moods of an audience whose expectations were shaped by capitalist social relations. Likewise, Brecht's rejection of the 'enemies of production' is about maintaining the ability of the cultural producer to operate in a radically engaged way. Here, the individual artist's relation to their society, while preserved, must not also reproduce the dominant forms of life that one is seeking to undercut.

The *Songs of Innocence* are constructed in a circular way to block out the work of totalising capitalist existence. Innocence acts as a bulwark against the threat of this world. It is a preserve against the danger of the outside. Innocence

---

127   Brecht 1978a, p. 6.
128   Brecht 1978a, p. 7.

is a refuge, but a knowing one. On the other hand, Experience is the warning of this world. Experience is not a harbinger of things to come but an identity of a spirit of a real existing world that is sold off and purchased piece by piece. Experience seeks to locate any activity, way of seeing the world or 'spirit' – such as the one that resonates in Innocence – and either block it entirely or usher it out of any sphere of influence. Innocence is knowing, is cognisant and aware, in that it sees the threat of these attempts to delegitimise and make it impossible. This dichotomy is the one in which Blake operates, and he does so consciously. His dilemma is then, how to maintain the individual's position while at the same time maintaining a connection to one's audience? Saree Makdisi and Jon Mee note how central this question was to Blake's overall aesthetic strategies:

> ... Blake refused to endorse wholesale the Orientalist discourse distinguishing between a virtuous, disciplined, productive, sober, rational Western Self, and a delinquent, undisciplined, unproductive, unregulated, and irrational Eastern Other. Moreover, he refused to distinguish between Self and Other in the first place. Not only is such a rigid contrast not something that we can find anywhere in Blake's work, early or late: it is the very antithesis of all his work, the concept that he most fundamentally struggled to resist and subvert ... *This* is why Blake refuses Orientalism: because he utterly refuses the logic of individualism predicated on an opposition to otherness – the logic that Orientalism fundamentally requires as its motives force.[129]

Blake's refusal is a step further away than Brecht's strategies allow and marks out a disjuncture between the two. In order to divine more closely in what this

---

129 Makdisi and Mee 2012, p. 16. Yet we should be clear that the rejection of the present did not result in a retreat into the past. Martin Bidney also uses Benjamin's 'Theses' in his essay on Blake, but contrary to the position I have sought to put forward, Bidney argues that to 'counteract the seeming threat of a relentless speeding up of modern industrial time by nostalgically envisioning a dream-like slow-motion medieval world where time is comfortingly relaxed, or even brought to a halt. Both the historical, socioeconomic problem and its attempted poetic solution can be expressed in terms of ontological psychology as involving each poet's attempt to protect himself against the overwhelming pressures of chaotic Becoming by imagining a more blissful alternative condition of purer, simpler Being. The paradoxical trap is that such an imagined freezing of life and action in static Being makes palpable the even graver menace of a deadening Nothingness' (Bidney 2002, p. 102). While the notion of counteracting the time of capitalism is part of Blake's oppositional aesthetics, to suggest that his poetics leads him to a position of stasis seems to be a rejection of the thesis of potentiality put forward by Makdisi, and against the spirit of referenced authors such as Erdman, Thompson, Mee, et al.

disjuncture consists, we must first think in terms of what possibilities have been opened by the understanding of the contemporary moment, and what options there are in an alternative future. Nevertheless, it is for this reason that Brecht relies on a far more clearly co-ordinated response than Blake's. For Blake, as Thompson points out, there is something far deeper required. He notes: 'There must be some utopian leap, some human rebirth, from Mystery to renewed imaginative life. "London" must still be made anew as the New Jerusalem'.[130] This leap though does not move us away from connection with the world, or put us in a holding pattern while the Utopian leap approaches. To the contrary, 'Blake's innocence is more than a cultivated state of inner warmth, however, for the cultivation of innocence is itself a form of social criticism'.[131] Critique exists so that we may make future possibilities possible. Critique exists so that good spaces can remain and be potentially harnessed for a redemption of the present for future purposes. Whereas Brecht seems to take in all he can in order to engage more fully within the frameworks available to him, Blake understands what is dominating his society in order to remove himself and his work, to maintain what is fundamentally good from the clutches of the totalising system. In this sense, individuality (as understood in relation to Makdisi and Staehler above) and a rejection of alienation are fundamental. A central focus for Brecht, from *Mann ist Mann* forward, is to map out the seeming impossibility of individuality. This could, in part, be a difference of historical moment, but it also underlies the notion of reproducibility. For Blake, the artwork bore the necessity of individual input, whereas Brecht's work – fully immersed in the moment of no return of technical reproducibility – locates the death of the individual and the need to embrace this and respond in collective fashion.

---

130   Thompson 1995, p. 193.
131   Erdman 1969, p. 117. Likewise, as Northrop Frye noted of the *Songs of Experience*: 'Contempt and horror have never spoken more clearly in English poetry'. Yet despite this, 'The reason will not take us far. Only vision helps us here, and vision helps us here, and vision shows us the tree of mystery and morality growing inside the human skull; it shows us the prophet calling to the earth to herself and earth answering with a groan to be delivered; it shows us our accusing enemy who frightens us out of Paradise behind the menacing blaze of a tiger's eyes'. 'This is the only world the child can grow into, and yet the child must grow. The *Songs of Experience* are satires, but one of the things they satirize is the state of innocence. They show us the butcher's knife which is waiting for the unconscious lamb. Consequently, the *Songs of Innocence* satirize the state of Experience, as the contrast which they present to it makes its hypocrisies more obviously shameful. Hence the two sets of lyrics show two *contrary* states of the soul, and in their opposition there is a double edged irony, cutting into both the tragedy and the reality of fallen existence' (Frye 1969, pp. 236–7).

Despite the ways in which they present their cases, both Blake and Brecht present us with a world that is always changing. In Blake we see more clearly how those in power seek to extinguish the fires of change, and likewise in Brecht we see the ways in which change has been used by those in power for their own purposes. This posits a conception of change that is reliant on a notion of 'messianic time' where other worlds are possible. As Peter Fenves argues:

> ... messianic time is not another time; it is just time – time and nothing else but 'plastic time'. The paradisal character of space, toward which the painterly plane tends, accords with the messianic character of time, which is thus charged with tension and can be called 'full' because every stretch of time contains all of time. In 'World and Time' Benjamin says of the first category 'there is nothing continuous'; the opposite condition characterizes the other concept under consideration, namely time, which, as Benjamin briefly suggests, should actually be called 'the coming world'. By virtue of its nondirectional continuity, time – 'turned' by 'now' – is the 'coming world'.[132]

This coming world requires for Blake and Brecht opposition and experiment in the present for its eventual manifestation to be even remotely considerable, were a 'Utopian leap' possible.[133] If this is not deemed possible in the present, if the time of the now provides insufficient nourishment required for the rich veins of experiment, then the move towards the past and historical redemption, the focus of the next two chapters, becomes the hope for the future.

---

132   Fenves 2011, p. 244.
133   Benjamin himself expressed this relationship to the present. Michael Jennings states: 'Life as an experiment: Benjamin's restless travelling, his problematic friendships and alliances – all can be seen under the category of experiment. "When it comes to the most important things," he wrote to Scholem in 1926, "I always proceed radically, never consistently; this would also be my attitude, were I one day to join the Communist Party ... The possibility of my remaining in the party will have to be determined experimentally"' (Jennings 1987, p. 8).

CHAPTER 4

Brecht, History and the Productive Past

Much has been made of the period of Brecht's exile and the ways in which this move abroad, or more accurately *moves* (given the many countries he sought refuge in before arriving in the United States), shaped his politics and the nature of the work he produced.[1] In what follows I examine these exilic works and the nascent relevance of history in his writing. I am not, however, arguing that the move towards history was in any way unheard of for Brecht. His work in Weimar Berlin was marked by an interest in historical themes. For example, there was *Leben Eduards des Zweiten von England*, not to mention the celebrated reworking of John Gay's *The Beggar's Opera, Die Dreigroschenoper*, perhaps his most well-known work. During this period, however, historically reimagined works were the exception and not the rule. While Brecht's connections with the working-class movement in Germany did a great deal in shaping his response to the particular social and political situation in Germany, as shown in Chapter 2, the imposition of successive exiles ('changing countries more often than our shoes'[2] was his deft description) saw Brecht resort to using history and historical themes as a means of returning to the present conjuncture.[3] This is not to suggest that Brecht eschewed political intervention. On the contrary, his more considered and fully-formed turn towards history and historical themes was specifically an attempt to make a political impact in a different manner than was previously the case, given that connections to oppositional cultural producers and to socialist social-political movements were now thin on the ground, and the receptions of Brecht in the United States were mixed at best.[4] Although more could be added to the list, John J. White notes that:

---

1   An important contribution on the successful work of Brecht while in exile is White and White 2010.
2   Brecht 2019, p. 736. Galvano Della Volpe refers to this poem as 'Marxist', writing that the 'moral and ideological climate which constitutes the poetic "tone" is, unlike Rimbaud's *Ouvriers*, revolutionary' (Della Volpe 1978, p. 147).
3   Just as Brecht offered little fidelity to other texts, so too did he view history. As William Burling notes: 'Brecht routinely thought of all history and all earlier cultural production as grist for his mill' (Burling 2007, p. 173).
4   On Brecht's exile and his search for a new project, Theodore Rippey writes: 'From this we conclude that art, while not necessarily subject to social context in its self-forming, is nonetheless dependent on (thus bound to) that context because art is incapable of *sustaining* itself. Art divorced from social reality will deplete itself; poetry is a social practice,

'Two factors weighed heavily with Brecht in the mid-1930s. The first was knowing that ideologically progressive theatre-groups could also fail to grasp Epic Theatre's innovative approach, and the second, an awareness that the American stage was becoming dominated by Stanislavskians to a far greater extent than he could have suspected from his European vantage point'.[5] Given this context, it is telling that during his period of exile, a period which stretched from 1933 to 1949, his most direct form of political writing – wherein there was scant effort to mediate his political interventions via history and historical themes (despite a few exceptions) – is located in his poetry.[6] Yet it is in Brecht's plays, which included other post-1939 texts and re-workings such as *Die Verurteilung des Lukullus, Die Judith von Shimoda, The Duchess of Malfi, Antigone,* and *Coriolanus,* that the historical focus (both as a device and as a strategy) offered him a means to continue his political aesthetics productively in order to intervene in the contemporary moment. In this sense, the 'time of the now' still operates as a guiding principle for Brecht, but with historical settings and motifs used as vehicles to shed light on the present. This historical turn, although a continuation of the political trajectory of his earlier work,[7] a process that Brecht himself termed *Historisierung,* marks his Brecht's 'final – and most political – major new term in his conceptual arsenal of the late 1930s',[8] which used so effectively and plays such a dominant role in his work in the German Democratic Republic (GDR).

His time in the GDR, from 1949–56, was fraught at best. During his exile period he wrote the three plays under discussion in this chapter, but it was only when he was back in (now-East) Germany that he gained sufficient control

---

even if not a politically catalytic one. This, not the fantasy of social intervention, is the *Gegenwartsbindung* that becomes clear in exile' (Rippey 2009, p. 53).

5 White 2004, p. 84.
6 A collection of essays that speaks directly to the political nature of his poetical work during the period of exile is Spiers 2010.
7 There is a stream in Brechtian scholarship that has sought to divide Brecht into a younger and older version, with each position defined by decidedly contradictory political positions. As Betty Nance Weber has argued, what has occurred is a viewing of the 'young' and 'old' Brecht as two separate fields of cultural practice, 'as a backsliding on Brecht's part from the exciting experimental theatre of the 1920s to uninteresting, traditional, even simplistic plays for old-fashioned stages'. Much in line with my thinking throughout, she argues that these positions have 'hindered an appreciation for the strong continuity in Brecht's work, in form and substance' (Weber, 1980, p. 61).
8 White 2004, p. 126. While White's highlighting of history is useful, his portrayal cleaves an unnecessary split between Brecht and Benjamin's notion of progress. 'Moreover, his various explanations of "Historisierung" are clearly based on a dialectical materialist conception of history and not on some simple appropriation of Walter Benjamin's more mystical concept of "Jetztzeit"'. White argues that 'The "Jetztzeit" concept plays a central role in Benjamin's attempted dismantling of historical progress. The pessimism that informs this focus is the

over his theatre and the conditions that would make it possible. This control relied on involving a large network of cultural producers with whom he had variously worked prior to, during and after his exile. This collaborative form was essential to his work in the GDR, as David Barnett explains: 'From the very beginning of the enterprise, Brecht was keen to turn the BE [Berliner Ensemble] into an institution that empowered as many of its workers as possible to make positive contributions to the rehearsal process'.[9] Autonomy of production was not completely possible, and there were clear tensions with the East German state.[10] There was no easy balance to strike, given that the leading figures of the East German state, and the Soviet Union, treated him cautiously at best, even if they had to acknowledge that his presence in the GDR leant them significant legitimacy. In the nascent GDR, Brecht's inside position allowed him (and arguably politically obliged him) to establish a longer position of making arguments about the dangers of the potential resurgence of fascism coming from the West, while also trying to resuscitate a worthwhile socialist intervention. Compared to the position in which he found himself in the GDR – where he both had serious misgivings of the present functioning of Stalinism, yet also saw its potential willingness to produce a socialism worth fighting for – Brecht forged a politics of lesser evilism. As Laura Bradley argues, this was an especially difficult task: '... Brecht struggled with the challenge of defending and improv-

---

      diametrical opposite of the premises of Brecht's conception of "Historisierung"' (White 2004, p. 128). Such a view unfairly assigns Benjamin to a resigning position, and not one that in fact calls into question the liberatory potential of historical understanding, even if that historical understanding leads to disheartening truths.

9   Barnett 2011, p. 26.

10   The question of Brecht's autonomy in the GDR was posed by Hannah Arendt in her famous 1966 New Yorker article. The article 'struck many readers as a bitter attack on Brecht for his postwar accommodation with the Stalinist regime in East Germany', as Patchen Markell writes. This was particularly notable in Arendt's assertion that Brecht composed 'odes to Stalin'. Markell argues against a highly critical interpretation of Arendt's piece, stating that 'Arendt's defense of Brecht was both powerful and vulnerable to misunderstanding, I propose, because it operated within but also cut against the grain of the dominant problematics of its time, implying a critique of the forced choices and forms of thoughtlessness that Arendt found pervasive in Cold War political culture' (Markell 2018, p. 507). While Wizisla's text has gone some way towards establishing the importance of the Brecht / Benjamin relationship, Arendt was an early supporter of the combination. As Wizisla notes, 'Hardly ever has the friendship between Benjamin and Brecht been assessed as positively, even euphorically, as by Hannah Arendt ...' (Wizisla 2009, p. 20). Arendt nevertheless offered a critical perspective on Benjamin, as Wizisla continues, describing Arendt's view of Benjamin as a 'failure, an isolated figure, and she imputed to his thinking a resistance to any form of ideology which corresponded to he own anti-authoritarian concept rather than to his own political intention' (2009, p. 21).

ing a socialism that was ordained from above and implemented by politicians who did not necessarily view him as an ally'.[11] Brecht was not wrong in his suspicions. Although he enjoyed some political freedoms that others were not granted, the leading cultural authorities were quick to criticise his work. His first production of *Mutter Courage* in the GDR, for instance, in January 1949, was met with the accusation of 'formalism' by the critic Fritz Erpenbeck. Erpenbeck had previous public disagreements with Brecht. During his time as editor of the influential *Das Wort*, Erpenbeck sided with Lukács against Brecht in an important exchange on Expression and Realism.[12] That this was the reigning cultural ideology of the Sozialistische Einheitspartei Deutschlands (SED) – the Socialist Unity Party of Germany, the governing party in the GDR – on the matter was hardly a secret, yet Brecht saw sufficient hope that over time this could be changed. As Peter Harkin argues, 'Brecht viewed the SED's approach to cultural policy as wrong but as an understandable product of his time'.[13] Needing to work within a system that was suspicious of his political and cultural work was something Brecht got very used to in his time in the United States, while he wrote the plays discussed here.

The plays *Mutter Courage und ihre Kinder*, *Der Kaukasische Kreidekreis*, and *Leben des Galilei* are constructed in such a way as to continue the political uses of estrangement effects while using the historical past as a means to stretch the political expectations and ways of seeing of an audience subjected to a dozen years of fascist propaganda. Yet history is not meant to act as a mirror of the present, but to skew it slightly, giving it distance or 'perspective', as a means of establishing a productive memory that continues to make itself useful in the present rather than repress the oppositional energies that could be unleashed by going against the grain, in the sense of Benjamin's Brechtian maxim. Indeed, the new maxim, after Benjamin, is more akin to 'start from the bad old times *for* the bad new times'. In order to demonstrate this, the present chapter will first show how *Mutter Courage*'s historical backdrop helps frame the lead character's inability to see the system which feeds on the destruction of her family, and that this ultimately propels the audience to learn from that bad history. I will illustrate how the 'Little Monk' character in *Leben des Galilei* is emblematic

---

11   Bradley 2011, p. 1.
12   Gardiner 2015, p. 632.
13   Parker 2011, p. 71. Harkin usefully notes the bind that Brecht saw himself as being confined by, while also recognising the hope that he saw as deeply latent in the GDR. He writes, '... Brecht knowingly accepted the toils that the socialist state would surely have in store for him at a time when he could have chosen a much less arduous path for himself in the west of the German-speaking world. Yet Brecht found the challenge to participate in the establishment of a socialist Germany irresistible' (Parker 2011, p. 69).

of the importance of the larger struggle for justice by those who are deemed to have little power. In this regard, although key historical targets for Brecht's play were both Stalinism and capitalist war, the backdrop of Renaissance Italy provides the opportunity to explore the deeper question of how an audience can learn from history and historical themes. In the third section, the usefulness of historical learning for the present, especially as regards the ingenious strategies of productivity and historical planning, will be shown in the *Die Kaukasische Kreidekreis*. Perhaps fittingly, given that infidelity to history is a focus of this chapter, I will eschew chronological order and begin with the role of memory and forceful forgetting in Brecht's *Mutter Courage*.

1 And the Cart Rolls On ... *Mutter Courage* and Learning from Those Who Don't

> WHAT IS A PERFORMANCE OF MOTHER COURAGE AND HER CHILDREN PRIMARILY MEANT TO SHOW? That in wartime big business is not conducted by small people. That war is a continuation of business by other means, making the human virtues fatal even to those who exercise them. That no sacrifice is too great for the struggle against war.[14]

Although others before him had discussed the long centuries of the wreckage of history, few have exposed the liberating potentialities of the past as sharply as Benjamin. Marx himself, who famous declared that the 'history of all hitherto existing society is the history of class struggle',[15] also acknowledged the grand scope of the reality of human oppression. But rather than exploring this potential for the contemporary conjuncture, Benjamin's position is to no longer take the past for granted, arguing that the sufferings of the past will not positively condition a future left without a radical resurrection of their victims. This was significantly the case with the largest German left movement of Benjamin's lifetime. As he writes in the 'Theses on the Philosophy of History', Social Democracy in Germany 'made the working class forget both its hatred and its spirit of sacrifice, for both are nourished by the image of enslaved ancestors rather than that of liberated grandchildren'.[16] By forgetting this anger towards historical injustices, the working class has become unmoored from the struggles of its past. This has been key to the suppression of opposition to war, most notably

---

14   Brecht 1978a, p. 220.
15   Marx and Engels 1985, p. 79.
16   Benjamin 1968, p. 253.

in the infamous vote in August 1914 by German Social Democratic Party deputies in support of 'War Credits' for the First World War. The fight against war for Brecht, as the above quote from his notes on the play makes clear, involves a sacrifice (of one's own life, even) in the present. The historical background offered in *Mutter Courage* enables a way of learning from the previous failures of others who have not acted against a similar threat. Perhaps the greatest and most pressing threat in this regard (despite being militarily defeated, fascism was bound to be resurrected) was Nazism's appeal to race, history and the nation, along with the change in worldview that emanated from this toxic mix. As Thomas Lekan argues,

> In place of what Walter Benjamin deemed modernity's 'homogenous empty time', the Nazis used organic metaphors of *Ewigkeit*, or eternity, to recapture what Benjamin termed 'Messianic' time, a simultaneity of past and future in an instantaneous present. The Nazis grounded their belief in racial character on supposedly objective laws of the natural world; Germans past, present, and future were thus eternally connected by blood. Though Germany's primordial landscape was gone forever, ecological restoration and spatial planning held out the promise that the natural balance in the contemporary cultural landscape could be restored.[17]

It is not surprising, in this context, that part of the European left cultural response was to connect the past and present. While the focus here is on Brecht and his response to the tragedy made manifest by Nazi atrocity, Alain Resnais's *Nuit et Brouillard* (*Night and Fog*) stands out as a singular achievement (Francois Truffaut famously called it 'the greatest film ever made'). Nora M. Alter has excellently laid out some of the connections between Brecht's productions and the film, tracing how the music for the film was not an original Hanns Eisler score, as Resnais believed, but instead was recycled from an earlier 1954 Berliner Ensemble production.[18] The overture for the film originally had been commissioned by Brecht for Johannes Becher's play *Winterschlacht* (*Winter Battle*), and before Brecht's death there were some suggestions that he could translate the piece into German, given the aesthetic political affinities between the projects.[19] The film's purpose, Eric Kligerman notes, is 'to uncover the remnants of the dead and to represent Europe's repression of the death camps

---

17   Lekan 2004, p. 251.
18   See Alter 2012, pp. 24–39.
19   As Ewout van der Knapp argues, Resnais 'strove to achieve the critical catharsis that Brecht espoused' (Van der Knapp 2006, p. 24). The term 'catharsis' is perhaps ill-chosen given

ten years after their liberation'.[20] *Nuit et Brouillard* counterposes both past and present through a contrast of black and white and colour film, brushing the two together to connect the profound horror of the Holocaust, on the one hand, and the current repression of its memory in contemporary Europe (the film itself was subject to attempted and actual censorships), on the other. These were key elements that Brecht, Eisler and the Berliner Ensemble were working on at exactly the same moment, in particular in the production of Becher's work. As Sylvie Lindeperg notes in her outstanding *Night and Fog: A Film in History*: 'To Eisler, the play's Gordian knot lies in the contradictory process that provokes critical reflection on Germany's past and history: Hitler and the savagery of war, the absurdity of death and the meaning of "military honour", the complex articulation between the defeat of the Third Reich and the question of Germany's possible future'.[21] How to make sense of the expanse of human destruction was a dominant concern for Brecht, particularly in the plays that received most attention during the post-war period. This is arguably most clear in his *Mutter Courage*.

There is a wealth of material that has been written on Brecht's *Mutter Courage*, and for an author whose works have been subject to an industry of investigation, few works have been so delicately (and at times indelicately) chewed over. Yet despite the proliferation of scholarly work on and translations of the play,[22] few have sought seriously to examine the role of loss in the work (and here loss means more than the sum of the parts found throughout, such as family members, capital, self-respect, etc.), and how that key theme of loss structures the work entirely.[23]

In Brecht's careful production of the play, special attention was given to clarifying the 'bare facts' of the work's background. For instance, maps of Europe detailing the progress and regress of various army movements were shown,

---

      Brecht's anti-Aristotelian sympathies on the subject, the underlying assumption regarding the political change aspired for is sustainable.

20   Kligerman 2011, p. 11. Kligerman's essay also connects the film with its date of release, suggesting that the role of the French government's colonial practices in Algeria were reflected in the film's less acute focus on Jewish suffering in the Holocaust.

21   Lindeperg 2014, p. 134.

22   See, for instance, Tony Kushner and Tom Kuhn's recent bilingual 2012 edition and David Hare's 2010 translation.

23   It is important to note that the character of Courage finds her roots not in Brecht, but rather in the work of the seventeenth-century German novelist Grimmelshausen in his *Der Abenteuerliche Simplicissimus* (translated as *The Adventurous Simplicissimus*). Grimmelshausen knew a lot about loss, having been stolen away from his family and rural life at the age of ten by the Hessian army. A comparison highlighting religion as a survival strategy in each is provided in Horwish 1997.

placards stating the year were used between scenes to give a sense of temporal fixation, and other visual markings were deployed. Such efforts may seem counter-intuitive for a playwright who is known, perhaps more than any other, for his work on distancing techniques, the *raison d'être* of which is the meticulous alienation of the trappings of realism and facticity present in what he saw as Aristotelian theatre. Yet the techniques Brecht used in *Mutter Courage* are not an eschewal of his formal practice, but rather an attempt to make the step backward in time clearer, so as to reinvestigate history in the present moment.

Through the use of these techniques Brecht sought to create a situation where audience members would leave their assumptions of the current period behind and move to a time which is not explicitly capitalist but is assuredly pre-modern. Without a doubt, we learn that Courage herself is engaged in the buying and selling of commodities and is a referent for the parasitical capitalist living off the proceeds of war. Indeed, so blatantly obvious are the historical markers provided that they are enough to establish that we are not in the present epoch, despite the obvious correlations for the audience of the original productions. We are invited to leave the moment of class conflict between proletariat and bourgeoisie and turn to feudal conflicts which, at least in terms of historical duration, outsize the relative newness of the two chief struggling classes under capitalism. This time conjures up the *almost* incomparable exploitation of the peasantry. Brecht wishes to mobilise this history. Jameson, in his 1998 work *Brecht and Method*, has written of this process of drawing back into historical time (more than history as such) in Brecht's work. He writes:

> This is the moment of freedom, the redemptive moment, in one of Brecht's temporalities: the moment of provisional change, the moment in which Azdak [the corrupt judge in *The Caucasian Chalk Circle*] can appear, no matter how briefly, before vanishing again into the mists of time and the immemoriality of peasant labour and oppression. It is the Xairos of Brecht's peasant history, and a temporality of pre-capitalism that is most often associated with the "populist" features in Brecht, and determines the chronologies of the great plays: the Thirty Years War in *Mother Courage*; a peasant Middle Ages shaking off its timeless lethargy in *Galileo* ...[24]

---

24 Jameson 1989, p. 139. While I am sympathetic to Douglas Kellner's attempt to situate rather than abstract (a very Brechtian impulse), I think Jameson's point here is at odds with Kellner's when the latter points out that: 'In his epic theatre built on the principles of historical specification and critique, Brecht sought to illuminate the historically specific

That Courage herself is not a peasant is not, strictly speaking, the point. It is rather the image and aura of the peasant, the larger 'structure of feeling', to abuse further an already-corrupted term of Raymond Williams, that is meant here.[25] A materialist analysis of the relationship between individual perception and social framing is attempted here, taking into account what Daniel Hartley describes as the 'realm of transindividual subjectivity'. The structure of feeling, Hartley continues, 'emerges from that permeable membrane of everyday life where the moment-to-moment affective shifts of subjectivity are fused with

---

features of an environment in order to show how that environment influenced, shaped, and often battered and destroyed the characters. Unlike dramatists who focused on the universal elements of the human situation and fate, Brecht was interested in the attitudes and behaviour people adopted toward each other in specific historical situations' (Kellner 1980, p. 31). Oddly enough, the notion of specific conditions is far too limited in a discussion of Brecht. For Brecht, the specific condition is the now, and the historical condition is that which is far more malleable in Brecht. This leads us to the point of change and performance in Brechtian theatrical practice. As Marc Zimmerman had pointed out, 'A Brechtian Theatre which represents a changing world implies that the theatre itself must change. A Brechtian production today which copies Brecht, or which adheres to his production models, is not Brechtian' (Zimmerman 1977, p. 125). In this regard the purpose is not to show historical truth or historical specificity for itself. Theatre does not seek to 'evoke feelings of compassion and pity in the audience, as in Aristotelian theatre, nor do they leave the audience purged; [the] aim is to teach the audience so that each member leaves the theatre a changed person' (Horsman, 2011, p. 92).

25   See particularly Chapter 9 of Williams, *Marxism and Literature*. On the connections between this longstanding feeling and historical knowing, Douglas Robinson writes: 'What for Brecht may in fact be *allgemein menschlich* is this hunger for progress, this instinct for the transitional moments in the dialectic, this shared kinaesthetic memory of our collective steps forward – this tendency, if I may generalize, to store in our collective regulatory knowing and deciding (our ideosomatics) the most important events in the long history of our learning' (Robinson 2008, pp. 227–8). This is a very fruitful thought, and one that connects our notions of learning and historical progress and crashes them to the ground of historical tragedy. For Brecht, accessing these moments of the grand sweeps of history was a playground of immense possibilities. And of course, the point was not merely to understand history, but rather to change it. As Robinson continues, 'The desire to alter the world is specifically a dialectical desire (a) to recognise (through identificatory empathy) one's membership and unconscious emotional and intellectual investment in that world, one's circulatory ideosomatic regulation by and of that world, and therefore the familiarity and "ownness" of that world, and (b) to feel (through estranging empathy) the discomfort of alienation from that world, the strangeness of alienness of that world from one's own best interests, and yet at the same time the anxiety caused by any thought of separating once from it, precipitating (c) the discovery of another (Marxist) channel of ideosomatic regulation, which offers models for the *Umfunktionierung* of the world from a (de)alienated standpoint, a standpoint incorporating both the belonging of (a) and the alienation of (b)' (2008, pp. 228–9).

the historically variable rhythms of social life'.[26] Expanding further on Williams, Christian Fuchs argues that our reception of the world, within which I would include the history which we inherit and to which we contribute, 'conditions individual experience and vice versa'. While Fuchs' specific concern is the way that communication functions as 'a social process', this is nevertheless a useless lens for understanding how this process, as he writes, 'organises the relationship of individual and social experience and relates the individual to other individuals and thereby to groups, organisations, social systems, institutions, social spaces and society'.[27] Knowledge of these forms of social determinism is a means of drawing one into history and exacerbating its tensions.

Brecht draws into historical time and brings with him, as Jameson writes, the 'immemoriality of peasant labour and oppression' as a means of emphasising the dire situation of this form of expropriation and exploitation. Yet this critique does have limitations. Whereas a defining feature of peasant labour is its specific involuntary nature – the peasant is forcefully tied to the land – Courage's 'enslavement' is neither enforced by, nor the fault of, others, at least not directly. Her relationship to her own exploitation is very much of her own making. While one should be cautious in limiting her struggle as one solely concerning her own 'freedom' – she is compelled to reproduce herself and her family under threat of starvation – she is given the possibility of not relying on war profiteering. Ultimately, she embodies most importantly the contradictions of her own exploitation. The exploitation is largely of her own devising, albeit unintentional, as it is not her surplus value (or all of her produced value) that is stolen from her. What Courage is robbed of is her children (and thus her store of labour power), stolen away by the war upon which her material existence is based. Brecht here is mobilising the fresh memory of the World Wars and the destruction that they wrought. By doing so, he confronts the mindset of those who can neither face the truth about what they are/were involved in, nor recognise the conditions which make such destruction possible. Further, this exposes the contradiction that Brecht presents between the feudal relations of production that existed in Germany and Europe during the first half of the seventeenth century and the capitalism of his day. This Germany (or if we take the borders of twentieth-century Germany and read them back to the seventeenth century) was not a capitalist society, and would not fully establish the capitalist market as such for some time.[28] Yet while history is not treated

---

26 Hartley 2016, p. 221.
27 Fuchs 2017, p. 755.
28 On this point I would follow the historiography of Blackbourn and Eley 1984. While the authors famously reject the 'Sonderweg' Thesis (wherein Germany's capitalist ascent

by Brecht as a 'series of neatly composed and finished episodes', this does not mean that there are not, as Tom Kuhn notes, 'active analogies between past and present'.[29]

It is useful here to pause and think back to the lines of Benjamin's essay to capture the political reasoning of Brecht's historical positioning of the play. Brecht's gesture matches Benjamin's urging to remember the hatred of exploitation that can be drawn from the image of the 'enslaved ancestor'. In Benjamin's Thesis XI, he writes that 'Nothing has corrupted the German working class so much as the notion that it was moving, with the current'.[30] The idea of a rupture in the notion of progress raises the question of movement away from this 'progression'. This rupture transforms the idea of a steady climb of prosperity into something akin to the *longue durée* that is represented by peasant suffering, but is visible in this specific form of exploitative, commodified relationships. The *gestus* (and perhaps as well the *habitus*) of the peasant, coupled with the immense chronicle of loss that defines *Mutter Courage*'s personal narrative, sets in motion a past wherein the oppressed protagonists have been unable to shake themselves out of their dire situations. Benjamin's 'Angel of History', looking back on the destruction behind it, is mirrored in the moment of recognition entailed by the part that Courage plays in the death of her son, Swiss Cheese. This was made famous by Brecht's lead actress and long-term collaborator and partner, Helene Weigel, in her performance of Courage, inspired by a newspaper photo of an Asian mother 'screaming over her son's dead body'.[31] This usage reminds us to hold in contrast historical portrayal as a distancing device and the brutal reality of the continuing relations of war production and profiteering. When Courage is forced to deny knowing the identity of her dead son, whose death wears especially heavy on her because she haggled too long over his ransom, she lets out an inaudible scream. The scream punctures the air through silence. Even in the moment of tragedy her voice is not heard, just as the peasant history is silent in the annals of official history, despite its ubiquitous historical presence throughout the centuries of feudalism. For Brecht, the silent scream of the past, that history of pent-up anger, must be made audible.

---

occurred only in the late nineteenth century due to a political push from the state), even they do not acknowledge a capitalist hegemony during the Thirty Years' War. David Blackbourn later argues that, far from a direct shift from feudalism to capitalism, the transition was uneven, and there are several examples that during this time there was an expansion of nobles' direction of the economy. See Blackbourn 1997, p. 19.

29   Kuhn 2013, p. 105.
30   Benjamin 1968, p. 255.
31   Honegger 2008, p. 100.

The question, though, is why Courage seems unable to recognise the rather simple logic that her parasitic existence on the war is slowly but surely killing off her children. If she were to resurrect the past, what is the value in her inability to change her circumstance? It is this problem that Brecht seeks to make apparent in the play itself, but more so in its reception. Dealing with this dynamic in correspondence with the playwright Friedrich Wolf, who asks if *Mutter Courage* would not have been more successful if there was some sense that *Courage* had learned from her behaviour, Brecht responds:

> As you quite rightly say, the play in question shows that Courage has learnt nothing from the disasters that befall her ... But even if Courage learns nothing else at least the audience can, in my view, learn something by observing her. I quite agree with you that the question of choice of artistic means can only be that of how we playwrights give a social stimulus to our audience (get them moving). To this end we should try out every conceivable artistic method which assists that end, whether it is old and new.[32]

The link between historical time and the trajectory of her downfall, the loss of all but her own life and her wagon, are presented not just in the content but also in the formal strategies that Brecht employs. They shape the way in which the audience learns, in the particularly Brechtian constellation of didacticism,[33] i.e. through learning from others' mistakes. The key idea of learning, and its absence, is crucial here. In this regard Jameson writes, 'But in Brecht what is fatal is always the failure to learn: as witness the alleged tragedy of *Mother Courage*, for Brecht a fundamental illustration of the deadliness of the idea you can't give up (the little nest-egg, the capital of the wagon that cannot be lost, hanging on to your investment no matter what happens)'.[34]

---

32   Brecht 1978a, p. 229. In part this was a difficulty for Brecht as the actresses were successful in the Aristotelian tradition and audiences became too connected with them. This raises other issues of the type of theatre that Brecht put forward in an institutionalised GDR theatre, although as David Barnett notes, a technique used in another production with Therese Giehse as Mother Courage, produced the effect that despite her hope, 'the audience knows it is mistaken' (Barnett 2015a, p. 177).

33   While Brecht's didacticism clearly does not sit entirely well with Raymond Williams, Williams felt most drawn towards how Brecht constructed a way of so-called 'complex seeing'. This form of seeing develops the mediation of the complex actions that are present on stage. As Alan O'Connor writes, 'This separation between action and consciousness is the actual history that Brecht's plays live out' (O'Connor 1989, p. 89).

34   Jameson 1998, p. 91. Courage's problem is that she tries to sneak through the gaps, to be that lucky one who escapes war's total destruction while profiting from it. In contrast to this, 'Brecht contends that survival tactics, if practiced collectively, can undermine oppressive

Despite the feeling of historical accuracy – the firm dates listed throughout the text, the map that was originally used to show Courage's movements across northern Europe, the backdrop of an historical war, etc., – the lesson is to learn from the person who cannot themselves learn from their own exploitation despite massive personal loss. This trope is useful for Brecht because this figure in the popular imagination (especially as an historical figure in the guise of the peasant) is enmeshed with decidedly clear forms of exploitation and oppression as the object of historical suffering, while also being the terrified subject of war and famine. Despite the fact that Courage is not herself a peasant – her particular lesson is that of the historically represented peasant turned small businessperson – the play relies heavily on the forms (or depictions of historical forms) of this oppression and exploitation. Brecht's historical work demands what Sarah Bryant-Bertail has discussed as the dialogical model wherein a particular theatrical piece is 'multitemporal and multispatial in itself, able to stand independently' from its direct content while also making productive use of a recognised history.[35]

The first version of the play was written in 1939, at the dawn of World War II, and the allegory[36] of historical loss would have been all the more prescient as the plague of Nazism was to project its havoc outward after years of doing so within its own national borders, even though the most famous productions of the play, save a 1941 Zurich version, came after the war. Most notable here was the international production in Paris in 1954. This production was witnessed by, among others, the French theorist Roland Barthes.[37] What influenced Barthes so immensely was the practice of *gestus*, fundamental in Brechtian theatre. While gestus is notoriously hard to define, Bryant-Bertail has noted that 'Gestus may also be a nexus where contradictory spatio-temporal dimensions and

---

strategies. The *details* of material, tactical existence have revolutionary potential, which is why epic theatre tries to single them out' (Bryant-Bertail 2000, p. 70). While I am sympathetic to aspects of this work, especially as it locates how very often female characters in Brecht are depicted as marginalised and left to manage the 'tactical' issues of everyday (eternal) survival, one should not confuse all 'strategies' as oppressive ones.

35   Bryant-Bertail 2000, p. 22.
36   Examining the formal role of allegory, Alan Ackerman notes that: 'Allegories collapse aspects of the present and the past, as Miller did in The Crucible or Brecht did in *Leben des Galilei*, redeeming the past for the purposes of the present' (Ackerman 2006, p. 151). While Ackerman does not delve further into *Leben des Galilei*, his comment is useful in diagnosing the purpose of the Allegory for Brecht's play. This basic point is often lost on critics of the play. This could be equally applied to the other texts dealt with in this chapter.
37   A useful analysis of the history of the play and its popular productions is found in Thompson 1997.

their ideological valuations cross paths at one material object'.[38] One example of these 'contradictory spatio-temporal' moments that impressed Barthes was the moment in *Mutter Courage* where Courage bites down on a coin to test its authenticity. The dual moment of the hardness or materiality of money, in contrast to its abstract quality in capitalism, is a useful and informative contradiction. There is a dual moment involved here, which involves a recasting of the moment of historical reality in Brecht. On this formation in gestus, as regards the particular and the general, Jameson notes: 'What has not yet been added is that *gestus* clearly involves a whole process, in which a specific act – indeed, a particular event, situated in time and space, and affiliated with specific concrete individuals – is then somehow identified and renamed, associated with a larger and more abstract *type* of action in general, and transformed into something *exemplary* (even if archetypal is no longer the word we want to use about it). The theoretical viewpoint required by *gestus* is therefore one in which several "levels" are distinguished and then reassociated with each other ...'.[39] What is refreshing here is Jameson's emphasis on specific concrete individuals and instances, as this is something which he is at times not as willing to address, in part as his otherwise immensely valuable text does not take seriously Brecht's engagement with Benjamin.[40] Yet what is interesting is that both Jameson and Bryant-Bertail used similar words – 'concrete' and 'material', respectively – in relation to gestus. What should be taken from this is that those who attempt to place Brecht as a formal practitioner above all else miss that. Brecht's formal practice is realised only with reference to concrete and material practice and situations.

It is for this reason that gesturing in Brechtian theatrical practice is such a vital entity. Gestus is so fundamental in his work as it is a means of locating a specific point in the body that is the irreducible locus of human life. Des-

38 Bryant-Bertail 2000, p. 22.
39 Jameson 1998, 103.
40 Indeed, the sparse references to Benjamin contained in Jameson's text speak solely to Brecht's work before the historical works under investigation in this chapter were written. In part, this seems to reproduce the notion – much harder to hold after Wizisla's text – that any influence between the two was unidirectional, from Brecht to Benjamin. This may in part be in relation to Jameson's presentation of Benjamin's aesthetics as too influenced by 'mysticism', unlike Brecht's supposed hard-nosed, almost vulgar, materialism. Jameson would not be alone in this reading (with which I disagree). For instance, Stanley Mitchell in his introduction to *Understanding Brecht* notes: 'In one respect, by eliding the politicization of art with the use of artistic "means of production" or apparatus, Benjamin and Brecht at times constricted the relationship between politics and art. Brecht, in his later theory and practice, was able to clarify this confusion. Benjamin died before he could completely think through a new materialist aesthetics'. Mitchell in Benjamin, 1998, p. xv.

pite capital's wish to attempt to abstract away from the body, gestus brings the materiality of the body back into play. As McNally argues, 'The drama of gesture is an historical one – an index of what has been lost with the decorporealization of language and culture'.[41] What capital attempts to be rid of – the body as a site where its effects cannot be gotten rid of – is the place where Brecht attempts to dwell. As much as capital seeks to exist in a world divorced from material labour and in a 'monetary universe that knows no social fixities or stable identities',[42] it cannot occupy that space without exploiting human, corporeal labour. Brecht realises that this tendency is unsustainable (one can only *attempt* to abstract away from the body) and brings us back to the ground zero of the body found in each moment of time, making them dialectical. McNally explains:

> Such gestures are dialectical because, by disrupting the flow of scenes and actions which recreate the time of everyday history, they cast light on the space of the body and its desires. In so doing, they give rise 'to the dialectical at a standstill', the dramatic entry of that which has been repressed – body, Eros, *mimesis* – onto the stage. Gesture is the language of the body and things.[43]

Gestus is an oppositional practice. And what one learns from this material practice is the importance of giving up on things that bring nothing with them but misery. This is specifically a rejection of the notion of progress that Benjamin finds so central to German social democracy and detrimental to working-class activity. He writes, 'Progress, for Brecht, has a negative connotation as the *fortschreiten* (to strive forward; to advance; to progress; to pass; to proceed) from others; it implies moving ahead and thus destroying unity even when it is well intentioned'.[44] The lesson from this is clear. 'Theatre, then, can provide a site for tracing ideas back to their progenitors and to those affected by them. Tracing ideas back and forth forms the basic structure of Brecht's theatre ...'.[45]

The depiction of historical loss can be a useful force for opposition to contemporary forms of exploitation, oppression, and war. In Brecht's *Mutter Courage*, tragic history is (and was) therefore not that which has happened but that which will continue to happen, unless something breaks its rhythm. In part the

---

41 McNally 2001, p. 190.
42 Anderson 1998, p. 85.
43 McNally 2001, p. 190.
44 Oesmann 2005, p. 201.
45 Ibid.

tragic form lends itself to a form of teleology of the pre-ordained, to a kind of fateful outcome. For this reason Brecht was suspicious of the formal nature of tragedy. As Terry Eagleton notes, 'a rejection of metaphysical fate must be actually built into the dramatic form itself'.[46] Brecht addresses these traits by making it possible for the audience member to be a producer of alternate meanings and history for the present. In this sense Brecht's play is 'anti-tragic', as it argues that 'tragedy can be avoided'.[47] Yet for this to be avoided someone must act and be heard.[48] In this regard, the moment of Courage's pain over the death of her son is obviously insufficient, but this insufficiency is a design of Brecht's and is enacted as a means to encourage agency in the audience. As Elinor Fuchs notes,

> If Mother Courage achieves the political aim of Brecht's Epic Theatre, it is because the reverses of Courage's children's deaths do not function as reversals in the plot. The recognition scene that should classically follow on these losses is glaringly absent. In effect, that scene is transferred from the protagonist to the audience. If, as Brecht hopes, the spectator leaves the audience motivated to change the world, it is because Courage cannot see what needs to change.[49]

Courage, famous for her ability to talk around and fool others with linguistic trickery, is notably (and perhaps necessarily) silent in her scream. Yet silence, while the dominant response to a recognition of the barbarity of war, is not the only response the play offers.

---

46   Eagleton 2003, p. 126.
47   Eagleton 2003, p. 127.
48   This also involves a realisation of one's position in a politics of learning, and acting on that learning. On this question Julian H. Wulbern notes that there is a similarity in *Mutter Courage* and *Leben des Galelei* when each turns from the truth and reason: '... there has been a dialectical transformation quite akin to that which occurs in *Mother Courage*, when Courage curses the army for having killed her child at the end of Scene Six, only to proclaim in her next words at the start of Scene Seven that she won't have her war spoiled for her. Here Galileo has acceded to the demands of the Inquisition that he abjure his astronomical and has turned to a considerably safer field of investigation, the study of floating bodies' (Wulbern 1971, p. 163).
49   Fuchs 2007, p. 540. A similar point is offered by Susan Cannon Harris. She writes: 'Courage knows, as the audience knows, that if she betrays her relationship to him by expressing emotion, she will be killed. Brecht would also seem to have known, by now, that forcing Courage not to express grief was the surest way of inducing spectators to feel it. Brecht enforces another such divergence by informing the audience of Eilif's death while Courage is offstage. Since Courage never learns of Eilif's death, she cannot grieve for him; the

By the end of the play Courage is alone, having witnessed the death of all her children. Yet only one of her children, her daughter who was deemed not to have been militarily useful due to her gender, has died in anything resembling noble circumstances. Courage's daughter Kattrin sounds an alarm in the early hours of the morning and wakes a town that will otherwise be sacked. She nevertheless does so in the full knowledge that she will be killed for her actions. In this way, 'Kattrin's death alone is also portrayed as an act of vital revolutionary resistance, and in this form it is positioned in the penultimate scene of the play as its climactic, defining event'.[50] Here, for once in the play, is someone who does not try to feed on the pain and misery of war. In her death, there is the ultimate irony that the one person who was deemed to be without voice (Kattrin is speech impaired) makes herself heard. The metaphor of those who are not heard and yet have agency has obvious parallels with the function of the audience, but also with Brecht's faith in the working class's ability to change the historical tides. It is they who have been hidden from and unheard throughout history and occluded in historiography. As the narrator asks in Brecht's poem 'Questions from a Worker who Reads', 'The great city of Rome / Is full of triumphal arches. Who set them up? Over whom / Did the Caesars triumph?'[51]

---

spectators have to do it for her. Courage hooks spectators as hard as any melodramatic mother ever did; but she is structurally prevented from making them her mirror' (Harris 2013, p. 54).

[50] Vork 2013, p. 33. While Vork's above point is valid, his work does betray a reductive notion that Marxism's radical notion can only lie within a narrow definition of class struggle, and this often leaves the complex relation to historical transposition buried under the presuppositions of what a Marxist playwright should be concerned with. 'At the same time, I will argue that this revolutionary power does not stem from the inherent inequity of class struggle' (Vork 2013, p. 35). Yet Vork is not alone here, as the most prominent postmodern appreciation of Brecht, provided by Elizabeth Wright, suggests that Brecht's plays 'cannot be reduced to any particular ideology, including those of Marxism or existentialism, because this would amount to an attempt to join up a deliberatively decentred view of reality'. Instead, Wright argues that: 'Their Politico-aesthetic function resides rather in the way Brecht manages to make the spasmodic, discontinuous perceptions of a reality-in-process into a theatrical object, thus challenging our automatic interpretations of the concrete and our assumptions that words are able to match that which we sensually perceive. Most of all, the plays are an attack on our assumptions of stable identity, our own and that of others, for in these plays no one has a fixed identity, least of all the "hero," who tries to wrest it from others in a ceaseless round of aggressiveness and exploitation' (Wright 1989, pp. 98–9). This position is counter-balanced by Dougal McNeill who states that 'We need to accept that Marxism, unlike measles or malaria, is not something one can isolate and cure a playwright from suffering under. There is no easy dissection possible to offer up Brecht the man and Brecht the Marxist militant' (McNeill 2005, p. 37). Another piece that dissects Wright's position is found in the aforementioned Silberman 1993.

[51] Brecht 2019, p. 675.

This reconsideration of those occluded or suppressed (or both) questions plays an important part not only in Brecht's concept of the gestus but elsewhere as well. While most of the earliest receptions of Brecht in English made much of his 'Alienation Effect', for some time Brechtian scholarship has opted for a more accurate translation of the *Verfremdungseffekt*, which is actually much closer to 'Distancing Effect'. Alienation should not be completely dismissed, however, as there is some sense that Brecht wishes his audience to take on a new role inside the theatre, alien in relation to their traditional role as passive consumer. This marks a new positionality for the Brechtian spectator. Similarily, Brecht has been depicted as encouraging an anti-emotional attitude in his work, in part due to this misleading translation. Brecht sought the opposite, as Anthony Squiers notes in the following:

> In fact, Brecht wanted the audience to be engaged with the performance. He required attentiveness and personal, intellectual commitment to it. The estrangement Brecht desired was an internal estrangement from one's current *Weltanschauung* or worldview.[52]

The shift in emphasis is vital here, as we move away from the caricatures of Brechtian theatre as austere and anti-emotive to a space wherein complexity of positionality and emotion are central to any production of his work. As Angela Curran notes in her useful 'Brecht's Criticisms of Aristotle's Aesthetics of Tragedy', 'The play does represent the individual suffering and loss Mother Courage experiences from the death of her children in the war. But this loss is presented so that the relationship between Mother Courage's individual loss and her occupation as a businesswoman whose livelihood depends on the war is made clear'.[53] This loss conflicts though with Kattrin's outburst. The loss is accepted and predictable. In order to fully understand it we must have a critical attitude to this historical loss. Brecht made explicit reference to how this could be achieved in his instructions to the play:

> Three aids which may help estrange the actions and remarks of the characters being portrayed:
> 1. Transposition into the third person.
> 2. Transposition into the past.
> 3. Speaking the stage directions out loud.[54]

---

52 Squiers 2015, p. 244.
53 Curran 2001, p. 172.
54 Brecht 1978a, p. 138.

While the first and third aids give the impression of specific tactical use, the second extends beyond the confines of a single production. Together they go a long way in determining the content of the play itself. Indeed, while aspects of the production were changed given the location of production (important here are the productions in Berlin, Munich, Paris, and London), the field of historical transposition marks the work's *sine qua non*. The shifting to another historical time allows for the further distantiation of action and thought in the play.[55] As noted previously in Jameson's comment that learning from errors is vital, the inability of Courage to learn from her actions is a further sign that the benefits of war are only available for those at the very top of the economy. As with the case of Mauler in *Die Heilige Johanna*, it is clear that through crisis there are those that win and those who will (continue to) lose. The point of Courage's example is that it should have been learned as a specifically historical lesson. This is not an abstracted exercise, an *Aesop's Fable* of instruction, but one which involves an emotional *and* critical tie to historical learning and transformation. By seeing what has failed before, and by understanding the reasons for this, we also understand what will be a dead end. The resonance for a German audience of the time, their memories fresh with the barbarity of Prussian militarism, the immense carnage of the First World War, Nazi rule and their role in it, would have been stark.[56] The implication of the audience was

---

[55] Part of the role of distantiation and history must be understood in relation to the intellectual environment within which Brecht was working. It is safe to say that although Brecht's works and aesthetics came to be seen both in the North and then later in the Global South as *the* committed response to the arts, this is not to suggest that such a state of affairs was present at either the time of Courage's writing or at the first production. What is more, the opposite was in fact the case. By far the dominant literary position of the left at the time had been expressed via Zhdanov and Lukács, which stated that art must eschew 'subjectivist tendencies' and aim to present a clear wholeness of the contemporary situation. Writing on the Lukácsian phenomena that 'It just is the case that art which gives us the "real" is superior art', Eagleton shows how the emphasis on displaying history as real is problematic for Brecht. He writes: 'Now there is a sense in which Brecht would agree; but his sense of "rationality" surely differs in important respects from Lukács's. For Brecht, it is not quite that art can "give us the real" only by a ceaseless activity of dislocating and demystifying; it is rather that this *is*, precisely, its yielding of the real, not a mere prelude to the dramatic moment when the transcendental signified will emerge in all its glory' (Eagleton 1994, p. 85). This should not lead to the position that Brecht saw no hope in Lukács. Rather than a rejection, his critical engagements with Lukács are more properly seen as an encouragement, even if one with 'misplaced' hope that 'could be corrected' (Slaughter 1980, p. 129).

[56] As Michael Richardson notes, 'Brecht's ending, however, derives its potential prophylactic power from a different sort of identification with Courage, one in which the audience is forced to come to terms with its own possible guilt with respect to its actions (or inactions)

also, particularly in those versions of the play performed after 1949, pushed to counteract the Nazi ideologies of the world war's origins, and the lived realities of Germans under the Nazi dictatorship. Locating a means by which one could become both critical of the collective process, as well as of the part played in it by the Nazis' concept of the 'people's community' (*Volksgemeinschaft*), was key, especially in the new-born GDR. As Geoff Eley argues, the effects of Nazi lived ideology should be expanded to examine how 'the moral boundaries of national belonging, civic obligation, social responsibility, and human intercourse could be coercively remade under the aegis of the *Volksgemeinschaft*'. This remaking of national identity borrowed much from Germany's colonial history, but highlights the more practical process of reframing the idea of a national morality and purpose. 'This again broadens the concept of ideology by following the impact of ideas *into* society and seeing how they became converted into *practices*'.[57] Perhaps the clearest practice in this regard, and what most spurred Brecht into writing the first draft of the play, is the military expansion into Poland and Eastern Europe. The practice of expansion was justified with recourse to race (which religion in the play stands in for, however insufficiently). The Nazi ideology of racial superiority was deeply connected to the notion of space and, in the drive to occupy Eastern Europe, was motivated by what David Blackbourn terms the 'mystique of the frontier'. The parallels to manifest destiny were not far from the minds of leading Nazis themselves.[58] The move east provided a means to cleanse eastern Europe, but also to fulfil a destiny of spatial expansion. The ideology of racial superiority was entwined with expansion, particularly by military means.

It is doubly important that Brecht understands Courage's downfall is not due to her individual choices. Courage follows the logic of capitalism transposed

---

during the war years. In implicating the audience in this way, Brecht is able to activate the audience to ground their conclusions about the future in a specific moment in the past' (Richardson 2007, p. 168).

57   Eley 2013, p. 141. On the longer trajectory of viewing the eastern frontier, Birthe Kundrus writes that during '… the Wilhelmine period, there was considerable interest in those regions in central and eastern Europe in which Germans had formerly settled. Sine 1900 representatives of the political right, especially those with a *völkisch* orientation, had called for the annexation of these regions, but their demands remained without substantial political results' (Kundrus 2014, p. 331). Summarising Jürgen Zimmerer, she states quite categorically that, '… one can trace strands leading from the structures, attitudes, and practices of German colonialism to Nazi imperialism and, in particular, to Nazi modes of warfare an occupation in the East' (Kundrus 2014, p. 338).

58   See Blackbourn 2009, pp. 141–70. Also useful, on the comparison of the American move to occupy native land and the Nazi conceptualisations of their territorial conquests to the east, is Kakel 2011.

onto a peasant past and thus what is often framed as an 'opportunity' to profit in capitalism is understood here rather as an imperative. She must keep moving, following the war in order to sell her goods. This imperative offers no choice outside of its own logic and thus defines who one can be or become. Darko Suvin articulates this dynamic:

> *Mother Courage* is a union of opposites; even her nickname (or man-made name) testifies to it. It was earned when she saved her little wagon business by running a corridor of gunfire. Ironically, the 'courage' came from her being more afraid to lose her profits than to face the shells. (It is, of course, a 'courage' which will lead both her financially virtuous and her ruthlessly warlike sons to face the firing squads.)[59]

The imperatives, as opposed to opportunities, imposed upon Courage's family necessitate the risk-taking that will eventually lead to her inevitable downfall.

This is a thoroughgoing radical critique of the present.[60] The excursion into history which marks Brecht's period of exile involves a fundamental understanding of the present condition. This includes coming to terms with the knowledge that a simple reproduction of the past, were that even possible, is not what is required or desired.[61] Brecht's formal strategies are not peripheral to his political strategies but rather are integral to the same process. They are devised in tandem and work to make the links between forms of oppression and exploitation and material and concrete consequences as clear as possible. The 'spirit of sacrifice' of Kattrin's actions ultimately upsets the prevailing historical narrative, and is a key feature in rejecting the continual process of the business of war, of which there are few winners but many losers. The question of the losers in history, and the extent to which they have been let down in moments of (perpetual) crisis, problematises faith and its rupture in Brecht's *Leben des Galilei*.

---

59 Suvin 1984, p. 65.
60 As David McNally has noted, *contra* Adorno '... Benjamin's dialectics at a standstill, like Brecht's epic theatre, was not about an adequate depiction of an historical totality, but about puncturing the flow of everyday experience' (McNally 2001, p. 219).
61 *Pace* the above footnote, a similar point was expressed by Theodor Adorno as well. Writing on *Mutter Courage*, Adorno states: 'Because the society of the Thirty Years War was not the functional capitalist society of modern times, we cannot even poetically stipulate a closed functional system in which the lives and deaths of private individuals directly reveal economic laws. But Brecht needed the old lawless days as an image of his own, precisely because he saw his own could no longer be directly comprehended in terms of people and things'. See Adorno in Adorno et al. 1998, pp. 186–7.

2 The Religion of the Now: *Galilei* and the Knowing Science

It may be heretical to speak of the religiosity of Brecht's commitment to the now, especially in relation to a play that provides such a resounding critique of the Catholic Church. What exactly the now is depends on the version of the play that one refers to, but that is as essential a Brechtian problematic as it gets.[62] As in *Mutter Courage*, Brecht uses an historical backdrop, in this case a retelling of Galileo Galilei's well documented battle with the Catholic Church, to arrive at the centre of political questions of his time.[63]

Galileo's struggle with the Church held great importance for his society, as did the consequences of the hopes and disillusionments that Galileo's work and renunciation forced onto the stage and into Brecht's time.[64] This point has been misunderstood by Keith A. Dickson, who mistakes the clash of two historical moments for the privileging of one over another. He writes that 'The

---

[62] The play has been recognised for its radical nature, and Benjamin Bennett goes as far as to state that it 'is as close to a demonstrable instance of revolutionary theatre as we are likely to find' (Bennett 2005, p. 73).

[63] It is interesting to note that in a production of the play in Toronto, the director of the production finds it necessary to claim that 'As a piece of history, it's [*Galileo*] horribly inaccurate' (Zimmer Kaplan 2010, p. 39). This is stated even though the one-off production was itself utilising Brecht's work to make a comment about the present, in this case the private sector infiltration and commercialisation of university-based scientific research. Much more productively, Betty Nance Weber argues that 'Brecht's strategy of composition in the play is to interlace moments of authentic seventeenth-century history with anachronisms and invented history to create a consistent set of parallel between two epochs' (Weber 1980, p. 62). In Weber's essays she analyses the parallels with Galileo and Trotskyists in the Soviet Union. It is interesting further to consider that Weber sees a connection between many of Brecht's history plays and the 'need to counter the falsification of history', particularly as there was a progressively greater 'distortion in official Soviet record' (Weber 1980, p. 62).

[64] For a more general philosophical examination of the reasons to underline the specific historical contradictions that Brecht sought to highlight, see Ray 2010, pp. 3–24. It is important not to fall into the 'argument' that Brecht used history as an attempt to sway his dim-witted audience, a position advanced here: 'The problem is, of course, as Brecht's own Marxist analysis shows very clearly, that appetite for illusion and fetish flourish under the conditions of capitalism, creating a gullible mindset that makes room for the uncritical acceptance of representation. The capitalist spectator-consumer is not simply stupid, but in need of magic and illusion' (Von Held 2011, p. 59). In fact, as Laura Bradley notes, Brecht's project moved in the opposite direction. Writing on the context of Brecht's *Die Mutter*, Laura Bradley writes: 'Brecht's emphasis on the historical context of the stage action must not be confused with his own use of theater, *Historisierung* (Historicization). In a postscript to the *Messingkauf* Brecht explained that *Historisierung* destroys the illusion that familiar phenomena are eternal: 'was ist, war nicht immer und wird nicht immer sein.' [What is, was not always so, and will not remain so forever]' (Bradley 2006, p. 71).

present is weighed and found wanting by a pointed comparison with the past ...'.[65] Rather, it is *not only* that the present has been found wanting: the past and the present have both been found wanting. Historical transposition brings this contradiction out. To this end, I will not investigate the importance of Brecht's work for his time as manifested in the play but rather examine what Galileo's crucial failure, backing-down in the face of pressure from above, means in relation to the peasant 'Little Monk', a character who well understands the politics of history and the politics of the now, more innately than any in the play. Indeed, the Little Monk represents the vital intelligence and, problematically, the repeated Brechtian trope of the simplicity of working-class intellectuals.

These intellectuals are fundamental to radically altering and fulfilling a project that shuns the pacific notions of official historiography and works for a politics of the now, which seeks to produce from history something burning in the present. The term working-class intellectuals should be read in connection with the theorist Antonio Gramsci's description of 'organic intellectuals', a group that, unlike traditional intellectuals who can be won over to a cause, arises from within and is born with a movement.[66] Such intellectuals are intimately related to their moment and in establishing a counter-hegemonic project.

My concern here is not to rehash the surplus of academic work which makes the connections with the actual historical reference points with which the play is, loosely put, 'in conversation'. Rather, my focus is to broaden the discussion so as to take into consideration the larger implications of these reference points for an often-overlooked character in the play. By using the Little Monk as an example of that comprehension of history (he, of course, is not named, but is defined by his social category), in contrast to the definitive dates that are offered throughout the play chronologising Galileo's life, Brecht simultaneously counteracts the many necessary omissions that comprise the 'great man' theory of history. This also brings to the fore the important question of social transformation and class.[67]

---

65 Dickson 1978, p. 61.
66 Gramsci notes that 'One of the most important characteristics of any group that is developing towards dominance is its struggle to assimilate and to conquer "ideologically" the traditional intellectuals, but this assimilation is made quicker and made more efficacious the more the group in question succeeds in simultaneously elaborating its own organic intellectuals' (Gramsci 1999, p. 10). The organic intellectual reflects in part the newness of the class formations from which they originate. As Peter Thomas notes, 'It is for this reason that the specificity of the organic intellectual is integrally linked to the specificity of the class project from which they emerge' (Thomas 2010, p. 416).
67 On the importance of the Little Monk, Terry Holmes argues that 'In his argument with the little monk he even asserts that the problem of social justice is the real point at issue

There are two historical events which are normally brought up when one examines the contemporary inspirations for the writing of the several versions of the play. The more popular interpretation sees in the work a condemnation of Oppenheimer and the Manhattan project, which involved the discovery of the technology behind the atom bombs that was horrifically put into practice on the cities of Hiroshima and Nagasaki. The lesser-known interpretive example and also 'the least mentioned', argues Jameson, 'no doubt for all kinds of reasons, although Brecht himself mentions it, is the submission of Bukharin in Stalin's show trials'.[68] It stands as a testament to the strength of the play that its function could be switched from a critique of the punishing of oppositional theories and practices in the Soviet Union and, a few years later, to the nuclear politics of the post-war era.[69] The common thread which binds the two separate histories is important here. At the centre of both is the responsibility-shirking of naming the proven truth, whether of science, in Galileo's case astronomy, and in Bukharin's case the 'science' of Marxism. Here, following Jameson, '... the notion of Marxism as a science, and, indeed, as the well-known "science of society" is a secondary signifying move which also corrects and limits itself: it says, yes, Marxism really is a science in that sense, but *only* in that figurative sense of what accompanies and theorizes the New'.[70] This 'New' is both the

---

behind the cosmological disputes ... Galileo's retraction of this insight, a retraction in effect of his own commitment to the cause of humanity, is a much more serious and fundamental betrayal than his later repudiation of the scientific facts' (Holmes 1998, p. 154). This is a useful analysis and similar to my position, but is unfortunately not taken up further by Holmes. Rather, Holmes relies too often on preserving a sense of 'orthodox Marxism' in Brecht's work, even when that may not be the playwright's purpose. Note for instance Holmes' argument that Brecht had wished to have Galileo ally himself with the bourgeoisie, hastening the bourgeois revolution and thus communism. This stagist approach often found in Marxism has been powerfully criticised throughout the work of Ellen Meiksins Wood: see Wood 1995 and 2002.

68 Jameson 1998, p. 123.
69 While I would not take the position that Bukharin represented a fundamental change of direction for the Soviet Union, it is enough for our present purposes that Brecht thought so. On Brecht's attitude to the Soviet Union, Peter Brooker accurately refers to Brecht's anti-Stalinism as 'indirect, cautious and delayed'. Brooker also refers to the Soviet Union as a 'type of socialist society', a point with which I would also take issue, arguing instead that it was state capitalist (Brooker 1988, p. 6). Brooker's text is very useful in pointing out how critics have often sought to divide Brecht between a young period (sometimes 'anarchistic', less rational and more overtly political) to an older (often rational, 'humanist') version. These latter interpretations often picture Brecht as being at odds with his own work, bursting through the confinements of his 'unsustainable Marxist' politics (1988, pp. 182–5). A remarkable study that depicts the downfall of the hopes and utopic inspiration of the Russian Revolution is Buck-Morss 2000.
70 Jameson 1998, p. 126. Brecht's theoretical work is often underestimated. Wolfgang Haug

immediate present which unfolds from insoluble contradictions, and also the present to come, that which is both presented, and gestures at future directions.

I have already argued that, for Brecht, a 'transposition into the past'[71] was a key strategy in establishing a critical distance in his history plays. In a similar way religion stands in for other, established forms of dominance and is simultaneously a prism through which to understand the new. Yet despite his significantly over-stated 'hyper-rationalist' politics, Brecht does not dismiss the question of religion as false consciousness or as a way to cast a shadow over a society's ability to use logic. Rather, understanding that the new is riven with contradictions, Brecht is clear that even within the church there are instances of struggle for good and ill, not least represented during the time of Galileo's birth in the Peace of Augsburg of 1555 (Augsburg is also Brecht's birthplace and this history would have been very familiar to him). The Little Monk is the prime example of this as, coming from the peasantry, he believes in the power of the Church to relieve suffering. In this instance winning him over to a position of science over religious authority must deal with the consequences of its success, and ultimately the circumstances upon which the success is founded.[72]

The Church of the Little Monk is not the Vatican and its institutional force, but rather a 'little church and Bible texts' of Sunday's devotion.[73] In the Monk's presentation, the Church's standing comes from its ordering of life: in making sense of the poverty and degradation that are integral to peasant labour. In this sense religion's usefulness is to rationalise all forms of life, no matter how abhorrent. Thus, the Church here represents a very real, material operation in the lives of peasants while also providing a way of viewing the world historically. Given the long traditions of Church orthodoxy and of the Church's daily practices in the world, a mere dismissal of these would be too much for the Little Monk to bear, producing too great a vacuum in his worldview. As Wolfgang Sohlich notes in his analysis of the play, 'Faith, at least, gives meaning to suffering and redeems death'.[74] Galileo himself has a coterie of true believ-

---

argues that: 'behind Brecht's world fame as a playwright and poet it is still a widely kept secret that he was one of the most outstanding Marxist philosophers' (Haug 1999, p. 113). Anthony Squiers partially addresses this considerable gap in his 2014 text.

[71] Brecht 1978a, p. 138.
[72] As Peter Smith notes, '*Leben des Galilei* suggests that scientists should not view themselves as operating within a metadiscourse isolated from external influences'. This is no doubt a complex problem, and a general one in the play. Smith's interest is in the history of science, and he continues: 'Galilei warns that a pure science risks becoming an exploited science, as happened in Germany under the National Socialists' (Smith 1997, p. 406).
[73] Brecht 1966, p. 83.
[74] Sohlich 1993, p. 57.

ers, but these are educated men whose links to the poor are non-existent.[75] This separation is notable, and Brecht is clear as to what transpires on the ground: the torture of the people by the Church and the ways in which it expresses dominance. However, he is also aware that a simple dismissal of God is dangerous for a counter-hegemonic politics. It will, for instance, not win over those who, like the Little Monk, are necessary to win Galileo's larger struggle against the Church.

The Little Monk position is precarious, balanced between the reproduction of the 'orderly' society and the potential of the peasants who, for the moment, believe in the rightness of the established Church. This Church has the power to structure the worldviews of peasants, and this cannot be forgotten by Galileo in his dealings with the Little Monk. Yet this must be balanced by the Little Monk's response to Galileo's assistant Federzoni when he cries that the established families 'who ordered the earth stand still because their castles might be shaken loose if it revolves ...'. The Little Monk interjects, stating '... and who only kiss the Pope's feet as long as he uses them to trample on the people. God made the physical world, God made the human brain. God will allow physics'.[76] God may be something different from the Church, yet God's institutional presence is felt in ways that must be taken into account. This is both a lesson that Brecht leaves for Galileo, and the audience. Indeed, the philosophy of meeting people where they are in the moment, and acknowledging these contradictions, seems to be the point that we (and Galileo) are to take from this interaction.

As so often in Brecht's work, and as shown in the above section on *Mutter Courage*, we learn from those who do not. Galileo is a complex figure in this regard, as he is one of the most knowing characters in Brecht's oeuvre, yet he is as vulnerable as others in not learning. At the beginning of Scene Seven of the play, when his findings have been ratified by the Papal Observatory and things seem to be turning in his favour, Galileo engages in a conversation with the Little Monk. Troubled by Galileo's material facts that conflict with his theological texts, the Little Monk resolves to resign from his pursuit of astronomical truth. Galileo's response, perhaps emboldened by this official validation, is arrogant, suggesting that he can only see the Little Monk as a loyal officer of the Church hierarchy. Galileo states 'Your motives are familiar to me'.[77] The Little Monk engages in a full-blown response, which links Galileo's facts to the world with which he is most familiar: peasant life in the Campagna. After hav-

---

75 There is a serious gender problem here, as the few women portrayed in the play lack the ability to think outside of their perceived respective positions and gendered stereotypes.
76 Brecht 1966, p. 96.
77 Brecht 1966, p. 82.

ing listened to the complexity of the Little Monk's honest statement, and the genuine experience on which the Little Monk draws, Galileo is embarrassed to realise he has overreached in his assault against the Little Monk.

Viewed without the Little Monk's intervention, *Leben des Galilei* can very easily be read as a struggle of one man's ideals against the powers that be. The Little Monk's intervention deftly challenges this reading, and the central problem becomes the scientist's arguments against the established Church, balanced against the concrete situation of working people. Witness for instance the Monk's statement that 'Too often these days when I am trying to concentrate on tracking down the moons of Jupiter, I see my parents. I see them sitting by the fire with my sister, eating their curded cheese'.[78] The distinction here between heaven and earth, between abstract struggle and the lived lives of peasants in the Campagna is not nearly as severe as has been presented thus far. Indeed, they are presented as if an understanding of one is necessary to understand the other. The 'curded cheese' also stands in contrast to the wonderful meals and wine to which Galileo is accustomed, a pleasure he rates as highly as his research.

In the discourse between Galileo and the peasant, the former is taught another lesson by the latter. After Galileo has heard of the penury of the Little Monk's devout parents, he asks 'where is their divine fury?'[79] The Little Monk's response that 'They are old' leaves Galileo 'beaten', and unable to 'meet the Little Monk's eyes'.[80] The multiple forms of abuse that Galileo will take from those in positions of power has been the focus of much of the criticism of the play. The intellectual defeat and shame that Galileo experiences from someone occupying such a lowly social position, as evidenced with this statement, has been pointedly absent.[81]

Galileo's embarrassment points to a key problem in Brecht: individual self-criticism, but also how intellectuals operate within Stalinist societies, given that for Brecht they carry an increased level of responsibility in order that socialism is properly defended from bureaucratisation and betrayal of socialist principles. Brecht was keenly aware of this, as Benjamin notes in a conversation between the two in August of 1938. 'In Russia a dictatorship is in power *over* the proletariat. We must avoid disowning it for as long as this dictator-

---

[78] Brecht 1966, p. 83.
[79] Brecht 1996, p. 85.
[80] Ibid.
[81] Thus, the problem is not one simply to be placed on him alone. Brecht does not wish to isolate the problem but rather, as Darko Suvin explains, 'Brecht's *Life of Galileo* melds in the protagonist both individualist and societal failure' (Suvin 1994, pp. 530–1).

ship still does practical work for the proletariat'.[82] Galileo's difficulty is that he prides himself most on his material well-being (with eating emphasised as the chief form of such pleasure). Brecht brings together the problematic nature of an individualist material focus and brushes this against the historical ramifications of such behaviour. Two points in particular stand out here. Firstly, the Little Monk notes that this materiality is expressed in specifically historical terms. The depiction of the ceiling beams 'which the smoke of centuries has blackened' evokes Jameson's clever depiction of the 'Xairos of Brecht's peasant history'.[83] Secondly, the Little Monk's father who 'did not get his poor bent back all at once, but little by little, year by year, with unfailing regularity ...' illustrates again the *longue durée* of the peasant. Yet the example of the peasant is also more largely an opportunity for learning. This is expressed especially in Galileo's own case but also in terms of his teaching.

Despite being twice humbled by the Little Monk, Galileo ridicules him again for taking an interest in his new manuscript, despite his misgivings about Galileo's relation to the Church. The Little Monk pays no attention to Galileo but, coming across a difficult passage, states: 'I don't understand this sentence'. Galileo's response is a practical one. 'I'll explain it to you, I'll explain it to you', he responds, as they are both sitting on the floor. The symbolism of the basic question, the simple repeated answer and the fact that they are working together on the floor is telling. The problematic idea of high-mindedness that was present before, of a battle between the noble, great, individual and the political machine, is deconstructed and ridiculed here.[84] In this scene the Little Monk has established the inefficacy, or even the uselessness, of knowledge that is out of reach to those who most need it. Again, he brings Galileo back to earth. It is highly significant that Galileo's single moment of non-coerced submission, free of physical or economic compunction, comes in the moment where is he forced to acknowledge the larger social importance of his actions. Sat on the

---

82 Brecht in Benjamin 1978, pp. 218–219.
83 Jameson 1998, p. 139.
84 An attempt to examine this relation between individual and the social has been presented in Merriam-Paskow 1992, pp. 42–56. Merriam-Paskow's contention is that rather than the historical figure of Galileo being a divided subject, straddling the lines between the truthfulness of his political position and the social implications of that position, the play is in fact a deconstruction of the idea of the rational scientist in the Western tradition. My use of the term deconstructed is much different than the meaning provided by Merriam-Paskow and the postmodern trajectory to which it is arguably indebted.

floor, closest to the base elements which Galileo's study has only been able to come to terms with in abstract theory, Brecht invites an inventive contrast between idealism and materialism. Jameson examines the complex materialist/idealist contradictions in the play using Hegel's Master/Slave dialectic. He writes:

> The Master is willing to sacrifice his life for Honour (for a Recognition that will later include power and material privilege as a bonus and a supplement). It is this willingness to sacrifice his own life and living body that distinguishes him from the Slave, who is supremely unwilling to lose the one good he already has. The Slave is the materialist; the Master the idealist: materialism, then, is the ultimate unwillingness to let go of the body as such, no matter what the promises of reward (and those are, in any case, generally paid out in idealistic rhetoric and in a hollow language of honour a good deal less "materialist" in the long run than the Master's feudal privileges).[85]

This only partly fits, as it is clear from the play that the mark of Galileo's famous submission is that he does not wish to give up his life for his cause. Yet the conversation with the Monk nevertheless illustrates a central intentional omission in the play. Galileo's war with the Church is not at all sympathetic to the actual concerns of the peasant class; his war is merely abstract, utopian in the sense of not existing in a specific location (note again the embarrassment and submission of Galileo when the Little Monk raises basic questions of material circumstances). In this respect, the 'good that the Little Monk already has' may not in fact be all that productive. The Little Monk is himself deeply conflicted, and despite his concerns about the repercussions of Galileo's new book, he nevertheless 'wolfs down' the text.[86] The reasons for his devouring of Galileo's work is that it has an understandable purpose. How one learns and is taught to learn will shift just as the 'ground on which you stand', as *Mann ist Mann* teaches. In this regard, as Freddie Rokem notes: 'Learning and pedagogy are for Brecht also a form of interaction with the world that is *revolutionary*, both in the sense of contemplating a particular phenomenon from constantly changing perspectives moving "around" it, but also by changing the world itself through revolutionary social change, which as Brecht's Galileo also argues, is based on the new forms of knowledge he propagates for'.[87] Learning must respond to

---

85 Jameson 1998, p. 124.
86 Brecht 1966, p. 85.
87 Rokem continues: 'In order to achieve this dual goal, not only the world as we know it,

the world it finds itself in. Learning conditions new thought, but it is limited in that it is itself shaped and determined. As Galileo notes in his *mea culpa* to his lifelong assistant Andrea in the penultimate scene, 'Even a man who sells wool, however good he is at buying wool cheap and selling it dear, must be concerned with the standing of the wool trade'.[88] To tear a world asunder one must understand and have connections to the lived realities of material existence.

After Galileo's recantation, his many followers flee from him.[89] Of the Little Monk, Andrea notes: 'Fulganzio, our Little Monk, has abandoned research for the peace of the Church'.[90] In this sense the centrality of the Little Monk for the majority of the play, and the centrality of his sudden and distinct withdrawal from political life, recalls the idea of something missing ('etwas fällt') of Brecht's earlier piece *Der Aufstieg und Fall der Stadt Mahogonny*. The meaning of this loss, and the potential that it could have unlocked, is made clearer in the final scenes of the play. Galileo is visited by Andrea, who is on his way to Holland to spread the word of Galileo's works. Attempting to reflect on his part in the larger attack on science, Galileo states:

> As a scientist I had an almost unique opportunity. In my day astronomy emerged into the market place. At that particular time, had one man put up a fight, it could have had wide repercussions. I have come to believe that I was never in real danger; for some years I was as strong as the authorities, and I surrendered my knowledge to the powers that be, to use it, no,

---

but also the activity of learning itself – in this case, from and through the theatre, as well as the pedagogies of studying theatre – must also be constantly investigated and radically critiqued and restructured' (Rokem 2015, p. 57). This text also is useful in articulating novel ways in which the Brecht and Benjamin collective path began before the two began their friendship.

88   Brecht 1966, p. 123.
89   While her article is useful in examining the interrelation between ideology and scientific reason in Brecht's play, Anne Moss's analysis seems to overstate the reliance on the reasoning in Brecht, stemming from what she sees as Brecht's 'predilection for a utopian vision of *reason* as man's unique capacity for practical intelligence, cognitive acuity and ideological thinking – none of which may necessarily be informed by sound judgment' (Moss 1998, p. 141). Such a viewpoint abstracts away from the principle of applied reason in Brecht's work and, as with *Mutter Courage*, the usefulness Brecht locates in learning from those who do not learn. This also separates the meanings of truth in differing social settings. 'Truth must never be regarded as an absolute content of writing but must always be treated as a function of the responsible social action of individuals here and now' (Bennett 2005, p. 62).
90   Brecht 1966, p. 120.

not *use* it, *abuse* it, as it suits their ends. I have betrayed my profession. Any man who does what I have done must not be tolerated in the ranks of science.[91]

This may sound like an extreme burden to be placed on one's shoulders, yet such a concern is not a new one, and Brecht goes to great lengths to make this clear. As I have already established, the idea of suffering – especially for the cause – is omnipresent in his work. This is not always unproblematically formulated, for instance in his infamous *Die Massnahme*.[92] Nevertheless, what Galileo's failure produces is not merely the absence of the Little Monk but the unrest that is belied by his return to the Church and its version of labour peace. Here we have a rejection of peace as an abstract category. Peace in the material sense does much to produce and reproduce the material destruction of the timeless peasant who along with Galileo could be blown out of History's continuum. That Galileo's work 'could have had wide repercussions', coupled with the blow that the renunciation of politics had for the Little Monk, the figure for whom these repercussions would be most keenly felt, is clear for Brecht.

Yet recourse to history here is also the potential liberation of that weight that is placed on the shoulders of those in the present. Yet as Benjamin notes, disrupting this past is dangerous for all involved. The Little Monk is clear on this when he asks,

> How could they take it, were I to tell them that they are on a lump of stone ceaselessly spinning in empty space, circling around a second-rate star? What, then, would be the use of their patience, their acceptance of misery? What comfort, then, the Holy Scriptures, which have mercifully explained their crucifixion?[93]

Something must stand in for this missing piece, which will offer a way out of the 'happy peace' of the Church's chronology. As stated earlier, the Little Monk's future is delicately balanced. The religion of 'our Little Monk', a name intended to be worthy of great compassion rather than condescension, is one of feeling

---

91   Brecht 1966, p. 124.
92   This play, commonly translated as *The Measures Taken or The Decision*, centres around four Soviet communists on a party mission in China. In the fulfilment of their duties, the four feel it necessary to kill a communist who was unable to control himself as he was threatening the secret nature, and ultimately the fulfillment, of their mission. The play sought to reinforce the notion of sacrifice, and in particular to justify extreme acts in order to push forward the cause of Chinese/World communism.
93   Brecht 1966, pp. 83–4.

towards working people. Working people are knowing subjects who are experts in their own struggle, even if they do not always arrive at the right answer, just as Galileo may be the knowing subject who has the right answer, but is not an expert in the struggle which surrounds and consumes him. Thus falls the great man theory of history and a renewed interplay of agency and structure comes to the fore. The emphasis on agency and division is central to the play, as Michael Bennett notes: 'Thus, *Galileo* examines the point in human history where narrative and the idea of motion intersect: forcing the audience to be aware of conflicting narratives; forcing the audience to realize that their own narratives about the world are just socially and culturally constructed (i.e., artificial, in the broad sense, and human-made, in the more general sense); and forcing the audience to accept that both narratives and society is not a given and is not unchangeable'.[94] For *Galilei*, the knowledge of science is useful. However, crucially it is not the only form of knowledge that counts: there is also a knowledge joined to practice. Practice, its implications, and what confines it, will be the focus of the next section on *Der Kaukasische Kreidekreis*.

3 The Chalk Lines of History: *Der Kaukasische Kreidekreis*, Productivity and the Past

I move now from the historical investigation of *Galilei* to *Der Kaukasische Kreidekreis*, where the transposition into the past has a more open, directly strategic, use. In some ways the movement is very similar to that in the previous chapter on Brecht. As in *Kuhle Wampe* and *Mann ist Mann*, Brecht uses the trope of a play within a play. Here, though, there are two uses of this device, firstly with the story of the rescue of the child, and also in the story of the Judge, Azdak.[95] Indeed, the principle of moving and shifting terrain structures the

---

[94] Bennett 2013, p. 61. Also useful in this regard is Bennett's argument regarding the link between the moment of the now and historical consciousness. He notes: 'Confronting these memories not only takes us "back" into our individual and collective consciousness but also, importantly, simultaneously makes it "anew", so as to alienate (to use Brecht's idea that will be articulated near the end of "modern drama") the familiar, making the "past and the strange" come into contact with the "near and the present": making us encounter and question our deep-seeded individual and collective assumptions and memories' (Bennett 2013, p. 15).

[95] The origin of Azdak, argue Neil Brough and R.J. Kavanagh, is possibly found in a Persian religious figure called Mazdak. See Brough and Kavanagh 1991, pp. 573–80. This adds to the complex make-up of the play's origins, and points towards Brecht's use of various historical trajectories in the play.

play, not only formally but also with regard to content. Important in this sense is the connection between Grusha's development from obliging servant to self-conscious actor,[96] a dynamic which mirrors that of Joan in *Die Heilige Johanna*. Continuing in this vein, *Mann ist Mann* and *Die Kaukasische Kreidekreis* have similar trajectories wherein the lead characters set out on a journey not of their choosing, forced to carry a burden (another identity and social role for both Galy Gay and Grusha, with the latter taking on the responsibility of a child besides) before ultimately accepting and making that burden their own. The point here is that there are major structural links to be made between the works written before Brecht flees Germany and those written in exile. The major distinction here is the specific use of history as it occurs in the later work (as opposed to the scant use of history in his Weimar days) through which Brecht articulates his politics of productivity in the now. History here is productively employed, both in the sense of the oppressed peasant as well as a false/failed utopian past. As a correlative, in *Der Kaukasische Kreidekreis*, the possibility of building socialism is seen simultaneously as productive and utopian. Brecht's use of peasant history makes this odd linking possible.[97] The specific question

---

[96] Given the potential misunderstandings that are possible in Grusha taking the child, Brecht sought to formally divide the moment (and any flippant connection) involving 'innate' behaviour. In this regard, a deep problem for Brecht was to prefigure Grusha as a product of a class divided society with its own inherent determinants. As Meg Mumford notes: 'Not only did Brecht present Grusha's behaviour as socially derived, but he repeatedly sought to avoid the presentation of her character as a fixed entity. For example, by foregrounding Grusha's long hesitation before taking the abandoned child he interrupted the idea that her decision was a spontaneous impulse born of an eternally honourable character' (Mumford 2009, p. 119). With this stated, however, in an important essay Iris Smith pays attention to the role of women's sexuality in Brecht's later works. She writes: 'The crux of the problem is the representation of the mother's desire. In *Mother Courage* (1939), *Caucasian Chalk Circle* (1944–5), *Good Person of Szechwan* (1939–41) and *The Mother* (1930–1), the female subject is identified as an asexual mother, or as a sexual being that willingly abandons her sexuality and self-definition for the sake of children. These characters' social and economic positions are determined through their roles as mothers, and their sexual identities are correspondingly stunted. None of this can be explained by the flattening of dramatic character normally seen in Brecht's epic theatre, for the sexual identities of male characters are not similarly foreshortened' (Smith 1991, p. 496). There is no doubt validity to this point, and it perhaps for this reason (and the stereotype of the 'sexless' mother) that audiences identified so strongly with the principal characters (to Brecht's bemusement). This said, it does need pointing out that Brecht focuses more on the social effects and problems that women (as mothers particularly) have to deal with as primary caregivers and providers for children and the elderly, and that their involvement in this day-to-day struggle often means putting off meeting their own needs.

[97] While the pretext of the play is the decision-making process of collectivisation in the Soviet Union, there is a real question as to whether Brecht felt such freedom in deciding

of historical positionality in *Der Kaukasische Kreidekreis* is key to understanding the play's political and aesthetic relevance.

Brecht wrote the play when his political relevancy was at a low ebb. His work in the United States with college and labour organisation productions was fraught with problems and often quickly abandoned. His one other significant work during his time there – the film *Hangmen Also Die* – was both a limited and limiting production given the restrictions of working within the Hollywood system, even though the film bears some Brechtian marks.[98] Nevertheless, devoid of a political-aesthetic organisation with which to work, not to mention a large group of committed cultural producers like himself (Eisler and Weigel being the major exceptions), Brecht turns to the parable as a means of providing a productive distance to his work.[99] However, as with his other historical works, this parable relies on a distinctly different use of time than the frantic, ear-to-the-ground movement of his earlier works.

---

one's future was in fact possible in Stalinist Georgia. While Brecht may have held a sincere hope that the economic successes of socialism would destroy the necessity or possibility for Stalinist-type rule, he himself expressed sincere misgivings about the rule of Stalin: he referred to him as the 'great murderer of the people' and expressed as early as 1936 the point that Leon Trotsky's devastating criticisms of the Soviet Union may very well be valid. Nevertheless, it is worthy to note that the expert in the Prologue – the Delegate – is from Tiflis and his role is that of a Bureaucrat. Stalin was himself from Tiflis and in the Prologue there is a sly criticism of the Delegate. When, for instance, he asks for the play to be shortened to fit his schedule the Singer responds bluntly with 'No'. For more on the critique of Stalin, see Holmes 1977, pp. 95–106.

[98] Among other examples, the character Professor Stephen Novotny states the Brechtian formulation found at the beginning of Chapter 2: 'Don't start from the good old times, but from the bad new ones'. Lang 1943. On the subject of the United States, J. Chris Westgate humorously notes: 'If Brecht had lived long enough to consider the history of his plays on Broadway, he would have known that he made the right decision in settling in the GDR' (Westgate 2007, p. xii).

[99] Long-time Berliner Ensemble member, Manfred Wekwerth, constructively delineates the parable as form and ideological content. He writes: 'If the history play contributes to the construction of ideologies by encouraging activity on the part of the spectator, the parable makes ideology itself into its subject. It critiques ideology. It is not primarily concerned with discovering people or processes, but rather discovering discovery itself' (Wekwerth 2011, p. 157). Wekwerth qualifies his notion of Brecht's work: 'This does not refer to the history play as a literary type, but to a mediating form in theatre' (2011, p. 156). 'The history play is a suitable way of confronting the individual in the audience with the individual on stage. Its technique resides in highlighting the individual' (2011, p. 157). And here: 'Likewise, if you want to question the present – with old or new plays – and "mercilessly" criticize it, dehistoricization in the end leads to the opposite – to adaptation. Because it deactivates the spectator' (2011, pp. 37–8).

The play begins with a discussion of the future of a Georgian field that was operated by the 'Galinsk goat-farming commune', before the Nazis had taken over and subsequently expelled the local inhabitants. The question presented to the nascent 'Rosa Luxemburg fruit-growing commune' is how to convince those who wish to return to the pre-Nazi goat farming days that the land should be collectivised. The strategy that the commune devises is to invite a group of actors to produce a play that will clarify the notion of productive 'ownership', showing how those who work together *productively in common* deserve their rightful reward. Clearly, the specific deployment of art to actively engage with material questions, something *Kuhle Wampe* also exhibited to maximum effect, is still present in Brecht's work. Yet, lacking an organisation devoted to making such a politics a possibility (an organisation like the *Red Megaphone*, for instance), Brecht uses history to make an argument for the present. In order to provide an answer to the collectivisation problem, historical representation is used to illuminate the present circumstance, both via transposition into the past and by resurrecting the content of a biblical parable (although the reference given in the Prologue is that the legend 'comes from the Chinese').[100] The immediate fascist history, and in particular the Nazi conception of the 'integrity' of labour, had to be challenged, particularly as they had attempted to reframe the national mythology of the German nation-race, but also as they sought to reframe the centrality of benefits of exploitative practices as ones that could be shared along racial lines. This was attempted by 'unifying an otherwise disjointed ensemble of discontents within a totalising populist framework – namely, the radicalized ideological community of the German people-race'.[101] This vision of labour that was initiated from above was both ideological and heavily enforced through state repression. As Alf Lüdtke notes,

> The field of force in which men and women workers and working-class wives found themselves in Nazi Germany was transformed. Silent as well as open violence increased perceptibly. But at the same time, a multitude of symbolic practices and presentations facilitated an altered self-perception.[102]

Coupled with the state's 'open violence' was an attempt to reconfigure the socialist ideology of workers' solidarity which stood in opposition to the nation

---

100 For an overview of the history of the Chinese versions of the *Chalk Circle* play see Du 1995, pp. 307–25.
101 Eley 1986, pp. 269–70.
102 Lüdtke 1994, p. 98.

into one in which workers' value was in what they produced for the national collective. Yet inscription into the collective narrative demanded obedience, not only to ruthlessly crushing opposition within, but also without. This process of invitation was not merely to a better life, but a better life through an adherence to open barbarity, particularly that experienced through the east. Lüdtke continues:

> Equally decisive were concrete, sensual, as well as general-rhetorical, reinforcements of the 'honor of labor'. The diffuse rhetoric of the sense of 'community' in the factories gave industrial survival interests in the work-places – and in fact the self-assertiveness of the 'quality worker' – increased legitimacy and opportunities. In this way, in an unprecedented fashion, hopes for a "good life" could be sensually experienced and felt to be justifiable. ... Survival and enjoyment of the 'honor of labor' thus also meant becoming an accomplice to criminal policies.[103]

Culture fields were a vital accomplice in this regard, particularly in eliding the long history of exploitation that the time of the peasant so deftly signifies. While the Nazis borrowed from a long-standing strain of cultural conservativism in the arts that distanced itself from the experimentation of the Weimar era, they broadened and institutionalised these movements (including an opposition to a supposed 'Feminization of Culture') into their own cultural dictatorship. Towards the beginning of Nazi rule especially, the classics were relied upon to forge a new national ideological community. As Adelheid von Saldern notes, 'The Nazis used the classics to foster a new sense of national identity with strong heroic streaks. The classics also served to legitimize the "*Volk* community" and place it on elitist, racist foundations suffused with the autocratic *Führerprinzip*, which underlay the political and social structure of the Third Reich'.[104] This is not to suggest that this was the only terrain deemed fit for Nazi cultural purposes. The Nazis made forays into 'those elements of popular culture that were deemed acceptable to make the general population feel comfortable with the new system'.[105] As the war progressed, the Nazi culture industry forged new identities that were amenable to the practical purposes of the regime, and it also helped restore 'a patina of normality to society beneath which the terrorist Prerogative State could carry on'.[106] Brecht was aware of

---

103 Lüdtke 1994, p. 98.
104 Von Saldern 2002, p. 325.
105 Von Saldern 2002, p. 332.
106 Von Saldern 2002, p. 333.

the extent to which these forms of understanding had been driven into German society, and 'his poems and journals show he was acutely aware of the hold that Nazi attitudes still had on the population, and of the unpopularity of the occupying Soviet forces'.[107] It was necessary to show that not everyone joined in in the celebration. The peasants, for instance, are never invited to join in the plunder. They are the universally plundered. As argued before, this is specifically a peasant history in the general sense, not merely focused on exploitation of the land as such but on the entirety of social oppression of that time. Jameson has argued that this vision of the peasantry represents an almost heuristic vision of historical exploitation before capitalism. The peasantry epitomise exploitation taken to its most exaggerated state, without even the weak freedom of workers under capitalism. Likewise, the capitalist class (as opposed to the Feudal ruling elites, etc.) represent the clearest example of parasitic life. As Marx famously describes them in Volume I of *Capital*, 'Capital is dead labour which, vampire-like, lives only by sucking living labour, and lives the more, the more labour it sucks'.[108] This is the choice that Jameson sees Brecht making. How to represent the systems of exploitation most clearly involves a blending of historical periods and their particular forms of surplus extraction. He writes:

> For in the peasant works – and above all in the *Chalk Circle* ... – peasant time is *par excellence* the time of oppression: in the great class struggle of human history as a whole, now defined not by the specific modes of production as such but, rather, as the immemorial relationship between exploiters and exploited – yet not a relationship of sheer power and domination only, as in the anarchist tradition, but as a very general economic relationship between those who produce and those who enjoy the products of that production – in this vision of human history, as Brecht sees it and is able to represent it, or perhaps as he sees himself able to represent it, peasant life is the great vehicle through which one is able to represent the experience of the exploited and the oppressed; while the life of the capitalists is the form through which one can best represent the exploiters ...[109]

What we have here is a compression of history into a compact form. This means a cursory summary of human history reduced to its basic (exploitative) impulses that is, once compressed, more easily explored for its being therefore

---

107   Bradley 2011, p. 3.
108   Marx 1990, p. 342.
109   Jameson 1998, p. 138.

generalisable. And while Jameson may object to the Benjaminian possibilities that such a compression leaves open, there is nevertheless in this an historical politics which allows for a highly redemptive hermeneutic. This is not merely one of subject matter but also especially of linguistic form and content. Indeed, Brecht's language choice in the text matches this turn towards a long view of history and the reduction of dialogue and emotion.

Of special importance here is the reliance on the axiom in *Die Kaukasische Kreidekreis*. There are numerous examples of axioms throughout the text, but there is a particularly enlightening episode found in Scene 6, wherein the Judge Azdak and the Ironshirt Simon debate the fate of Grusha. In this debate/challenge the two exchange the following salvos:

> Simon *loudly*: 'When the horse was shod, the horsefly stretched out its leg', as the saying is.
> Azdak *eagerly accepting the challenge*: 'Better a treasure in the sewer than a stone in the mountain stream'.
> Simon: 'A fine day. Let's go fishing', said the angler to the worm.
> Azdak: 'I'm my own master', said the servant, and cut off his foot.
> Simon: 'I love you like a father', said the Czar to the peasant, and had the Czarevitch's head chopped off.[110]

The purpose of this exchange is to reproduce the play's key notion of suffering – of injustice from above meted out on those below, as well as the parasitical nature of those who live off of those who labour – on the level of aesthetic representation.[111] These exchanges excel in their purpose of historical reduction, yet they are by no means the only such devices found in the play. Another example in this vein is found in the following insertion from the 'Singer':

---

110 Brecht 1988, p. 91.
111 Yet this basic anti-oppression politics is at times lost on some important readers, including Jean Genet. A particularly shocking 'understanding' of Brecht's play is delivered in Carl Lavery's essay on Jean Genet and commitment. In this piece, Lavery shows how Genet took Brecht's argument about productivity (the land 'belongs to those who are good for it') and twisted it into pro-colonialism, its opposite in intent and theory, while then suggesting that this is Brecht's position. Lavery notes that Genet '... uses Brecht's commitment to Marxist ideals of progress to justify colonial violence. This is an apt demonstration of Genet's point about ideology, for it shows that Marxist ideology does not interrupt bourgeois oppression; rather, it repackages that suffering under a different name' (Lavery 2006, p. 226). To reiterate, Brechtian reception is at times subject to seemingly wilful misrepresentations, and these examples show up their limitations.

> When the houses of the great collapse
> Many little people are slain
> Those who had no share in the fortunes of the mighty
> Often have a share in their misfortunes. The plunging wain
> Drags the sweating beasts with it into the abyss.[112]

These axioms not only sum up the key problems of the play but direct it irrevocably. The axiom as strategy in the play is symptomatic of a type of gestus that seeks to link historical forms of oppression and reconstruction and recognition of this former 'attitude' for the present. Sean Carney has expanded on this double movement in the following passage from his *Brecht and Critical Theory*. He writes:

> The most important thing to draw from Brecht's play, then, is the attitude that it displays, which Brecht also calls a kind of wisdom that is performed or staged for us. It seems important here to distinguish between the form of wisdom, and the content of wisdom. Brecht, for his part, is concerned only with the former, the posture of wisdom, wisdom as an action. The form of this wisdom is dialectical and historical. As the storyteller himself says, 'It may be mistaken to mix different wines, but old and new wisdom mix very well' (148). The message of *The Caucasian Chalk Circle* is found in the 'mixing' of old and new wisdom, and what matters is not the moral of Grusha's tale, but that we perceive the dialectical relationship between past wisdom – the traditional Chinese tale and its biblical counterpart – and present wisdom, namely Marxist reconstruction and innovation.[113]

Carney's contribution here is valuable, not least for the emphasis on historical understanding and its implication in contemporary situations. However, I find the latter half, dealing with 'present wisdom' and 'Marxist reconstruction and innovation', less convincing. History and its relations to the present cannot be

---

112 Brecht 1988, p. 13.
113 Carney continues: 'As a dialectical, eminently Benjaminian storyteller, the singer is the emblem of the play itself, for he produces something new through his transmission of the old. Past wisdom, decayed and historicized, is produced in the present in the form of a new historical attitude' (Carney 2005, p. 56). Yet this learning always takes place in a social setting. As Markus Wessendorf writes: 'Brecht the dramatist prefers to put his characters into social situations in which they are compelled to produce attitudes and gestures that reveal who they are as social beings, for example when standing trial, conducting a business transaction, reporting a traffic accident, going on strike, or teaching a lesson' (Wessendorf 2016, p. 123).

read merely via a simple philosophical procedure, staging an ancient legend as a means to smuggle in Marx. In fact, this relation structures the text in a far more dramatic and *immediate* way than Carney allows. The most vicious group of the play – the *Panzerreiter* in Brecht's original but often suggestively translated as the 'Ironshirts', an obvious reference to the Brownshirts of Hitler's Germany – are modelled on the *Sturmabteilung* (SA), the predecessor to the *Schutzstaffel* (SS). This makes the link with historical forms of oppressive governments and those that were for Europe at the time an immediately pressing concern. These are yet again examples of the 'directness' that is key to Brecht's works. Yet perhaps the most important point here is that the introduction of the 'mixing of old and new wisdom' is worth little if it is not ultimately joined with an philosophy of action in the present, essentially a principle of judgment.

Grusha's tale is a harsh one, mirroring the reduced history of exploitation of which she is part. She is bullied and cajoled at almost every point in the play because, like Galy Gay before her, she is a far too willing and perhaps naïve soul who often considers those she comes across as equally well-meaning, hard-working and altruistic and thus is unable to say no. While smuggling the child across borders, her situation is constantly compromised and she often is subjected to various forms of indignity. Despite all the personal sacrifices she has made, when Grusha is called to bring her rescued child to its biological mother, she bucks this demand, and with it her own history (and the compressed history of exploitation), declaring the child rightfully hers. At this impasse Brecht resolves this situation by opting for a trial to be led by the woefully corrupt and imperfect Azdak.[114]

The move towards a moment of judgment is vital in this historical recovery if it is to be meaningful. Yet the material conditions of this particular judgment are highly questionable, as Grusha would normally simply be dismissed or killed for her 'impudence'. What makes this moment of judgment possible is the fact that Azdak believes *History* has been arrested, the peasants have taken over and that restorative judgment can be highly productive. The parable form liberates the audience from the necessity of following official historiography. For this brief utopian moment, a space has been carved out on stage, albeit in chalk, impermanently, and we are able to discern that by learning to judge historically, we can effectively judge in the now, although with different weapons.

---

114   Marc Silberman has noted of Azdak that he is 'the judge despite himself who knows how to exploit the disorder of a revolution when it is opportune but never takes a risk otherwise. Such figures do not represent class positions but rather move between them, and hence they are able to undermine both class solidarity and social hierarchies' (Silberman 2012, p. 178).

Good judgment relies on having good justices in positions of authority, aiding those who contribute.[115] As Darko Suvin notes: 'In fact, this is an aesthetic correlative to a salvational perspective in which history has no end, so that the kolkhoz story is simply a *presently possible* society in which Azdak's exceptional drawing of a chalk circle has become the normative or dominant use of pencils instead of pistols'.[116] Yet in order for this to happen, we must first have the example *par excellence* of Grusha as the framework or backdrop of historical class memory, and of the historical figuration of the time of the peasantry that she embodies. This moment of 'making succinct', which seems endless, is a productive use of history. As Brecht notes, '... the kolkhoz story assigns a historical localization'.[117] Grusha and Azdak offer this localisation but this should not be confused with the form of localisation that takes place in a specific moment in the play, when a concrete historical situation is analysed. Because the play is in itself a mode for learning (it supposedly has a specific motive – to convince the peasants to collectivise the farm), it necessitates a focal point in history. From this position Brecht is also able to articulate a moment outside of historical-chronological order and requires that history itself offer up an 'exemplary "case" calling for judgment'.[118] This judgment of the exemplary case (which follows from Andre Jolles's notion of *casus*)[119] allows Brecht to make history more malleable and generalisable. This double yet linked procedure is one in which the past is made plastic and therefore accessible, so that which needs to be made strange – the present forms of exploitation and oppression – can become that much more visible.

Yet we must warn ourselves not to reduce the problematics laid out above to merely a formula wherein the mystery to Brecht's genius is revealed and easily duplicated or, on the other side, tossed away as mechanistic (the latter of the two is much more common). Instead, the chief conjunctural tensions of the day need to be connected more fruitfully with those that have historically determined the individual moment. This is a philosophical question for Brecht, which reasserts the principle of usefulness in the present moment. Jameson writes: 'Brechtian storytelling, looked at in this way, is indeed informed by something like a "method", but one which is rigorously non-formulistic, and

---

115 This is also notable in 'The Democratic Judge', a poem that Brecht composes around the same time as *The Chalk Circle*. Brecht's judge rewards the sincerity and hard work of an Italian innkeeper by manipulating immigration law in his favour. See Brecht 1979, p. 385.
116 Suvin 1984, p. 179.
117 Brecht in Suvin 1984, p. 179.
118 Jameson 1998, p. 28.
119 Ibid.

thereby evades the philosophical objection to sheer method as such which have been outlined above. Casus, in other words, must be shown to be a form with genuine content, not merely an abstract frame into which narrative content of all kinds can be neatly arranged and subsumed'.[120]

If we follow Jameson, this moment of judgment suggests a philosophical trajectory of judgment in Brecht, but the judgment never allows itself to be fixed. This draws out the metaphor of the chalk circle as an heuristic tool that makes judgment possible. A chalk circle is easily rubbed away. It is not meant to be a permanent fixture, but rather a sketch that will require rewriting, as in a liberated classroom where teachers and students work together to produce knowledge for themselves, or as in Brecht's work, where the ensemble creates meaning firstly for itself, and then more broadly for the audience. The result is an internal education that is as important as that made for others. The chalk circle is that possibility, outlining something that may be theoretically possible and demonstrable in the confines of a play, but that is as yet unattainable in broader society. In this sense Brecht leaves his most furtive and speculative moments for the future.[121] The moment of judgment can, at least for now, be merely a suggestion based on a type of guidance, as laid out by Mayakovsky: 'The home of the soviet people shall also be the home of Reason'.[122]

As decision-making of the sort in the Prologue did not take place in the Soviet Union,[123] we may read this as an implicit critique of that Stalinist sys-

---

120 Ibid.
121 Where we are left at the end of the play is not resolved, given the play-within-a-play movements that come at the beginning. As Caroline Rupprecht points out, '... since the play does not return to the action of the prologue but rather ends with the play-within-the-play, we do not see their reaction. What we are left with is a happy ending, and at the same time, an open ending, since Brecht never closes the "frame" established in the prologue'. The implications are that 'Brecht works with two competing versions of reality to show the discrepancy between what is and what might be' (See Rupprecht 2006, p. 39).
122 Brecht 1998, p. 6. It may have hoped to be the home of reason, but also, in Brecht's text, there is an attempt to rescue this project. As R. Darren Gobert notes, 'The framed story of the chalk circle test, [Brecht] claims, demonstrates for the kolkhozes not a just verdict but "a certain kind of wisdom" – "an attitude" that might help produce a verdict in the still-undecided argument over the valley's ownership' (Gobert 2006, p. 21). This emphasis on a critical attitude, something that is just as fundamental to Brecht's earlier theatre as to his later theatre, is fulfilled by an estrangement into (and by) history. Yet while this 'attitude' relies heavily on a reasoning subject (and not a 'consuming object' of culture) this need not eschew the use of emotion.
123 Part of the problem in this line of work is that Brecht, particularly after he departs the United States after 1947, is caught between the two dominant spheres of his age. Despite this positioning, the dialogue between audience and producer remains the fundamental productive nature of Brecht's works *specifically* as it relates to the activation of the audi-

tem. The choice to name the fruit-growing commune after Rosa Luxemburg suggests that Brecht was siding with that particular revolutionary instead of many other Soviet rulers after whom the commune could have been named.[124] Nevertheless, Azdak's decision to grant custody to Grusha, to side with use over ownership, is a utopian one. It is hopefully assigned to the next generation, as the child hints towards a future world and its potential for an alternate material/social existence. His request that the estates of the rich be made into a playground for the children of tomorrow – to be named 'The Garden of Azdak' – is humorous, and yet also suggests that this parable needs finishing by those in a position actually to make history in the now. The principle of usefulness needs resolution. The time of the now is still the question, yet at this point the question is addressed through the prism of historical chalk lines.

4 Concluding the Historical Brecht

Chapters 2 and 4 argue that there is a dominant motif running through Brecht's work, beginning from earlier pieces such as *Mann ist Mann* and continuing into

---

ence in making sense and fulfilling his project. Often Brecht's note that he simply 'made suggestions' is not given its full due, or perhaps it is not given the importance that it requires. Ultimately, that was the self-set limit of the project. Brecht's project is one that must always be fulfilled in practice, and practice has no template. For this reason, both political and aesthetic, Brecht was wary of Stalinist orthodoxy (and not only how it applied itself to the arts) and fought to encourage openness and debate. This is why Brecht added the vital introduction to the *Kaukasische Kreidekreis*, in order to make clear the open, productive politics that the play ultimately suggests. Loren Kruger recognises this deep connection between politics and aesthetics: 'It is this particular experience of defending pluralist socialism against a monolithic socialist party at the historical moment of postimperialism, rather than a generalized Marxist attitude, that enabled Brecht to refine the theoretical as well as the political point of his key terms, estrangement and realism, and their critical relation, and to argue convincingly that estrangement was under the circumstances the most realistic method' (Kruger 2004, p. 16). Yet this open political aesthetics is often lost on contemporary readers. Some strangely have read Brecht as a pure propagandist for a Stalinist politics. The revolutions of 1989 have therefore made the later works dealt with in this Chapter 'in the canons of modern dramatic literature a conspicuous anachronism'. Calabro 1990, p. xiii. Calabro's text is motivated by a reaction against the political trajectory of Brecht (as much of Brecht is equivalent to Stalinism, the failure of Stalinism means the necessary failure of Brecht). For a good (and often seething – perhaps necessarily so) analysis of the (mis)interpretations of Brecht's works by American critics, see Westgate 2007.

124 As Sascha Bru and Anke Gilleir, Brecht '… had a lifelong fascination with Rosa Luxemburg and planned as late as the 1950s to write a drama about her …' (Bru and Gilleir 2017, p. 467).

plays such as *Mutter Courage und ihre Kinder*.[125] This motif – that the oppositional text must be as attuned as possible to the demands of the present, and that this requires a commitment to experimentation and revision – is focused on making the audience as active a critic of Brecht's arguments as possible. Far from diverting from this path, Brecht's move into historical settings and formal strategies is a continuation of his earlier work and marks a continuation of a fundamentally productive aesthetic. A key aspect in this chapter has been to show how the suffering of the peasant, and especially the time of peasant suffering, was utilised by Brecht to make a political aesthetic argument for the present, chiefly about the importance of learning from those that do not. In this regard, much of this chapter has focused on the way in which this suffering has come about and played out in the lives of the chief characters. We have the Little Monk (and his absent family) and the disillusionment that comes from Galileo's retreat; Grusha's self-sacrifice in keeping the small child alive; and Courage's lifelong struggle to maintain her family, and more importantly, her business. Yet through this depiction of struggle the audience is invited not to be a mere recipient of the characters' stories. Rather, the question of political decision, which we will see again in Blake's texts, is a constant in Brecht's understanding of his position as a cultural producer in the now, and this was present in his work even before his exile. Benjamin explores the question of political decision, and its importance in Brechtian oppositional culture, by critiquing dominant literary trends found in Brecht's contemporaries:

> I have spoken of the way in which certain modish photographers proceed in order to make human misery an object of consumption. Turning to the New Objectivity as a literary movement, I must go a step further and say that it has turned *the struggle against misery* into an object of consumption. In many cases, indeed, its political significance has been limited to converting revolutionary reflexes in so far as these occurred within the bourgeoisie, into themes of entertainment and amusement which can be fitted without much difficulty into the cabaret life of a large city. The characteristic feature of this literature is the way it transforms political struggle so that it ceases to be a compelling motive for decision and becomes an object of comfortable contemplation; it ceases to be a means of production and becomes an article of consumption.[126]

---

125 My argument stands in contrast to that of James Lyon who argues that there were 'almost as many Brechts as there were people who knew him' (Lyon 1980, p. 205). This is a problem in Brecht scholarship that attempts to resurrect aspects of Brecht 'for today', but to varying degrees offer less in an overall understanding of Brecht.
126 Benjamin 1998, pp. 96–7.

There is a connection that Benjamin makes between the political significance of a work of art and the way in which that work is received. This link was understood by Brecht, whose historical turn aided this purpose.

An integral aspect of this turn is its fundamental rejection of fidelity to history: that is, an adherence to the process of analysing a moment of history, as Benjamin notes, 'how it really was'. Instead, Brecht follows Benjamin. The latter notes in 'Theses on the Philosophy of History', 'To articulate the past ... means to take control of a memory, as it flashes in a moment of danger'. To do so results in an urgency of agency for the materialist aesthetic producer. 'For historical materialism it is a question of holding fast a picture of the past, just as if it had unexpectedly thrust itself, in a moment of danger, on the historical subject'.[127]

It is notable that a dominant theme of danger occupies each of the plays. Courage is constantly in fear of her life, her family and her capital. Grusha rescues the child as the castle she works in is being sacked, and afterwards she continues to move with the child, even though death seems to be only narrowly evaded. And finally Galileo, despite his status, has his life threatened by the brutality of the Inquisition, to whose power he ultimately bends. Brecht's history plays, stitched together, bear a striking resemblance to Benjamin's reception of Paul Klee's *Angelus Novus*.[128]

In the central metaphor that Benjamin takes from Klee's painting, we see a reduction of history as well. The Angel of History, while gazing towards the past, is propelled forward by the storms from Paradise and in so doing witnesses that 'the pile of debris grows skyward'.[129] To acknowledge this process sets the historical materialist apart from the rest. To not set one apart from the story of history 'as it really was', leads to empathy for the historical victor. This has repercussions for the contemporary moment. As Benjamin notes, '... if one asks with whom the adherents of historicism actually empathize the answer is inevit-

---

127   Benjamin 1968, p. 255.
128   Brecht himself suggested that 'Theses on the Philosophy of History' had been written after Benjamin read a fragment of his 'Caeser' project. Wizisla suggests that this was unlikely, as Benjamin had been thinking about the same issues for 'some twenty years', and further suggests that Brecht was most likely thinking about the proximity of the ideas to each other and 'probably did not mean his statement quite so literally.' That said, there are striking resemblances between the texts. Wizisla notes that '... the correspondence in intention and concept between *Die Geschäften des Herrn Julius Caesar* ("The Business Affairs of Mr. Julius Caesar") and the theses ... is by no means accidental. Brecht's sentence, 'The triumph of the commanders were triumphs over the people', is reminiscent of the 'triumphal procession' of the rulers' (Wizisla 2009, pp. 176–7). Paul Haacke has also covered the connections between Benjamin and Brecht on the philosophy of history in Haacke 2012, pp. 65–6.
129   Benjamin 1968, p. 258.

able: with the victor. And all rulers are the heirs of those who conquered before them. Hence, empathy with the victor invariably benefits the rulers'.[130] Thus, the historical materialist must acknowledge history and make use of it in the moment of the now: 'The awareness that they are about to make the continuum of history explode is characteristic of the revolutionary classes at the moment of their action'.[131] Yet just as history in Brecht necessitates a contraction, a process of making more finite the seemingly infinite history of catastrophe, so the moment of the now contains an exaggeration, an exploration of the present that demands experimentation. In this regard the compression of history is not a failure of Brecht's (the inability to fully understand the precise terms of a specific historical period) but rather the strength of an aesthetic project that aims for precision in the moment of the now. For Brecht, history offers a means to depict the present conjuncture more clearly, and thus to reach back into the past to salvage something for the time of the now. As McNally notes, 'Rather than something laid down once and for all, the past is a site of struggle *in the present*'.[132] By seemingly moving away from his own time, Brecht is actually, as I have tried to argue throughout this chapter, making himself productive in the present.

130   Benjamin 1968, p. 256.
131   Benjamin 1968, p. 261.
132   McNally 2001, p. 191.

CHAPTER 5

Blake, *Milton*, and Historical Redemption

This final chapter will be drawing on many of the central ideas and authors of the previous ones, particularly Walter Benjamin, Michael Löwy and E.P. Thompson. I will be arguing that the alternative understanding and usages of history as seen in Brecht and Benjamin are also to be found in Blake's epic poem *Milton*.[1] Blake's return to history is geared towards offering a source of inspiration, a sense of a direction out of the current impasse, that the present is currently lacking and cannot provide for itself. The present more broadly, but Blake's present specifically, is engulfed by a failure, a failure which keeps being repeated. Given history's determining influence, it is in constant danger of beginning itself anew (indeed is actually doing so), repeating the past's injustices that were themselves often caused by the political errors of those trying to change systemic abuses. In this sense, history is not only that which we can learn from, but also as a means to create a redemptive hermeneutic in the present.

Unlike in Brecht, where the historical setting of his plays acts as a backdrop to illuminate the present, for Blake history and/or the backward reference is mobilised to access that which the present is unable to, given that the organisational patterns of society (capital, exploitation, a life-destroying and -quantifying rationalism, mind-manacling ideologies, the tradition of Newton) section off humanity from its potential. Whereas for Brecht history was mobilised to more deeply access the present, Blake looked to history to fill in for that which was absent in his own world. Despite this different emphasis, both Brecht and Blake believed we are not dealing with 'history as it really was' and saw in their presents a lack of those energies required to enrich and produce a comprehensive oppositional aesthetics. In the move towards history, both Blake and Brecht disregard a realist, naturalistic fidelity to the past.

While in this chapter I will be investigating the way in which Blake uses and develops a conception of history in *Milton*, I will also be drawing on Thompson's work on the historical legacy of Blake's work. Thompson wrote relatively little about *Milton* in his text on Blake, and for that reason I will attempt to apply his important insights to Blake's later work. My purpose is not

---

1 Few historical writers stand as high for Blake, as Jackie DiSalvo notes: 'Blake's poetry is scarcely comprehensible outside its Miltonic context' (DiSalvo 1983, p. 5).

to be overly exegetical in trying to parse out how the work's characters relate to his earlier writing, but rather to explore how *Milton* is structured as a text of redemption. This redemption does not seek to make peace with historical events, but rather to negotiate with these unresolved tensions for contemporary purposes.[2] In what follows I will not be restating the complex mythology of Blake's poem, as that field is very well tilled; multitudes of Blake scholars have already sketched this out (sometimes producing internecine fallout). Rather, I will focus on the importance of previous historical moments and artists for Blake's conception of history. Here, the question of labour in Blake's text is important, particularly as it is coloured by a strongly redemptive vision. That is, in this text labour redeems the past and makes possible a future that leaves behind the ways in which it is currently conceived, in particular as a source of value for capitalism. The focus on this basis of material reproduction has often been lost from academic view (essentially a self-annihilating project, given how vital the importance of his own material practice was to his way of analysing and producing his reality).

1   Blake Contra Newton

To begin the discussion of Blake's use of history and historical figures, I should first disabuse the reader of the notion that Blake was a solitary figure, operating outside of his social or political spheres as a hermit-like figure creating mystical interpretations of scripture.[3] Although this has not been argued as such, it is important to note that Blake's usage of the Bible cannot be read merely as metaphorical. Rather, it seems appropriate to describe Blake's reading and faith in the Bible as itself a radical practice whose logical conclusions extend bey-

---

2   Makdisi has argued in a different context about Blake's strategy of drawing on historical traditions for his own ends. Makdisi's thesis articulates the same idea that is being presented here. He writes: 'What I want to propose is that through this investigation of Blake's anti-imperialism we will discover how he found a way to draw on and reformulate certain premodern traditions in order to produce a critique for his own time – rather than as a quasi-reactionary attempt to return to some lost original fullness – both of the *ancien regime* and of the bourgeois radicalism which attacked it; a way to refuse the logic of the State and of the discourse of sovereign power itself in the name of what he would call "Immortal Joy"' (Makdisi, 2006, pp. 20–1).
3   While Ian Balfour notes in his own text on 'Milton' that there is a long tradition behind this notion, he argues that later generations find it easier to understand Blake due to 'the greater availability and circulation of his texts, and the critical and scholarly efforts of a large community of readers who have elucidated literary and historical contexts framing Blake's works' (Balfour 2002, p. 128).

ond the text itself. The text, whether historical or contemporary, is very much a living one for Blake. For this reason, I think we should take seriously Blake's criticisms of Newton who, beside Milton, is the historical figure with whom Blake concerns himself the most. Donald Ault, in his analysis of Blake's dialogue with Newton, notes that despite his death in 1727, 'Newton's centuries of triumph were the eighteenth and (in a fuzzier way) the nineteenth'.[4] The figure of Newton as he appears in these 'centuries of triumph' may in fact be quite dissimilar from his biographical record, but it is the figure of Newton and all it stands for that looms large for Blake. Other Romantics had gleaned something entirely different from Newton. Coleridge, for instance, in his *Religious Musings*, raises Newton to his 'elect' for his service to humanity.[5] For Blake, it is the triumphalist Newton figure (and the question of what it is exactly he triumphs over) that he engages.

As discussed in Chapter 3, in Löwy and Sayre's analysis, the Romantic criticism of the Enlightenment is not principally about rationalism in and of itself, but about a particular type of mechanical rationalism, on the one hand, and a rationalist abstraction, on the other. Attempts to cast Blake as anti-rationalist are thus wide of the mark. His seemingly exhaustive critique of rationality is a qualified one. In Blake's constellation, the figure of the rational intellect, Urizen, is criticised not *tout court*, but only because he is out of balance with the other Zoas.[6] The problem of Newtonian-infused Urizen is that he becomes over-extended and, therefore, out of proportion with his world.[7] Without being checked, rationalism in Blake's cosmology produces a self-generating process

---

4 Ault 1975, p. xii.
5 As David Collings argues, the poem 'shares elements of the Enlightenment science of figures like Darwin, Franklin, and Priestley (again) whose sympathy lies with social change, describing moral or historical processes in terms borrowed from meteorology, electricity, and the Newtonian sciences of optics and gravitation' (Collings, 1991, p. 171). For a broader context on this poem, and the philosophy of nature and God that underpins it, see Roe 2002.
6 Noting the effect of Urizen being so out of balance, Peter Otto explains that '… the end result of Urizen's activity, is to create a world of self-enclosed globes that outlaw all difference' (Otto 2000, p. 267). This text is heavily reliant on Derridean deconstruction, and thus difference signifies more to Otto than it would to Thompson or Erdman. In its usage above, depicting Urizenic methodology as blocking off other possibilities, there would most likely be little disagreement.
7 Urizen's consuming ways even go so far as to colonise religion. 'Blake's argument to the Established Church asserts that rationalistic moralism that governs atonement as they conceive it is the very thing that cannot possibly achieve it. If this is so even according to its own rules how much more does it fall short of accomplishing the kind of atonement that Blake envisions. A salvation obtained through mercy and forgiveness is wholly beyond the recognition of the satanic Urizen governing the Church' (Jesse 2013, p. 122).

of accumulation of other ideas, so much so that it begins to impose its worldview on all it surveys. And this brings us much closer to what Newton represents for Blake. Nicholas Williams notes that: 'Newton provides for Blake an oppressive model of self-motion, or rather an evacuation of self-motion in favour of an anatomizing view of the body as a collection of mechanically interactive parts'.[8] When Newton, coursing through the Urizenic world, operates out of proportion, or when Urizen becomes too powerful in himself, the effect is the creation of 'Newtonian Voids between the Substances of Creation'.[9] These voids are moments that block the ability of the artist to create, as they attempt to depict the creative process as irrelevant. Blake's worry, echoed in Ault's statement above, is that Newton *as spirit* becomes more than itself. It becomes Newtonian, and thus a movement springs up that aspires to something greater than it can contain in itself, and greater than even Blake himself can contain in his own poetry. The danger consists less in Newton as historical figure and more in Newton as 'world-spirit', an abstracting force whose distorted products become 'irrational' in that they are 'invisible to the Vegetable Man'.[10] Newton is opposed to that which is living, and his creations disguise from humanity its creative potentialities rather than open up possibilities for creation – and for Blake specifically, artistic creation inspired by the force of God's power. Indeed, Newton takes the potential of God's power and inverts it. The problem is that, as Balfour notes, 'Newton is systematically reviled in Blake's work as a proponent of mathematical reason, one who views God as the overseer of a machinelike universe devoid of living form'.[11] The absence of living form should ring alarm bells, for as I argued in Chapter 3, the eschewing of human 'living form' denotes for Blake a fundamental rejection of the divine image in which it exists. As the Newtonian worldview colonises ever more of social reality, Newtonian motion will become its opposite, seeing in itself its own rational and fully definable end.[12] In Blake's mythology, the figure of Newton is not only in and of itself

---

8   Williams 2009, p. 492.
9   Blake 1988, p. 138.
10 Ibid.
11 Balfour 2002, p. 142.
12 As in Blake's 'Holy Thursday', there is an open question as to whether the establishment that Blake skewers saw themselves in the evil that they, perhaps unknowingly, preached and performed. As Florence Sandler notes, these rulers '... were likely to wear the mask of bland civility and present their ideology as benevolence. They might even believe themselves to be benevolent and their Age of Opacity to be Enlightenment, like Satan in the Bard's Tale in *Milton*, whose demonic nature is not perspicuous even to himself' (Sandler 1990, p. 44).

devoid of living form. It must also become (through its own logic) an instantiation of the 'absurd', not in the sense of unusual but rather abhorrent in its destructiveness. In Plate 40 of *Milton* Blake pronounces:

> In Self annihilation giving thy life to thy enemies
> Are those who contemn Religion & seek to annihilate it
> Become in their Femin[in]e portions the causes & promoters
> Of these Religions, how is this thing? this Newtonian Phantasm
> This Voltaire & Rousseau: this Hume & Gibbon & Bolingbroke
> This Natural Religion! this impossible absurdity
> Is Ololon the cause of this? O where shall I hide my face
> These tears fall for the little-ones: the Children of Jerusalem
> Lest they be annihilated in thy annihilation.[13]

For Blake, Newton's 'Phantasm' is an 'annihilating' one which seeks to take over fully and extinguish the power of a strong messianic spirit. Annihilation is not solely a negative qualifier for Blake, as it is a necessary force that one must accept. As any being will be fundamentally fallible, they must be open to criticism that will require one's Self-annihilation. This goes a long way to explain why Blake has summoned Milton in the first place. Leonard W. Deen sketches this out nicely:

> In *The Four Zoas*, the true poet ceases to belong to the Devil's party. In *Milton*, he comes into full understanding. Milton becomes a true poet because he sees his error, which is his own distortions of vision and their effect on the religion that prevails in England. Inspired by a Bard's Song in which Los is divided in a family quarrel that issues in the warring nations of the fallen world, Milton descends from heaven to earth, annihilates his Selfhood by overcoming Urizen-Satan, and redeems his Emanation, Ololon … In *Milton*, then, a figure of identity is divided and falls as Los. As Milton, he is integrated with Blake, wrestles with his Spectre-Selfhood, and is reunited with his Emanation. Each of these events creates its appropriate human-centred world, fallen or redeemed.[14]

---

13 Blake 1988, p. 142.
14 Deen 1983, pp. 166–7. This humanising of the world also extends itself to engulfing 'natural processes' as well. 'In *Milton*, Blake substitutes an organic model of the city for the model constructed through labor in *The Four Zoas*. Conversely, however, *Milton* describes organic creations as works of art, thus further undermining the dichotomy between "nature" and

And this is precisely the problem for Milton. If his errors and their effects carry on – and not merely in his purgatory, where he mulls over his mistakes, but also through the errors they induce in those who follow in his tradition – then he must be absolved for those in the present. Errors compound themselves, and the dangers they breed are omnipresent.[15] These dangers never end, and self-criticism, even of those so important to Blake as Milton, must become an object of sustained focus. This unlocks a democratic model of criticism, for if such a monumental figure as Milton inspires and requires a fundamental critical reading, so too must readers of *Milton* draw critical attention to Blake.[16] Yet Blake's criticism of Milton is different in tenor to his criticism of Newton. Milton is among the cherished, and as Christopher Warley explains: 'Milton is a champion of the anonymous, but he never forgets that champions are always those with a name'.[17] While there are disagreements as to what exactly Blake wishes to redeem in Milton,[18] it should be clear that Newton- and Urizenic-inspired forces are another entity altogether. Redemption for them is debatable.

"art" or "civilization" ... The result is to humanise both nature and the city, so that the entire visible world becomes a product of human art, and the city becomes the body in which that art develops' (Michael 2006, p. 116).

15 As John H. Jones explains in his text, 'Yet, self-annihilation in *Milton* is not without risk and comes only after great difficulty. As Milton enters self-annihilation, he and the other Sons of Albion view his change as going to "Eternal Death". Since self-annihilation involves such a radical interchange between addresser and addressee to allow for the transcendence of the finite boundaries of Selfhood through dialogue, it implies a dissolution of identity that those in Selfhood see as death or worse' (Jones 2010, p. 137).

16 William Richey argues that Blake himself was implicated in his criticisms. 'For Blake, the Son's concession [in Paradise Regained] became symptomatic of the classic moralism that "curbd" Milton and thus prevented him from achieving his imaginative potential. But, as we have seen, Blake had come to realise that this failure was also his own. He, too, had failed to purge his pre-1804 compositions of their moral self-righteousness; he – no less than Homer or Milton – had celebrated the heroic individual's ability to assert his superiority over his rivals' (Richey 1996, p. 114).

17 Warley 2014, p. 122.

18 While this is a deep debate, this contrast falls into aesthetic ideology in the following: 'At some level Blake indeed saw *Paradise Regained* as more complete than *Paradise Lost*. However, rather than a perfect unity of iconoclasm and aesthetics in the later work, it is the perceived *lack* of unity between ideology and aesthetics that compels Blake's attempt to redeem the poet in *Milton*' (Marks 2011, p. 44). It becomes radical theology here: 'Notwithstanding his admiration, Blake felt Milton's radicalism to be compromised. His relationship to the poet was therefore one of creative antagonism. Blake sought to address this by re-writing and re-interpreting his predecessor. *Milton*, chiefly written between 1803 and 1808 (with a possible addition after 1815), is Blake's attempt to rectify Milton's theological errors by the substitution of a creed of self-sacrifice and forgiveness for one of punitive judgment' (Farrell 2014, pp. 136–7).

Coupled with Newton, standing as he does as the key English Enlightenment figure, is a conflation with the presence of the 'Natural Religion'. The critique of Natural Religion is profound for Blake, as it further removes from humanity any connection to the Divine.[19] This denies also the part that the corporeal was to have in maintaining this connection by establishing an 'increasingly remote and impersonal image of God'.[20] This phantasm seeks to deny the possibility of accessing God's presence. What is left then is a God at a (safe) distance, and this is exactly the problem for Blake and why one must have the connection between the material world and something which has the potential to transcend the world as we see it at any particular moment, including the factuality of the world. Safety does not seek to respond to Benjamin's notion of danger, that moment when memory explodes involuntarily onto the scene, exposing the fault-lines of repression. Safety is an attempt to further repress those fault-lines by removing the avenues through which the danger can be fully exposed. Donald Ault argues this point, making the connection between these 'safe' drives and the subduing of the potential for their unravelling (the Imagination): 'Blake never rejects his most basic conception that the crisis of process is rooted in the Satanic power to abstract static and dynamic elements from the interlocked structure of Eternity in order to construct a counter-system to Eternity to lure the Imagination from its true drives'.[21] The shift towards abstraction and the move away from 'the interlocked structure of Eternity' is a way to foreground a specific form of Blakean materialism that is expressly pronounced throughout the text, not least in the often repeated 'vegetation', with its attendant notions of being at once 'of the ground' (static)[22] as well as simultaneously growing and creating (dynamic). Given the prominence of this other

---

19 David Fallon convincingly rebuffs this worldview by locating the Divine principle driving Blake's philosophy. 'Blake, by contrast, denies that social feeling originates in nature: it is a divine gift requiring continual cultivation' (Fallon 2017, p. 260).
20 Thompson 1995, p. 111.
21 Ault 1975, p. 165.
22 On the interplay between the connection between the forms of stasis and dynamic change in Blake, John Hutton notes that 'Instead of reconciliation as stasis, as the end to change, Blake presents a constant negation of the negation, as a means to strip away barriers, to free all the *possibilities* for change'. As I shall later argue, Blake does not simply construct the final conflict in *Milton* as an end in itself, but rather suggests that the second coming opens up the space for productive change. In this regard, the wish to abolish poverty seems a precondition in Blake for the *possibility* to and for change. As Hutton argues, 'Blake's is a notion of change and existence which presents history as an open-ended spiral, a continuous and growing revelation which bridges a gap between metaphorical truth and that of lived reality'. John Hutton 1998, p. 161.

form of living, which ridicules the Blakean Imagination[23] through the dominant ideology of 'Newtonian Phantasms', Blake's question is how can we respond in ways such that our capabilities and rational usefulness are harnessed to halt this annihilation? The response in *Milton* is driven by that which the current capitalist-rationalist consensus cannot, through its own exclusionary nature, fulfil.[24]

2   The Importance of What Is Missing

If we accept that Blake's reach back to history in *Milton* is intricately tied up with the history of religious prophecy and action since the English Civil War, a position which is argued more generally by Thompson, I believe one must also accept that that history, defined by heightened class consciousness and a thoroughgoing struggle against the established powers, was no longer alive in Blake's England.[25] This, however, is not to dismiss this inheritance. As Aijaz Ahmad argues: 'The origins of English Romanticism are inseparable from the anti-capitalist passions of Blake, and it had the Cromwellian radicalism of Milton in its past …'[26] Yet while this was the historical backdrop that Blake sought to grapple with in *Milton*, his work was also immediately coloured by the relationship to 1789 and the subsequent failure of the revolution, as well as the after-effects that were felt outside of France. The shift must also consider the initial euphoric greetings (Wordsworth's 'Bliss was it in that

---

23   This is representative and provides an explanation of the *almost* dichotomous relation of the purely biological brain as opposed to the creative faculties. As Sarah Haggarty explains: 'Certainly, while Blake writes positively of the mind and the imagination, he represents the brain more ambiguously. Later in *Milton*, it will be the suspect Urizen who "stoop'd down / And took up water from the river Jordan: pouring on / To Milton's brain the icy fluid from his broad cold palm"' (Haggarty 2010, p. 149).

24   Coleridge also recognised that a gap exists between the more apparent world governed by what he termed the 'primary imagination'. Coleridge classified a 'secondary imagination' that understood and reasoned through the first, yet one that, Alexander M. Schlutz argues, 'serves to dissolve the illusory division of empirical consciousness in order to re-create an ideal unity in the work of art and is thus an aesthetic and poetic principle' (Schultz 2009, pp. 228–9). This division is perhaps a similar duality to Blake's division of Innocence and Experience in that it attempts to begin from a position not merely of understanding the world but trying to think of a space not wholly determined by that understanding.

25   For the definitive longer text on this see Hill 1977. Hill also argues that Blake is the inheritor of the 'dionysian freedom favoured by the Ranters' (the Ranters being an important part of the dissenting social forces of the time) (Hill 1991, p. 356).

26   Ahmad 1994, p. 50.

dawn to be alive', being the exemplar) and the effect on the ruling classes in England. This, Thompson concludes, consolidated 'landowners and manufacturers in a common panic',[27] prompting Sedition laws which aimed to crush nascent democratic and anti-capitalist movements struggles and speakers, including the popular preacher and friend of Romantic poets and thinkers, John Thelwall. These regressive reforms had an enormously disruptive effect across the literary and political landscape of popular democratic religious and literary sentiment. As Daniel White argues, 'If during the late eighteenth century many nonconformist writers associated themselves with liberal Dissenting denominations whereas others, especially lapsed Anglicans, embraced either non-denominational or anti-sectarian varieties of nonconformity, early nineteenth century literary culture saw a steady diminution of the former denominational mode. As liberal dissent gave way to Methodism, evangelicalism, and the missionary movement, and as the progress of the French Revolution and the Revolutionary war drove England into a period of political and religious retrenchment, the public viability of denominational sectarian identities dwindled in the minds of many heterodox nonconformist writers, and so did the possibility of literary affiliations rooted in the values and interests of these clearly defined religious organizations'.[28]

In Blake we see a unique acknowledgement of this predicament. Yet rather than becoming engulfed in the melancholic, he is driven by an understanding of the brutal realities of capitalist expropriation, and of the dominating logics that are meant to suppress the will of those who are expropriated, endeavouring to combine his rejection of these two heads of capitalism. As Thompson argues: 'After William Blake, no mind was at home in both cultures [fighting the machine world and "the exploitative and oppressive relationship intrinsic to industrial capitalism"], nor had the genius to interpret the two traditions to each other ... While Wordsworth and Coleridge had withdrawn behind their own ramparts of disenchantment'.[29] While Thompson's dismissal of Coleridge and Wordsworth may appear harsh, his reading of Blake's ability to be 'at home' fighting on two fronts is instructive. For this reason, the revolutions abroad continued to sustain Blake. As Susan Wolfson argues, 'energised' by the conservative reaction to what they saw as an 'apocalypse of wanton lawlessness', Blake 'launched a revolutionary poetics in *Milton* that outdid Milton'.[30] Wolfson contrasts this summation of Blake's work at the outset of *Milton* to the period of

---

27   Thompson 1982, p. 195.
28   White 2006, p. 182.
29   Thompson 1982, p. 915.
30   Wolfson 1997, p. 56.

Shelley's 'The Masque of Anarchy', highlighting the contradiction between the calls for radical change and the calls to nationalism. This also indicates a presupposed better past defined by 'The old laws of England'. This '... has to do with the way passivity, even (or especially) in a heroic masquerade, can serve the interests of tyranny. While Shelley never consciously put his art to such service, his anxiety about the historical processes of change is related to this effect'.[31] This is not to disparage the political potency of the injunction to 'Rise, like lions after slumber', but to caution against the redemption of a questionable past. He knows the importance of history as a battleground, and he chooses his inspiration far more carefully, even if he is not especially willing to completely condemn those with whom he disagrees or who have acted unjustly. This reluctance to assert definitive justice, which involves an act of expulsion, is reflected in Los's speech in Plate 25. The call to 'preach righteousness & punish the sinner with death'[32] is refused by Los, a figure so often connected with fire and judgment, who 'now moves history'.[33] Instead of opting for wrath, the watchword here is mercy, and redemption 'comes in as ecstasy'.[34] This world is full of division, and purity is in short supply. 'As it concerns Milton, the implication of the Bard's Song is that in *Paradise Lost* the source and father figure

---

[31] Wolfson 1997, p. 202. To re-iterate, this is not meant to cast Shelley as politically suspect *tout court*, but to provide daylight on the real political differences that existed between the two. Paul Foot's text on Shelley is excellent and illustrates the politically explosive power of much of Shelley's verse, while Mark Kipperman's work explores the ways in which Shelley's work was subject to a long-standing de-politicisation by, among others, his Liberal readers. See Foot 1982, and Kipperman 1992, pp. 187–211.

[32] Blake 1988, p. 121.

[33] The figure of Los is central not only regarding labour but also agency and the role of human potential in reorganising the social world. 'In *Milton*, which prefaces *Jerusalem*, Blake puts off apocalypse in order to prepare more carefully for the decisive role of the poet-prophet in its coming. *Milton* continues the account in *The Four Zoas* of the fall into the claim to be God and the rise into and recovery of the human. But the triumph of the human is greater and clearer now because *Milton* begins with a Los who retains the mature but beleaguered humanity he learned in *The Four Zoas*. Los now moves history by identifying himself with particular poets, with English prophets. The figure of the bard singing of a human Los leads to the figure of Milton and then to Blake, and finally to the forming of one man from the Bard, Los, Milton, and Blake. The result is a human poet-prophet, the Awakener, who unites myth and history and who prepares for apocalypse in a much more deliberate and internal and psychologically subtle way than Blake had ever done' (Deen 1983, p. 164).

[34] McGann 1998, p. 272. Instructively, McGann contrasts Blakean redemption with 'redemption pursued through logics of compensation' (McGann 1998, 272). What is more, it is important to differentiate Blakean redemption from those forms of European 'Romantic Orientalism', as Edward Said termed it: projects that sought to redeem Europe by thought-

is Milton, and that Milton, like Los, is divided'.[35] Given the poem's structure, and that a difference in chronological time needs to exist between Blake and Milton, the world that Blake inherits cannot be Milton's own, and thus the level of historical consciousness during Blake's era was limited (distance equals limitation). To judge those who merely went along with the current order, or even those who sought to continue the losses imposed on Milton's age, would be a penalty far outweighing the proportion of just judgment.[36] One must know one's crime to be guilty of it. Blake response is fitting with the larger framework not to condemn those who did not challenge the current order, and those that might have even supported it, judging in alignment with the divine position in the *Songs of Innocence*. It is for this reason that the group most anathematic to Blake's worldview, 'the Elect', must be ultimately saved.

> The Reprobate who never cease to Believe, and the Redeemd,
> Who live in doubts & fears perpetually tormented by the Elect
> These you shall bind in a twin-bundle for the Consummation –
> But the Elect must be saved [from] fires of Eternal Death[37]

The fires of 'Eternal Death', life as we know it, are not denied them even though they may, in Blake's worldview, reject that which will ultimately save them from damnation. This in part explains Blake's motive for moving back into/towards history. As Erdman neatly explains, 'The trouble is, however, that Blake is not content to formulate a message for the times …'.[38] Unhappy with his current consensus, Blake seeks to channel a different historical setting to get himself out of the limited possibilities of his own age.

There is something out of sync in Blake's mythology, which cannot gradually proceed from the current moment. The annihilating force of the quantifying logic of capital seeks to make the liberating potential of a return impossible. Those that seek to a 'make a Heaven out of our misery' need not only occupy the present, but are driven to eliminate the idea of the messianic impulse, especially as emanating from the danger that is the unoccupied past, as the idea of a

---

       fully studying Asian cultures and religions (India stood out as the exemplar) in order to 'defeat the materialism and mechanism (and republicanism) of occidental culture' (Said 1979, p. 115).
35   Deen 1983, p. 167.
36   Although the world he inherits is not similar, the desire to recreate and re-imagine is deep in the text. For an exhaustive examination of how deep this desire went – so deep that Blake is argued to be attempting 'to *outdo* Milton' – see Miner 2012, pp. 233–76.
37   Blake 1988, p. 122.
38   Erdman, 1969, p. 396.

moment of uncontrolled judgment terrifies them. In this regard, Los's reaction to what he mistakenly takes as the permanent absence of Rintrah, a symbol of revolutionary wrath, is instructive, as it seems to mirror Blake's own historically limited situation (minus the error in mistaking the temporary for permanence). Los sits down 'on his anvil-stock; and leand upon the trough. Looking into the black water, mingling it with tears'.[39] Given that the natural state of things is determined by God's benevolence, that which is love producing or life nurturing may be missing for a time (given the inequalities and injustices that capitalism and feudalism that produced), their absence is not irretrievable. This would be an historical slippage as great as if Milton had never existed in the first place. But Milton's existence, connected with Rintrah's, results in Inspiration being found in Prophecy. In a moment of desperation this prophecy hastens 'That Milton of the Land of Albion should up ascend ... and set free / Orc from his Chain of Jealousy'.[40] When confronted by absence, Blake reaches back into history in order to recall what is missing in the present, having found that there is kindling that he can ignite in order to make other possibilities actualisable, despite the fears that that such fires had been extinguished.[41]

The prevailing forces of Blake's social order define what is missing in the present. It is in this sense that Blake's particular use of prophecy is always looking backwards. As Balfour notes, '... if prophecy is always oriented toward a future – even when it does not take the form of prediction – it is also profoundly a thing of the past, an echo, a citation'.[42] The merging of prophecy and history should not be confused with nostalgia, a critique often levelled against the Romantics in general.[43] Rather, the attempt by Blake is to make the link to a notion of history that is fundamentally productive. In this regard, Makdisi

---

39   Blake 1988, p. 115.
40   Ibid.
41   Orc's enslavement points to the reason why Blake has summoned Milton, as Christopher Z. Hobson argues. '... in keeping with *Milton's* overall concerns, the hope is that Orc's imprisoned social and sexual energy will be freed by Milton in a larger liberation of human potentiality. Despite this shift, Orc's most prominent meaning in this poem is as imprisoned energy and elemental rebellion ...' (Hobson 1998, p. 22).
42   Balfour 2002, p. 129.
43   While the nostalgia critique is sometimes valid, it should not be used overused and generalised. For instance, Löwy and Sayre argue that 'In the constellation of Romanticisms, "restitutionism" occupies a privileged place ... In addition, it is obvious that the restitutionist perspective is in a way the closest to the essence of the overall phenomenon, given that nostalgia for a pre-capitalist state lies at the heart of this worldview. Now this restitutionist type is defined precisely as aspiring to the restitution – that is, the restoration or the re-creation – of this pre-capitalist past' (Löwy and Sayre 2001, p. 59). I think that in

is persuasive when borrowing Cesare Casarino's work to describe Blake's aesthetic practice as a 'philopoesis': a description of how life is a process or making and remaking (as well as being a process of consistently being under threat).[44] Makdisi emphasises the 'political and ontological' qualities of Blake's work, and the undergirding of how we exist and the quality of that existence. He writes that: 'For the question that Blake pushes us to ask is not whether life is made, but how, and under what circumstances; whether that making, and life itself, are to be sorrowful – a matter of lamenting, shrieking, howling, gnashing – or rather a matter of joy, celebration, piping and singing; whether life is to be dominated by "happy chear" which we "weep with joy to hear," as in the introduction of *Songs of Innocence*, by the "bells cheerful sound of" *The Ecchoing Green*, by the "tender voice" of the lamb, by *The Laughing Song's* "sweet chorus of Ha, Ha, He" or instead by the howling and shrieking of life perverted, abstracted, and stolen: the harlot's curse, the soldier's sigh, the chimney sweeper's "weep, weep, in note of woe!"'.[45] Following Makdisi, we can see that's Los's mourning and his being at his wit's end is clearly related to Blake's own desperation. Los is at his anvil and stops working when he fears the worst. The connection here with labour, as a creative and redeeming act – as opposed to labour as a stealing, oppressive entity from which we are or will be estranged – cannot be underestimated. The primacy of labour, of creation, is a structuring principle of Blake's thought. And it is for this reason as well that Blake should not be read as a forerunner of postmodernism, a *bricoleur avant la lettre*, taking a thing frozen in time for his own purposes.[46] Blake is not merely sampling, but taking from the historical past another conception of history itself, which is grounded in a conception of 'unfinished business' that art can channel and make real in the contemporary. This requires a different conception of historical time and an account as

---

Blake's case, it is better to focus on how and what he learns from history, particularly as he looks to take something useful from historical failure. Blake does not wish to merely recreate, but rather to take inspiration from the past in order to ultimately set it right. In so doing Blake looks to 'correct' the past while channelling it, a process which is far more akin to Benjamin's notion of history in the final thesis, rather than a process of mourning for mourning's sake.

44 Makdisi 2003, p. 265.
45 Ibid.
46 There is a belief in a sub-current of recent scholarship that Blake is a forerunner of postmodernism. It should suffice to say that his intervention into the political moments of his day did not rely on a sampling of different trends that he chose to tap into; rather, it was a targeted response to the deep structures of his society which were quashing, both literally and figuratively, the political and physical progressive spirits of his day. Jon Mee deals with this in the first section of his *Dangerous Enthusiasms*.

to why it is necessary: '... as William Blake reaches identity with Los, his function as the God of Time is emphasized. God's wheel of fate has Seven Eyes; each of the first six fails to serve as an eye for Albion, but the seventh, Jesus, comes at the right moment and thus marks or produces the complete revolution which makes any further rotation of human misery unnecessary'.[47] What makes this leap possible is an alternate conception of time (and historical time especially) that the established church and other authorities cannot accommodate. Blake's conception of time is highly influenced by his affinities with antinomianism, which, as Thompson notes, takes on an oppositional tone. It represents a position that dismisses the world that the present in Newtonian form dictates. Antinomianism 'is not a place at all, but a way of breaking out from received wisdom and moralism, and entering new possibilities'.[48] If we understand Blake as operating within this tradition, despite the caveats that were raised in Chapter 3, we see his approach to the historical world as deviating from those positions, especially the more dominant among them, that seek to make of it something safe, something that we can mourn over at the very best. This contested terrain is an example of the historical form Raymond Williams termed 'residual culture'. Terry Eagleton expands on this when he argues that 'A good deal of culture as identity or solidarity is in this sense residual – enclaves of traditionalist resistance within the present which draw their strength from "some previous social and cultural institution or formation"'.[49] In Blake's contesting of this 'settled' version of events, his radical poetics require, therefore, the 'rewriting of history' to make the residual apparent.[50]

3   Filling in That Which Is Missing

While Blake's Satan in *Milton* represents the established Church and the quantifying logic of capital, it is important to identify the historical boundaries of Satan's power. These delineate how his conception of life is different from Blake's worldview and also what the poet Milton offers that works against the aforementioned evils. The space in which the conception of oppositional time (in contrast to the dominant form) is stated most directly is in Plate 29. Blake lays out his conception of time:

---

47   Erdman 1969, p. 399.
48   Thompson 1995, p. 20.
49   Eagleton 2000, p. 123.
50   Thompson 1995, p. 20.

> For in this Period the Poets Work is Done: and all the Great
> Events of Time start forth & are conceived in such a Period
> Within a Moment: a Pulsation of the Artery.[51]

Blake's framework for revolutionary time is captured in the metaphor of the heartbeat, a pulse that operates in contrast to 'clock time' which 'is a mental nightmare like all other abstract ideas'.[52] Blake recovers the body's time, defined by its own needs and desires, from the quantifiable impulses of the capitalist age. In his commentary to Blake's *Milton*, Harold Bloom describes this and the above passages as 'a saving vision of time'. He continues: 'The poet's work conquers the Eternity that teases us out of thought, for imaginative time triumphs over clock time by denying its categories'.[53] Los, through his labour, creates and embodies a conception of time and space that refuses any attempt to quantify it. Los is also the creator of all that is truly visionary:

> For every Space larger than a red Globule of Mans blood.
> Is visionary: and is created by the Hammer of Los
> And every Space smaller than a Globule of mans blood. Opens
> Into Eternity of which this vegetable Earth is but a shadow[54]

Like time in the previous plate, Space is unable to be quantified. As Blake notes in a fairly deliberate jab at the 'Newtonian Phantasms': 'The Microscope knows not of this nor the telescope'.[55] As with Brecht, facticity is a betrayal of the possibilities for a time outside the seemingly immediately presentable. This is the case even though, as we see in the Galileo example, the telescope portends a world outside of the taken for granted and commodified place that we currently inhabit. Beyond the quantifiable vision of what exists before us operates another world of inarticulable power. The lineages to and from Blake on this point are considerable, but by no means do they necessarily have to pass through Blake. There are many traditions that prophesise transgressions of what for Blake would be clock-time. As Jordy Rosenberg writes,

---

51 Blake 1988, p. 127. Mark Bracher argues a similar point in his analysis of historical time and its reception in the poem. He writes, 'Everything remains because ontologically everything is interwoven with everything else from the beginning of time' (Bracher 1985, p. 128).
52 Frye 1969, p. 46.
53 Bloom in Blake 1988, p. 922.
54 Blake 1988, p. 127.
55 Ibid.

From the oracles of the ancients to the Dissenters of the English Civil War, enthusiastic prophecy is exemplified by a sudden, rapturous consciousness of future events, typically apocalyptic in nature. This concatenation of immediacy with an immeasurably long arc of historical time distinguishes enthusiasm from the time-worn truisms of priestly authority, and from the endlessly unfurling present of the status quo.[56]

And just as Blake cannot claim ownership of this tradition, nor was this the only form of opposition that the Romantics favoured, even for those who profoundly abhorred the destruction of nature.[57]

Blake is not arguing that a fundamental shift in human relations can happen at any moment of historical time. As Erdman's point above regarding his particularly war-dominated background illustrates, Blake knew that his England was not ripe for such a transition.[58] Rather, his argument is specifically against quantifying time. This formulation relies on a conception of recovery that closely resembles the logic in Benjamin's rejection of 'history as it really was'. The opening of Benjamin's second thesis reads:

> Like every generation that preceded us, we have been endowed with a weak Messianic power, a power to which the past has a claim. That claim cannot be settled cheaply. Historical materialists are aware of that.[59]

Benjamin's construction of the past as having a 'claim' on the present is powerful, and is useful in directing us towards locating in the past that to which the

---

56 Rosenberg 2010, p. 472.
57 As Adam Rounce argues, John Clare found refuge in other Romantic ideals more than in Blakean ones. He writes: 'This notion of domesticating the visionary, and concomitantly of finding the imaginative release in a sort of spiritual ecology, is the defining mark of Clare's unique aesthetic. The Protestant imagination too found the impression of divine wonder and purpose in nature, instead setting it apart and against the bourgeois encroachments of modernity, improvement, enclosure and other imaginatively and spiritually barren modes of thought' (Rounce 2015, p. 53).
58 On the question of a revolution in Blake's time, John Beer notes that in many of his texts dealing more directly with the French Revolution, Blake 'would not concern himself with chronological or geographical accuracy if change or invention provided a vivid means of suggesting a significance' (John Beer 1994, p. 159).
59 Benjamin 1968, p. 254. It would be a misreading of Benjamin to argue that any moment could be open to revolution, although it would not be too far to state, given the volatility of his own time, that the possibility of a revolution in his lifetime was something not to be dismissed. Rather, his point is to recognise and be open to this possibility.

present cannot fully respond. Without reckoning with our inheritance of previous social formations, we become stuck. As Balfour notes:

> The paradoxical task of politics, then, as of history generally, is to prophesy the present. And to make matters more complex, one achieves this visionary perspective on the present by turning one's back from one's own time to the past, not unlike the stance of Klee's *Angelus Novus*, whose back is to the future.[60]

What Benjamin is responding to here is his fear of 'political progressivism',[61] diluting the revolutionary potential of the workers' struggle. Yet the connection between the backward reference and the present as a necessary one is clear. While I agree with Balfour in noting the complexity of this task, it is necessary to acknowledge that it is only Blake's refiguring of time that makes history's reception in the present possible. Yet given these complexities, and Blake's acknowledgment of the inauspicious nature of his time, his goal was to counter the overwhelming tide that was clearly moving against him, not least since the demise of the early promise of the French Revolution. An argument could certainly be made that an achievable goal is to keep a heart of resistance beating in the present, so that even in situations where the possibilities for radical change are dim, there exists an element of carrying forward the possibility in future, but also in thinking through, or mapping out, some of the terrain for those who come after. David Erdman locates this in Blake's response to the Revolution's failing, which is not a rejection of revolutionary potential but its opposite, the criticism of the 'subversion of revolutionary force'.[62] The weak Messianic power that Blake saw at this stage of his life needed to find a long-term strategy. The move towards history and its opening up is both a theoretical strategy for his present and also for those who follow him. The former aspect is clearer in that Blake, furious at the weak opposition to the abundant injustices he witnessed and lived through, wanted a way of upbraiding his own time. Yet

---

60 Balfour 2002, p. 16.
61 McNally 2001, p. 217.
62 Erdman 1969, p. 376. It is useful to contrast this to the conclusion to Wordsworth's *Prelude* wherein 'any revolutionary process the worst are destined to win'. This is a conclusion which owes much to Edmund Burke's interpretation, and divorces the public from 'the possibility of rational affirmation action ... The very pretense of such aspiration is now presented as an object of scorn' (Thompson 1997, pp. 200–1). For a useful examination of the trajectory of Coleridge, who similarly to Wordsworth went from a supporter of the Revolution to dismissive of the notion of revolution itself, see Löwy and Sayre 2001, pp. 117–26.

the latter is also interesting in that Blake, by bringing in another notion of historical time and redemption, makes it possible for future generations in similar positions to explode the past in the name of a different present. This is a deeply Benjaminian insight. As Enzo Traverso notes in a discussion of Benjamin and what the past contains, 'History holds in itself the memory of the vanquished, the recollection of suffered defeats, and the promise of future redemption'.[63] As it goes for Benjamin, so does it for Blake. Precedence of previous social opposition to injustice, as in the example of John Milton, is vital.

4 Milton's Entrance

Milton's appearance in the text comes in two forms. He enters Blake's left foot in a moment of inspiration, again suggesting the importance of being grounded, yet also reminiscent of vegetative growth, as well as a reference to the conversion of Paul of Tarsus.[64] However, it is through Albion's heart that Milton first has to transcend Eternity in order to operate in the present world. Blake's movement into the past is not previous period as it is generally known – in that it is not a fixed item, a series of knowable and indisputable facts. This opening exposes the experience of the other and is reproduced in the other 'through the seemingly impossible yet necessary physical action of entering, and they "emit" one another by continued acts of inspiration ...'[65] Time is, as with Brecht, made plastic and available as a resource to those who aim to liberate both the oppressed groups of the past and the present.

The attempt to move into a new relation with the world, one available to him at any moment in time, is found in his attempt to eliminate any mediation between himself and the world he conjured. Rejecting the new consensus which broke up humanity's creative potentials, and severed any connection to a well-defined ordering of one's place in a rationalist calculation, Blake's sum-

---

63 Traverso 2016, pp. 202–3.
64 This refers to a conversion for Paul/Saul and Milton. 'As Erdman and other commentators have noted, the word *tarsus* punningly connects this episode to Saul of Tarsus's conversion into St. Paul. Much in the way that Saul suddenly renounces his self-righteous persecution of the early Christians to become an apostle of Christ, both Blake and Milton in the course of this poem cast off their judgmental neoclassicism to adopt a more genuinely Christian vision' (Richey 1996, p. 122).
65 Piccitto 2018, p. 116. This is a sincere willingness to understand another on their own terms, involving a compassionate observation. For an excellent brief commentary on John Clare's 'quiet objectivity', see the critical commentary by Merryn and Raymond Williams in Clare 1986, pp. 201–22.

moning of *Milton* begins his relation to the now in a form that expands our sense of what is possible. This involves a rejection of the 'mind-forg'd manacles': dominant ideologies with which he contended. Blake offers us a conception of experience that is similar to Benjamin's distinction of *Erlebnis* and *Erfahrung* in his 'On Some Motifs in Baudelaire'. In these texts, Benjamin distinguishes the two as follows: 'The Greater the share of the shock factor in particular impressions, the more constantly consciousness has to be alert as a screen against stimuli; the more efficiently it does so, the less do these impressions enter experience (*Erfahrung*), tending to remain in the sphere of a certain hour in one's life (*Erlebnis*)'.[66] In the realm of experience, we have two possible fields that dictate our relation to the world: how we process that which we inhabit, and that which inhabits us. As Thomas Elsaesser explains, 'Benjamin makes a distinction between *Erlebnis* and *Erfahrung*, the first associated with moments of sensation and the second with a more sustained texture of experience'.[67] There comes a moment, which Benjamin will note defines the Modernist experience of modernity, where *Erfahrung* disappears as a way of seeing or experiencing the world, as Esther Leslie notes: 'In 1933 he reaches the conclusion that conditions on the battlefield have made the continued existence of experience as *"Erfahrung"* – practised, well-established and continuous tradition – virtually impossible in this moment. The technological traumas of war confirm and kick home experience as *"Erlebnis"* – shock, adventure, disruption'.[68] Such technological traumas of war as seen by Benjamin were over a century away for Blake. Yet the entrance of Milton presupposes the access of an overwhelming flooding whereupon our traditional reception and expectation of experience (as ongoing over a lifetime) is ruptured by a need that cannot be satisfied by *Erfahrung*. A surplus of *Erlebnis* is required in the now to awaken the memory of long suppressed historical trauma.

In Blake, this resuscitated history is akin to inspiration, and thus often it is depicted as divine. And as God is omnipresent, history acts and attains meaning in the present. We must be careful here not to imagine that this shift to history is merely one reference, or one citation amongst others. As Balfour has written, 'the text [is] open for interpretation, open to an uncertain future'.[69] This open future would be possible only if what is denied in the present[70] could

---

66 Benjamin 1968, p. 163.
67 Elsaesser 2009, p. 294.
68 Leslie 2000, p. 38.
69 Balfour 2002, p. 172.
70 Makdisi usefully describes the tension between Blake and his own time and the desire to move outside of such a limiting historical period as follows: 'Blake's language of power

be fulfilled or enlightened by previous struggles. In this regard, the connection between the historical past and the moment of the now – in all its variant uncertainties – is one that Blake's poetics retains.

Yet while we can presume the political-aesthetic task at hand that makes summoning Milton possible and desirable, the question remains: who does the summoning, and to what end? While central questions, they pivot on a specific historical trajectory that is key to understanding the particular uses of Milton as a spirit made real, but also the importance of Milton as a spirit himself. There are overtones here of romantic *Naturphilosophie*, and in particular of a guiding impulse that is moving things into place, liberating those waiting to be rescued from their in-between (literal purgatory) state. History is linked to the present – through natural forces – by means of the activity of the person who summons that history. The link between Blake and Friedrich Schelling here is compelling. Brad Prager sums up Schelling's vision of nature as 'the progressive history of self-consciousness. Natural history was, in other words, the history of the world-spirit, or *Geist*, the divine consciousness developing through man'.[71] The development of mind as a means of accessing the world outside of its immediate grasp is fruitful, especially since the levels of demoralisation brought about by the failures of the French Revolution – and the promise that the Revolution symbolised – were more apparent. Many of those inspired by its prospect went in directions opposite to that which initially motivated their embrace of its logic. Alex Benchimol notes of Wordsworth, for instance: 'A key element in Wordsworth's vision of social landscape – one that would take on a new urgency after the conflict with Napoleonic France – is the emphasis placed on harmonious relations between the classes in general and the value of moral leadership from traditional institutions like the Church more specifically'.[72] That classes should exist in harmony would appal Blake, yet there is a strange connection with the acceptance of the existence of classes (as a norm, and, when in balance, a redeemable one) and central tensions that exist in *Naturphilosophie*. Whereas the desire for harmony papers over oppositions (requiring repression both of ideological and violent natures), there is a reliance on the necessity of these oppositions existing. As Joan Steigerwald notes, 'The *Naturphilosophie* that Schelling put forward in the *Ideas* was that all natural phenomena must be conceived as an interplay of attractive and

---

was obsolete by the 1790s ... only in the sense that it was allowed no room in the historicist discourse of modernity, and in the culture of modernization, which had to purge itself of such enthusiastic tendencies' (Makdisi 2003, p. 3).

71 Prager 2007, pp. 134–135.
72 Benchimol 2007, p. 94.

repulsive forces in varying degrees of complexity and activity. These opposed forces were not introduced as empirical concepts, or as the physical grounds of explanation like some form of occult qualities, but as the necessary conditions for the possibility of a world system'.[73] So here we see developing a key distinction between Blake and the fields of aesthetic and philosophic vision prevalent during his time. Blake is focused not on repairing class cleavages through harmonious compressions but on working through them and intervening. In his reconfiguration of worldly life, Blake emphasises the ability of the human mind to switch from a conception of life as a mere collection of experiences to something that is larger than the sum of its parts, and to control (and create the possibility for controlling in itself) a constituting spirit of experience and action. While '[Schelling's] *Naturphilosophie* had the character of Kant's first *Critique* and *Prolegomena*, works that showed how the fundamental laws of physics, though empirically established, nonetheless derived their universality and necessity from the transcendental categories of mind',[74] Blake's approach was closer to Goethe's, who argued that such strictures were meant as limits but not full determinations. As Christine Lehleiter explains, 'Each individual operates in a clearly delineated field within which freedom becomes possible. Although Goethe concedes that for some individuals ... this field might be extremely limited, he also demonstrates that such determinism will limit the possibility of selfhood only in the extreme case'.[75] Finding a way between the possibilities of creation and determination haunted Blake's *Songs* and guided his philosophy through *Milton*. Anthony Apesos's excellent work on the poem relates the heights and often abstractions that haunted the 'transcendental categories of mind' to what stood out most actively for Blake. Blake's project rejected a mechanistic construction of determination and replaced it: 'From this centre in his brain, open to Eternity, down the nerves to his writing hand, Blake informs us that his poem is both an inexplicable product of the imagination and a physical act performed by a living man'.[76] Blake's insertion of himself is a necessary one, framed to insert the reader as well. Blake 'places himself conspicuously at the centre of this drama. To overlook his presence is to edit his poem by half',[77] notes Paul Youngquist. Apesos extends this by arguing that *Milton* is Blake's clearest example of his own insertion into his world. This further draws the links guiding the inspiration behind the text that was dir-

---

73 Steigerwald 2002, p. 554.
74 Richards 2002, p. 128.
75 Lehleiter 2014, p. 149.
76 Apesos 2015, p. 384.
77 Youngquist 1990, p. 557.

ectly attributable to Blake's creative practice. He notes, 'Blake's presence as a character occurs so he can be depicted directly witnessing the poem's events and, paradoxically, to emphasise that Milton is not an account of actual events but the product of Blake's writing. The tensions between Blake's presence as character and author work together in Blake's effort to achieve his intentions of correcting John Milton and saving William Blake'.[78] This provides a framing for the text's reception, and draws out the political implications in taking up active readership. 'For Blake, the writing of Milton is a battle in that fight, and in reading it we must become brothers-in-arms [sic] with Blake engaged in mental fight'.[79] It is important then, given the limited agency presented in such a worldview – which is in peril of being shrunk even further – that Milton's presence in Blake's world comes at a moment of terror. This is reminiscent of Benjamin's notion of the past being taken hold of in a moment of danger, when the liberatory possibilities of Blake's contemporary world seem exhausted.

> The Sin was begun in Eternity, and will not rest in Eternity
> Till two Eternitys meet together.
> Ah! Lost! Lost! Lost! For ever!
> So Leutha spoke.[80]

What is interesting here, besides the provocative notion of two Eternitys meeting and that which is dominant being crushed, is that the denial of their meeting is put forward by Leutha, a character who in this plate is repentant but was once in the service of Satan. Her despair is expressed at a moment of shock at what she has done, and the feeling of hopelessness given her admission of guilt. Plate 13 continues:

> But when she saw that Enitharmon had
> Created a New Space to protect Satan from punishment;
> She fled to Enitharmons Tent & hid herself.[81]

There is protection for those causing damage, but that this is not universalised only further intensifies the havoc wreaked on others. In Plate 12, Blake moves through Harrow, London, which is reacting to pre-repentant Leutha's destruct-

---

78   Apesos 2015, p. 380.
79   Apesos 2015, p. 383.
80   Blake 1988, p. 107.
81   Blake 1988, 107.

ive movements. The situation here is 'A Hell of our making'.[82] Because of the problems of Theodicy (the explanation of evil in God's loving world), Albion is in a moment of flux, of dialectical anxiety. Blake expresses this contradiction in the following: 'To do unkind things in kindness! With power armd, to say / The most irritating things in the midst of tears and love'.[83] There is neither love nor care here, and the extinguishing of the radical power of God for those in need along with all manner of support for those in power is a galling contrast. Here, there is a profound twisting of power in the name of the 'Moral Law'.[84] But where to find succour in these moments? Blake is clear that it is certainly not in institutional learning.

> ... in Cambridge and in Oxford, places of Thought
> Intricate labyrinths of Times and Spaces unknown
> that Leutha lived
> In Palamabrons Tent, and Oothoon was her charming guard.[85]

In these passages we cannot be freed from the original failings of the historical fall and are left with the introduction of Oothoon, a figure of free love and of openness and compassion, as the only buttress against an almighty power. This is clearly not enough, and if we continue on this path, history as it has unfolded this will continue to maintain its course. If we are damned with this history, how do we make a break from this perpetual or 'Eternal' damnation? It is in this context that Milton arrives. In Plate 14 Blake writes:

> Shaking the roots & fast foundations of the Earth in doubtfulness
> The loud voic'd Bard terrify'd took refuge in Miltons bosom
> Then Milton rose up from the heavens of Albion ardorous![86]

The explicit identification of the Bard is at times unclear: he is seemingly a compilation of various figures in Blake's mythology, including Blake himself.

---

82 Blake 1988, p. 106.
83 Ibid.
84 Jennifer G. Jesse notes the distinction between what those in need *need*, and what they receive from the Established Church. 'By the time Blake produced *Milton* and *Jerusalem*, the primary activity he associates with Jesus is the forgiveness of sins and, more often than not, this is described in contrast to the Anglican interpretation of Jesus as a representative of the moral law' (Jesse 2013, p. 121).
85 Blake 1988, p. 107.
86 Blake 1988, p. 108.

However, it is instructive that at a moment of deep doubt, and unable to properly function, Blake summons Milton.

Milton arrives as a source of power, and he is among the greats to whom one may go back for inspiration. We should also note the connection between the move outwards for help when one is in need, as well as the stress on care, in *The Songs of Innocence and Experience*. Blake is not outside of this experience and when at his most desperate and in need he looks backward to Milton. Despite the complicated nature of 'The Bard', John Sutherland notes that in this position, 'the Bard himself seems to represent Blake at his most inspired'.[87] His summoning of Milton is significant for two reasons. First, Blake 'took refuge' at a moment when his conception of life was being threatened deeply by capitalism's quantifying logic and the 'Moral Law'. It was an impossible situation that required an impossible solution, in the notion of recorded time as put forward by the authorities of his day. Second, this introduction occurred during a moment of utter despair, when the almost complete abolition of hope prompted the need to take refuge in something that offered a way out of the current morass. This is recorded as a flash, which will radically alter the dangerous present from its unsettled history. Benjamin writes:

> The danger affects both the content of the tradition and its receivers. The same threat hangs over both: that of becoming a tool of the ruling classes. In every era the attempt must be made anew to wrest tradition away from a conformism that is about to overpower it.[88]

If we follow Benjamin in highlighting the importance of tradition on its receivers, and given that the focus here is on Milton, the question becomes: how does Milton figure in Blake's philosophy of intervention? Milton is a ready response to the conformism of the ruling-class attempt to 'make a Heaven out of our misery'. Yet his use here also is heavily indebted to the question of what he offers to the reception of religion in Blake's time. On the question of this tradition and Blake, Thompson is categorical. He writes, 'The strongest influence upon Blake comes from one major source – the Bible – but the Bible read in a particular way, influenced by Milton and radical Dissent ...'.[89] Such is the impact of Milton that, in Blake's framework, his presence becomes the fulfilment of prophecy. By creating the idea that Milton has been present from time immemorial, Blake

---

87   Sutherland 1977, p. 145.
88   Benjamin 1968, p. 255.
89   Thompson 1995, p. 33.

makes his summoning the potential for new forms of love. In order to make clear what Milton's purpose on earth is, Los states:

> O Sons we live not by wrath. By mercy alone we live!
> I recollect an old Prophecy in Eden recorded in gold; and oft
> Sung to the harp: That Milton of the land of Albion.
> Should up ascend forward from Felphams Vale & break the Chain
> Of Jealousy from all its roots;[90]

Blake conjures Milton, but only because Milton was in a state that allowed for him to be conjured. Milton was waiting for his summoning. His function resembles that of Jesus, as both were intended to live, die and then return. The connection between the three is no passing idea. As Makdisi notes, 'For on [Blake's] own account, his work is little more than dictation inspired by Jesus Christ, or John Milton, or the "eternals" …'.[91] What prophesying the past makes possible is that the true path of history may be understood, and thus the task before Blake is to be able to prepare oneself to be inspired by it. Only then can one be among those to receive history. As Blake notes in the Bard's Song:

> The Bard replied. I am inspired! I know it is Truth! For I sing
> According to the inspiration of the Poetic Genius
> Who is the eternal all-protecting Divine Humanity
> To whom be Glory & Power & Dominion Evermore Amen.[92]

Here we begin to see the fundamental importance for Blake of 'Poetic Genius'. Milton has been waiting for this time of inspiration, he who 'walkd about in Eternity / One hundred years … Unhappy tho in heav'n'.[93] Blake pictures Milton as unhappy because, as Erdman notes, 'history has not gone according to his vision of it'.[94] For Blake, Milton's return makes possible the illuminating process of fulfilling this lost history or, alternatively, of addressing this long history of loss.

---

90   Blake 1988, p. 119. One way in which we can read Blake's wish for the work to move beyond the text is suggested by the fact that, as John B. Pierce perceptively notes, '… the moment of action for the character of Milton in the poem springs from a specifically oral event – a Bard's song' (Pierce 2000, p. 449). And as Pierce argues, it is this making real (my phrasing), which translates into 'The union of thought and expression, inspiration and execution in turn prevents the work of abstraction' (2000, p. 458).
91   Makdisi 2003, p. 242.
92   Blake 1988, pp. 107–8.
93   Blake 1988, p. 96.
94   Blake 1988, p. 397.

Milton occasions a point of departure from the quantified temporality (clearly associated with Satan and his twisted invocation of God) as well as a passive, unresponsive reception of life. This contrasts with the conception of the poets' (Blake's and Milton's) reception of historical time. While not always accessible, this temporal framing nevertheless stretches beyond any quantifiable moment and is ever-present, if one is open to its reception. We do not make sense of raw material of history; rather, this conception of historical time is the key principle in understanding where we are at any given moment in time. Despite our predicament, it is always there. Blake notes:

> I in Six Thousand Years walk up and down: for not one Moment
> Of Time is lost, nor one Event of Space unpermanent
> But all remain: every fabric of Six Thousand Years
> Remains permanent:[95]

The reference to six thousand years, the time of existence according to scripture, provides an oppositional form of thinking and being in the world. It is a conception of time that rejects the facticity and capitalist temporality of Blake's present. As Frye notes, 'History as linear time is the great apocrypha or mystery which has to be rejected'.[96] Yet what is at stake here is partially the redeeming of another view of time for its own sake, although this is indisputably part of Blake's framework. It is not merely another version of time that Blake is looking to construct. Rather, the task is to create an oppositional form of life that offers a way out of the present distorting consensus. For this reason, the emphasis on creativity, and specifically labour as a broadly creative act, articulates a liberating politics for both Blake as an artist and for the world as a whole.

5   Blake *Labouring* in History

As with analyses of Benjamin that de-contextualise his work's explicit politics (in particular his rejection of social democracy in the *Theses*),[97] so with Blake's

---

95   Blake 1988, p. 117. While I disagree with S.H. Clark's argument that in this passage 'History becomes sealed and finite', his qualified notion that 'Time is the element in which constructive intervention becomes possible and so provides a merciful release from "eternal torment"', is nevertheless a useful description of the role of Los (historical time) in Blake's text (Clark 1997, p. 476).
96   Frye 1969, p. 340.
97   Although commenting on Blake, Julia Wright's following remark could equally be applied

texts it is important not to disregard the importance of work and workers and its/their representation. Labour in *Milton* is chiefly articulated in two ways. Firstly, labour is equated with work as it relates to all facets of human reproduction (not simply labour that is commodified), and particularly with agricultural work. Secondly, it is defined in relation to cultural production. In this second sense, labour is principally associated with Blake's own creative work. While in this second manifestation it is equally as valid as the first, labour often stands as a metaphor for a 'mental fight' necessary for the battle against Satan and for the inspiration to channel Milton to re-enter the world. The conduit through which Milton rushes is made up of several constituent labouring parts, but it fundamentally defines labour as a thinking, working, spirit.

> Properly understood, then, labor is not opposed to inspiration. … Invention, the labor of the mind, is coterminous with execution, the exercise of the hands. Copying is not a time-bound mediation (even though it benefits from practice), but an unmediated access, instantaneously, to a tradition of inspired originality. The spiritualization of labor, and as it were the bringing down to earth of inspiration, bring a capable, persevering humanity into contest with a captivating divinity.[98]

Early in the text, Blake makes an explicit distinction between contrasting notions of 'proportion': 'When Satan fainted beneath the arrows of Elynittria / And Mathematical Proportion was subdued by Living Proportion'.[99] Satan is identified with Mathematical Proportion, making this a negative reference, while Living Proportion is positive. The concept of Living is interesting as it has more than an undertone of being productive, as opposed to being overly abstract and thus non-reproductive and non-responsive to the current situation. Likewise, it is also concerned with its conditions and the manner of its historical reception. The centrality of living structures the representation of work in Blake.

In Plate 8, Blake draws a line between two places of labour. The first shows 'Satan returning to his Mills' where he does not see that he has 'opress'd nor injur'd the refractory servants'.[100] Satan possessing his mills and servants makes

---

to Benjamin. She writes 'Social and political change do not arise from historical evolution, the slow steady march toward civilization, but from beyond such chronological constructions …' (Wright 2004, p. 54).
98   Haggarty 2010, pp. 150–1.
99   Blake 1988, p. 99.
100   Blake 1988, p. 101.

clear that slavery still exists in capitalism, and with those subjects for whom enslavement determines their life. Yet Blake is quick to counter these 'Satanic Mills' with an opposition movement which was always there ('remained permanent'). Los, often depicted as a harvester throughout Blake's work, responds to the Satanic Mills as follows:

> Ye Genii of the Mill! The Sun is on high
> Your labours call you! Palamabron is also in sad dilemma;
> His horses are mad! His Harrow confounded! His companions enrag'd.
> Mine is the fault! I should have remember'd that pity divides the soul
> And man unmans: follow with me my Plow. This mournful day
> Must be a blank in Nature: follow with me, and tomorrow again
> Resume your labours, & this day shall be a mournful day[101]

There is no arguing against the idea that mills, plows, and labour are metaphors deeply imbedded in Blake's references to redemptive religion, and to a God who is active in the material world. The point is that the predominance of these metaphors is just as meaningful in articulating Blake's worldview as is their place in religion more broadly. The fact that Satan returns to 'his Mills' locates a sense of ownership and materiality (of property and labour time), while at the same time the reference to those working at the Mill connotes a magical note, which squarely identifies the workers as the creators of all wealth. As Makdisi notes, 'Who works, how he or she works, and the conditions under which she works are all inextricable questions for Blake'.[102] As Los calls on the labourers to leave the Mills, this raises the question as to the nature of their Labour under Los, and to how it prefigures the industrial nature of production that Blake criticises in the poem.

Los himself suggests how he is identified within this unique labour process. In Plate 25, he cautions against vengeance 'till all the Vintage of Earth was gatherd in'.[103] Yet while Los calls to wait for vengeance, for the reasons Erdman suggests, how he frames his call is instructive. 'And Los stood & cried to the Labourers of the Vintage is now upon Earth / Fellow Labourers! The Great Vintage & Harvest is now upon Earth'.[104] Los is the leader of the harvest, one of the dominant metaphors throughout the poem, but allies himself clearly with the 'labourers' in his rallying cry to action. Los stands here as a sort of vanguard,

---

101 Blake 1988, pp. 101–2.
102 Makdisi 2003, p. 113.
103 Blake 1988, p. 121.
104 Ibid.

but a vanguard that is not separated from the workers, but rather stands as one of them. Further, his caution recognises the potential of the former slaves to *not* heed his call. They have the agency to seek vengeance, and it is necessary to guard against it. Agency places everything in play. As Sarah Haggarty notes, this means dictates from above will not wash. 'The struggle dramatized by *Milton*, then, is not quite between God and man, dictator and secretary, but between the capacity of a man to act divinely and his corporeal aspect. And it is precisely a struggle'.[105] These labourers possess the possibility of making history, and are in agreement with Los in this creation. It is at the moment that 'fellow labourers' are summoned to take part in making history, as opposed to being passive pawns in the history of their own lives, that we should reflect that this process has occurred before.

On the link between labour and past history in Blake, Thompson's work is most convincing, as he places Blake's 'very unusual and probably unique, position' in an 'obscure antinomian tradition'.[106] While Thompson focuses on a crucial developmental period in Blake's work between 1788 and 1794, his argument concerns the structuring of Blake's key ideas, which carry forward particularly from this period. While the antinomian tradition had 'become obscure by the 1790s',[107] by '1810 Blake's views had become so strange that Henry Crabb Robinson could comment that "his religious convictions had brought on him the credit of being an absolute lunatic"'.[108] The disjunction between this tradition and its potential reception demonstrates how unfashionable Blake's adherence to this tradition had become, but it is interesting nonetheless that there is something that is consistent in Blake's oeuvre.[109] Thompson definitively provides this consistency in the last two lines of his text. He writes, 'But there is never the least sign of submission to "Satan's Kingdom". Never, on any page of Blake, is there the least complicity with the kingdom of the Beast'.[110]

---

105 Haggarty 2010, p. 150.
106 Thompson 1995, p. xix.
107 Thompson 1995, p. 62.
108 Thompson 1995, p. 63.
109 This thesis is in direct contradiction to Nicholas Williams's work, who attempts to construct, not unlike Althusser's reception of Marx, with which he is sympathetic, an earlier and mature Blake. See Williams 1998.
110 Thompson 1995, p. 229. Following Thompson's point that Blake never wavered, Jon Mee writes that, far from there being a 'break' between the 'radical Blake' of the 1790's and of that in the time of writing *Milton*, '... After 1795 Blake published nothing of his own work till *Milton* in 1804, there is little evidence in either his annotations or notebook that he renounced his political perspective on state religion' (Mee 1992, p. 213). This text also provides a useful analysis of Blake's work during that decade, while highlighting the formal developments therein, not merely their historical significance.

In part, this helps illuminate the above quoted passage wherein Los, entering Blake in a moment of inspiration, declares that all time 'remains permanent'. Nothing can slip outside such a framework, even though it is seemingly not always accessible.

This compressed time is chronology that discernibly works in a continuum, but it also operates within a level of continuity that allows it to work outside of its own assumed properties. For this reason, Milton is positioned as a Reprobate while Cromwell, given that he did not fulfil his role, is only ready for redemption (that is, a member of the 'redeemed' class). Kings Charles and James are positioned as members of the 'Elect'. This may not be the capitalist working class as it will later be defined in the Marxist tradition, chiefly because it is not defined by its relation to capitalism. It is fully exploited labour yet it also includes labour from pre-capitalist social formations. In the same way, however, that this 'working' class produces in the continuum and in the instance, so too does the Elect 'class'. What the Elect in *Milton* repent is instructive. Blake writes:

> Charles calls on Milton for Atonement. Cromwell is ready
> James calls for fires in Golgonooza. For heaps of smoking ruins
> In the night of prosperity and wantonness which he himself Created[111]

The 'fires of Golgonooza' are meant to burn up and cleanse the errors of the past, yet the notion of prosperity as a negative qualifier allies Blake with an oppositional understanding of history and the present. This raises the question of who benefits from the creation of wealth. There is a good deal of wish fulfilment as Kings James and Charles are both confronted with the wreckage of their own disastrous histories and held to account, although how far Blake could have gone in this regard is an interesting question, as the royal descendants are sure to have profited from the original theft, and offer further support for the system which upholds their power.

While Blake would not have been alone in presenting this disastrous history and its contemporary manifestations, the form in which he does it – the Daughters of Albion 'sing Creating the Three Classes among Druid Rocks'[112] – is unique. As Makdisi notes, there is a '... distance between Blake and the hegemonic tendency in 1790s radicalism. For the latter, as indeed for the conservatives themselves, "labourer" and "employer" are categories to be taken for granted; whereas for Blake, they are socio-bio-psychological organisms, the products of a particular social organization'.[113] If they are both products of a

---

111 Blake 1988, p. 99.
112 Blake 1988, p. 99.
113 Makdisi 2003, p. 113.

particular social organisation and socio-bio-psychological organisms, then this offers up a very interesting question about what specifically this era, the era of Milton, of the English Civil War, the advent of capitalism, means for Blake. This seems to suggest that Milton is something larger than a mere reader of the Bible. The fact that Blake looks for redemption and inspiration in Milton concretely offers a way of getting at the heart of the predicament in Blake's age, in particular the ways that past crimes continue to determine the forms of oppression and exploitation during his time.[114]

The way in which Milton makes himself known in Blake's world is instructive in framing both his introduction and what he offers as an alternative to the social and political construction of Blake's time. Blake compares Milton entering from a high position with the heavenly 'in the Zenith as a falling star'.[115] Yet he enters Blake through his foot – where he stands – 'And on my left foot falling on the tarsus, entered there'. Together, the connection between the two symbolises the process of something organic, in a similar sense to Makdisi's 'socio-bio-psychological organisms', and also further articulates a specific moment. In other words, the two worlds of God and the physical universe are important for highlighting the moment of the now in the process of historical reception, as well as in a history that is always waiting to be received. This possibility of historical redemption comes not as something alien to the universe, but rather as an entity that is foundational to earth's own essential character. This essential character is itself essentialist. While Blake is considerably ahead of his times in presenting a more nuanced and positive representation of women and their agency than was normally offered by male writers of his era, the mixture and manipulation of genders and gender norms is a core ingredient involved in the advancement of humanity's broader commonality. To be clear, one side is still more equal than the other, as David Shakespeare notes:

> In *Milton*, a mix of vision and concealment, and an accompanying mix of genders, are what lead to redemption. This gender mixing is less "sexual" than it might be both in the modern sense of sexual acts and in the sense contemporary to Blake that Susan Matthews delineates – heterosexual

---

114   Describing the way in which Blake contrasts the mythology of the essay in comparison to the second coming of the end (of which more later), Andrew M. Cooper argues that '*Milton* strives toward an unqualified affirmation of concrete human life'. While this essay is heavily indebted to a Freudian structuralism (note the title), the article, as evidenced in the above, is unwavering in its emphasis on human agency as vital for Blake in the poem (Cooper 1981, p. 88).

115   Blake 1988, p. 110.

gender roles. It is not copulation, nor even a joining of properly male and female figures, but an ideal of androgyny where the feminine remains subordinate, but makes a tangible contribution.[116]

Yet this essential character that brings together Blake and Milton is coloured by a specific return to a definitive place. While Milton returns to 'eternal death', our lived reality, he enters 'Albions land / Which is the earth of vegetation on which I now write'.[117] The literalness of this passage ('on which I now write') is out of place with much of the poem. Shortly thereafter, when describing Milton's entrance into Blake's world, he describes the connecting point as both of and outside the moment they live in. He notes:

> But Milton's Human Shadow continu'd journeying above
> The rocky masses of The Mundane Shell ...
> The Mundane Shell, is a vast Concave Earth: and immense
> Hardend shadow of all things upon our Vegetated Earth
> Enlarg'd into dimension & deform'd into indefinite space,[118]

The fact that space is 'deform'd' when made indefinite suggests the sense of urgency in location, as well as the importance in moving from abstraction ('mathematical proportion') to a vegetating or growing space ('living proportion').[119] There is a belief or doctrine of 'growing' in Blake that resists any attempt to provide a final destination point, where life will be fulfilled, and

---

116 Shakespeare 2013, p. 113. There is also a clear discrepancy as regards which gender and possession of knowledge and inspiration. '... throughout the poem the masculine figures not only have the privilege of access to visions divine and immanent, but they are often consolidating their privilege by doing the hiding' (Shakespeare 2013, p. 114).
117 Blake 1988, p. 109.
118 Blake 1988, p. 110.
119 The emphasis here on growing connects to Blake's critique of Urizen's over-rationalism and over-abstraction. As Mark Lussier notes, 'The emergence of consciousness into materiality is always an emergence into the field of the real as a specific perpetual location in spacetime, with only those willing to undertake what Blake later terms "self-annihilation" capable of perceiving the splendors of a complementary, undifferentiated experience' (Lussier 1996, p. 401). By reducing the self to something larger (the way in which Blake will distinguish himself from Satan), one opens up into a world of deep connection within itself and other worlds. This connection is deeply held in regards to nature. This adds to the anti-Newtonian aspects of the poem: 'Blake's signifying nature can be immediately distinguished from then current notions of the cosmos marked by the ascendency of a mechanistic worldview associated with Isaac Newton' (1996, p. 405). Further, he notes that 'Only through acknowledging the interpenetration of one another with and all with the world can the imagination truly shape a viable cosmological frame. The cosmos, for Blake,

this is made more democratic by being open for all to contribute to.[120] Raymond Williams notes that in Shelley's essay 'A Defence of Poetry', a text also concerned with proportion, particularly of sound, proportion is defined by the 'organizing principle' of synthesis, which, 'as the creative human act', marks the poet out as unique, in contrast to the 'child and savage'.[121] It is doubtful whether Blake would draw such a distinction, at the very least without first making clear a case against the impoverishment of the mind that is fundamental to capitalism. Likewise, the contrast of cultured and 'savage' is especially problematic, and doubly so given the work done in appropriating Blake with appeals to nationalism, given that Blake was well aware of how culture buttresses and promulgates imperialism. In *Culture and Imperialism*, Edward Said shows how the processes of imperialism manifested beyond economic and political formations and argues that these processes integrated culture movements in service to 'the national culture, which we have tended to sanitise as a realm of unchanging intellectual monuments'. Said quotes Blake's 'The Foundation of Empire', where he argues that were 'Art and Science' to be removed or degraded the Empire would be 'No more. Empire follows Art and not vice versa as Englishmen suppose'.[122] The framing of culture as a highpoint separate from the actual processes that make it possible is likewise also instructive, as it removes the processual and iterative nature of making. For instance, note how Mark Canuel explains the role of Beauty in Shelley's poetics:

> Beauty, for Shelley, is not quite the beauty of the eighteenth century – the beauty of symmetries and resemblances ... Shelley constantly draws attention to beauty as the product of human finitude. Beauty is a human "form" that strives to be more than human and seeks to encompass the full range of human and nonhuman living things.[123]

---

assumes an elasticity shaped by individual perception, fed by the imagination, and experienced beyond our own seemingly limited location in discrete spacetime' (1996, pp. 406–7).

120 This rupturing will tend towards removing oppression, not merely locating a space beyond – momentarily – the reach of Satan's destructive power. One such example of this necessity lies in sexuality. A Christopher Z. Hobson notes: 'Rather, as in *Milton*, Blake shows the disruption of same-sex subjectivity by outside enforcement and internal self-affirmation of social gender norms, leading to a different sex-subjectivity in which the repression of same-sex potential poisons personal life and helps form a world of gender and social oppression' (Hobson 2010, p. 32).

121 Williams 1984, p. 25.

122 Said 1994, pp. 12–13.

123 Canuel, 2012, pp. 141–2.

Blake's poetics seem to drag the form to earth and make it living, whereas for Shelley poetry seems to abstract humanity's form for greatest appreciation, as was the case for John Keats, and most other Romantic thinkers, whose focus was on the mind of the artist.

The larger metaphors of nature which abound in the text are deeply related to the possibilities of framing historical reception through the reliance on the labour of harvest. The notion of the end-point of the harvest cannot simply be viewed as a totality in and of itself. As Balfour has argued, 'The vintage and harvest are plausible as figures for the end because they mark the end of a given cycle of nature – and yet it is precisely the cyclical character of the seasons that prevents any harvest or vintage from being the last'.[124] While Balfour is absolutely correct in pointing out that the 'Last Harvest' is not at all 'the last'[125] (and in this regard it deserves noting that there are two 'Last Harvests' referenced in the poem), this should not preclude an examination of the importance of what the last represents in Blake for 'vegetating' and 'growing', which I am using interchangeably. There seems to be a correlation of the two that echoes Marx's famous statement that revolution will end humanity's pre-history, and thus our attempts to revolutionise – the summoning of Milton is for this purpose – our existence is about arriving at a truer 'nature'. That is a moment where our growing is no longer 'manacled' – that concept most hated by Blake – to Satanic Mills or Jealousy. That said, I am not arguing that it is within human nature to reach this point, as this would be to read Marx and Blake teleologically. It is enough to maintain that Blake's philosophy argues for the termination of something odious to human existence. That is, to echo Makdisi, we are able to see in Blake a desire for the true potentiality to occur, and to hope and work towards a moment where those fires which attempt to extinguish such potential are themselves snuffed out.

For this reason, until the 'Last Harvest' is behind us, Blake describes humanity on earth as living in 'sorrowful Vegetations'.[126] Without the second coming humans are literally grounded in historical structures of exploitation and oppression. Balfour has noted the comparative significance of Milton's intro-

---

124   Balfour 2012, p. 167.
125   Steve Vine describes the moment of the transcendent sublime in Blake not as a flight from the material world, so much as finding fulfilment in it. This links where one is and the direction where one will go. As he writes, 'The infinite is always in the process of (its) revelation, for Blake's corrosive designate a process rather than a product, a "displaying" rather than a display. The infinite resides in the corrosion and "melting away" of the material, but this process is internal to the material itself. The material is not so much sublimated as the sublime is installed in the material' (Vine 2002, p. 242).
126   Blake 1988, p. 119.

duction through the 'feet' and poetic structure (the foot as the form of metre in poetry). However, the resurrection will come not as something *merely* magical (falling from the sky) but rather through our fulfilling the base materiality coursing through us, arising from where we stand. Only once that has been done will we be able to fulfil the following lament: 'O when shall we tread our Wine-presses in heaven; and Reap / Our wheat with shoutings of joy, and leave the Earth in peace'.[127] Until that moment in time when the longing for fruition is fulfilled, Los stands as the 'Watchman of Eternity'[128] to warn us of the danger of repeating history's failing, principally from recreating a fall. Los warns us against this danger:

> Arise O Sons give all your strength against Eternal Death
> Lest we are vegetated, for Cathedrons Looms weave only Death
> A Web of Death: & were it not for Bowlahoola & Allamanda
> No Human Form but only a Fibrous Vegetation
> A Polypus of soft affections without Thought or Vision.[129]

There is a danger of negating or destroying the imagination that will fulfil our humanity and make us the materiality of our salvation. Ultimately though, Milton is the spirit of the Apocalypse, and his coming heralds the possibility of ultimate regeneration, a process that goes beyond merely shielding oneself and the broader community from the horrors of capitalism or previous exploitative systems. This regeneration prefaces the creative impulse in Blake and its importance in both making something grow, while at the same time highlighting the necessity of channelling history in poetry.

The notion of the Harvest is deeply implicated in the way in which labour appears in the text. Los's proclamation to 'Fellow Labourers' in the text is important, but the connection between labour and a larger politics of creativity also exists in the redemptive historical channelling that Blake desires. The final clash in the text between Milton and Satan is instructive. In this battle, and in the ultimate redemption of Milton, we see the primacy of a life of making, *philopoesis*, and how it is necessary to make this leap through labour into the moment of time beyond (perhaps an always penultimate) the Last Harvest. This perhaps always penultimate status was further featured in the reproduction of the illuminated works of the text. As Makdisi was quoted in Chapter 3, this indeterminacy was a conscious aspect of Blake's production, both visual

---

127   Ibid.
128   Ibid.
129   Blake 1988, p. 120.

and poetic. As Hélène Ibata notes, 'The renewal of the visual dimension with each new copy of an illuminated work is perhaps the most obvious aspect of the open-endedness of the designs: these well-known colour and graphic variations reflect the artist's continuous involvement in the visual aspect of his work, while they question the stability of the text itself in their shifting interaction with it. Even within a single copy, the illuminations are not static translations of the poetry'.[130]

Plate 38 witnesses the battle between Milton and Satan. The latter's description is telling, because Blake offers a clear binary of labour's competing states of being. The depiction of Satan's properties, that is, both his ownership and stewardship of things and what makes him what he is, stand against the notion of labour as a fulfilling practice. Blake writes:

> I also stood in Satans bosom & beheld its desolations!
> A ruind Man: a ruind building of God not made with hands;
> ...
> ... its ruind palaces & cities & mighty works;
> Its furnaces of affliction in which his Angels & Emanations
> Labour with blackend visages among it stupendous ruins[131]

The 'blackend visages' is a reference to industrial work performed in the 'Satanic Mills', but the fact that Satan's building is not made from human 'hands' demonstrates that it is divorced from the level of human creative (and also labouring) activity. Labour here is inclusive of mental strain or drudgery and especially cultural activity with Blake's own plates and poetry standing as the obvious case in point.

In his entreaty in Plate 39 to 'Awake Albion awake', Milton uses the common motif in inspirational thought to awake the recipient from sleep, yet the entreaty is not finished, as the way in which awakening comes about is dependent on the role of labour. The repetition of the word 'labour' and its variant forms in the following is striking. Blake writes:

> Urizen faints in terror striving among the Brooks of Arnon
> With Miltons Spirit: as the Plowman or Artificer or Shepard
> While in the labours of his Calling sends his Thought abroad
> To labour in the ocean or in the starry heaven. So Milton

---

130   Ibata 2010, p. 41.
131   Blake 1988, p. 139.

> Labourd in Chasms of the Mundane Shell, the here before
> My cottage midst the Starry Seven, where the Virgin Ololon
> Stood trembling in the Porch: loud Satan thunderd on the Stormy Sea
> Circling Albions Cliffs in which the Four-fold World resides
> Tho seen in fallacy outside: a fallacy of Satans Churches[132]

The repetition of the idea of Labour overcoming Satan in completing this redemption is significant. The reference to the Arnon is particularly fruitful, as Bloom notes in an early reference from Plate 19: 'The Arnon is a river of error, and like the Red Sea, its crossing symbolises a movement towards life, from Moab to Canaan, from Urizen to a redeemed Luvah who is Christ'.[133] To cross this river, becoming physically immersed in it, implies a judgment, a point of definitive departure.

A key feature of Blake's work is a compulsive dedication to democracy more generally and debate in particular. However, when the final moment approaches, and Milton is denouncing Voltaire and others, he cries out 'Obey thou the Words of the Inspired Man'.[134] Going further, he declares that 'the Reasoning Power in Man / This is a false Body'.[135] In a further attack, directed towards those who divorce theory from any form of beneficial practice, Blake attacks those whose 'Science is Despair'[136] by ridiculing the 'idiot Questioner who is always questioning, / But never capable of answering'.[137] Here not being able to provide answers should caution against accepting the notion that a moment of fulfilment is against Blake's 'nature'. Indeed, as we see in his final Plate, Blake suggests that labour is not only central to humanity and its liberation but also that its true fulfilment must be achieved rather than continually postponed.[138] In the penultimate verse, whilst travelling across the city, 'Los listens to the Cry of the Poor Man: his Cloud / Over London in volume terrific, low bended in anger'.[139] The anger of the London[140] labouring 'Poor man' is jus-

---

132 Blake 1988, p. 141.
133 Bloom in Blake 1988, p. 916.
134 Blake 1988, p. 142.
135 Ibid.
136 Ibid.
137 Ibid.
138 What I am arguing here is that there is something so rotten in the state of things that we require a new way of living that will aid us in removing us from our present misery. Yet as 'humankind can't live context-less' we must then resurrect other forms of knowing and living that pre-date our current, self-interested context (Thompson 1995, p. 221). This will require 'some utopian leap ... "from Mystery to renewed imaginative life"' (1995, p. 193).
139 Blake 1988, p. 144.
140 It is important to restate that London is not merely a setting defined by Blake's presence,

tified in Blake. It is they who create, and it is historically their labour which is in need of redemption.[141] Hearing this cry, Blake ends with the beginning of their redemption: 'All Animals upon the Earth, are prepared in all their strength / To go forth to the Great Harvest & Vintage of the Nations'.[142] The question of going forth and completing the act at hand necessitates that history be redeemed. To quote Benjamin on Messianism again,

> ... our image of happiness is indissolubly bound up with the image of redemption. The same applies to our view of the past, which is the concern of history. The past carries with it a temporal index by which it is referred to redemption. There is a secret agreement between past generations and the present one. Our coming was expected on earth. Like every generation that preceded us, we have been endowed with a weak Messianic power, a power to which the past has a claim. That claim cannot be settled cheaply. Historical materialists are aware of that.[143]

While I cannot argue that Blake was an historical materialist, I am on much safer ground in arguing that his aim was to resurrect the weak Messianic power, which at his time was being destroyed, in order to redeem those that have come before, and Blake and his own time as well. *Milton* shows how this is possible.

---

but as Makdisi points out, 'In Blake's geography, then, London is the spatial representation of the experience of the Universal Empire of modernizing capitalism; a process that was, in Blake's vision, gradually reterritorializing and transforming the globe' (Makdisi 1998, p. 157).

141 It is indicative of a real gap in Blake studies that in a work entitled 'William Blake and the Body' there is scant discussion of the role of the labouring body. See Connolly 2002.

142 Blake 1988, p. 144. Such statements may read as patriotic or as buttressing chauvinist politics. While Blake himself does not advance such a politics, for a contemporary examination of the uses of Blake's *Milton* and other texts in modern national myth-making, see Dent 2012, pp. 48–62. One need caution, however, that despite such readings, colouring Blake as a patriot in this conventional sense is wide of the mark. 'Blake seems to have been one of a number of republican writers who were seeking other ways in which civic virtue could be conceived and exercised' (Fallon 2009, p. 92).

143 Benjamin 1968, p. 254. Werner Hamacher also usefully notes how Benjamin opens up a new conception of time that is always struggled over: 'If the time-form of historical happening is the present – namely the past contracted to and fulfilled in the present – then the present is never a transition in a series of other presents and yet other ones, but always a singular moment in which the possibilities and demands of the past are contracted and fixed: the present is not the time-form of waiting for a better or simply different future, not the state of waiting that preceded the state of redemption, but the standstill where one no longer waits, a standstill into which even waiting itself is drawn and in which the demand associated with the waiting has fallen silent' (Hamacher 2005, p. 53).

6 Brecht, Blake and the Uses of History

As I have shown in this and the previous chapter, a focus on history can be an active way of moving beyond the 'merely historical' and accomplishing a realignment so that history can be brought into a productive conversation with the present. This is history as it is not commonly known and translated, written in a language unfamiliar to traditional historiography, which presents the catalogue of human relations as never pre-determined, and always, although structured and limited, open. Yet, even this is a pale incompletion of how both Brecht and Blake think of the past and its accessibility. History, as with the present, is never safe. In the times of capitalism and previous forms of oppressive social relations, the possibilities of alterity abound. While the movement of historical time shows it will always be contested, it is always also frozen as Werner Hamacher explains: 'When history occurs, it is only in its fixation to a moment and furthermore to an image. Whatever occurs, stands still. History does not have a course, it pauses'.[144] Brecht's and Blake's aesthetics are ingrained by precisely this version of history.

The moment of historical time in Brecht's later work always exists where appearance (in dates, in costume, etc.) is made to be in fidelity with factual events. Yet we are consistently invited by Brecht to renege on that allegiance to appearance, and operate on a level of historical understanding that demands a connection to the past so that historical wrongs are just as much part of the present as they were during their first occurrence. History is a continuum of articulations made at moments of danger, and often in the face of a threat the response is rarely to confront it head on. So often, excepting bizarre, tragicomic figures of justice like Azdak, those in moments of trauma recoil in the face of the truth that stares back at them.

Likewise, Blake will scour the past, and once inspiration is located, he'll move from a standstill – Milton waiting, unable to wake himself from the failures of his life (patriarchal, ideological, theological and aesthetic) – tearing us in a radical heartbeat into the moment of the now. The hand-brake of history is pulled so that another temporality can be made right by those that have wronged and been wronged by others. 'I in my Selfhood am that Satan: I am that Evil One! / He is my Spectre!'[145] exclaims Milton. This arresting of history provides a means

---

144   Hamacher 2005, p. 53.
145   Blake 1988, p. 108. 'In his epiphany, Milton sees that he yielded to pride, vanity, and power hunger, and consequently he emulated tyranny when he promulgated his unsavory portrait of God and, in patriarchal fashion, abused his wives and daughters. He became a despot in his home, a little Urizen' (Quinney 2009, p. 128).

to redeem it as well, as following the normal course of events will not provide any reasonable recourse to justice. As Michael Löwy argues in his reception of Benjamin:

> ... redemption/revolution will not occur in the mere natural course of things, by dint of the "meaning of history" or inevitable progress. One has to struggle against the tide. Left to itself, or brushed *with* the grain, so to speak, history will produce only new wars, fresh catastrophes, novel forms of barbarism and oppression.[146]

All these texts clearly show the result when one does not 'struggle against the tide'. The 'Little Monk' withdraws, casting aside the possibilities for those who could have been encouraged by a revolt against the church. Courage consistently meets horror after horror along the same path despite her silent scream, convinced that events will turn in her favour. Grusha finds herself played like a bargaining chip in her own life, consistently the subject of others' direction. Milton is left to wallow in purgatory which encourages those forces who seek, with an Urizenic impulse lacking control or proportion, to threaten the potential existence of a life informed by our relation and connection to the natural world. This provides at least negative hope for a world outside of a destruction of nature and humanity's life-giving qualities. In this, 'Blake's visionary poetry admonishes us to realise it is not really about technology; what ultimately matters in building our own *ecotopia* is the quality of human vision and the extent of our shared commitment to realizing human potential through creative endeavour'.[147]

Yet the object lesson here is that history must never be avoided, nor worked around as if it is something that can ever be passed by or de-materialised. Instead, rather than avoid history's lack of fulfilment and the way that dominant historiography cuts out the oppressed, both writers engage with humanity's creative faculties to produce new meanings from old truths. In this regard Benjamin is so vital because he 'retains a materialistic understanding of aesthetics by maintaining their connection to sensual perception, while also displaying

---

146 Löwy 2005, p. 49.
147 McKusick 2016, p. 239. McKusick further describes this ecotopia by noting that '... William Blake held the strongest commitment to such an idealised urban existence. In place of London's enormous factories and powerful steam engines, Blake envisioned the imaginary city of Golgonooza, powered by small, hand-operated machines, including a loom where women weave "clothing with joy & delight" and a wine-press where the sons and daughters of Luvah "tread the grapes / Laughing & shouting"' (McKusick 2016, p. 238).

the interactive relation between art and everyday life'.[148] This means attending to creative meaning but also to challenging and countering meaning 'from above', providing an oppositional hegemonic analysis of history and how it gets disordered following the needs of dominant ideologies: 'Benjamin cuts up preexistent creations that were believed to have been whole, reshuffles the pieces, and pastes them together in a new way. As a dialectical thinker, he sees aesthetic creation as a two-part process, being as interested in how meanings get created as in how meanings are destroyed ...'.[149] For both Brecht and Blake, the recreation of meanings, often but not exclusively as dead meanings resuscitated, provides opportunities for making political aesthetics in the now. Yet the manner of their resuscitation of labour does not match.

Labour holds a special place in the course of liberation in Blake, not as an occupation or a means to reproduce oneself but as an ultimate expression of the power of humanity to create and make new things and meanings. Labour is coterminous with ownership, not of another's labour but as the overcoming of alienation, understood in the Marxist sense of the theft of surplus value. On the one hand, it rejects the idea that a project of one's individual creation should enrich another, and on the other that a person would be alien to what they produce, that their creative connections would be severed from their creations. As S. Brent Plate argues, this is not – even in the resurrection of historical figures – a negation of the modern world and the technical means by which it reproduces itself. Labour creates a connection with the past as well as the present, and it aids in imagining worlds that had not yet existed. Jason Whitaker usefully translates this process in *Milton*. He notes: 'At roughly the same time as he was composing *Milton*, Blake seems to have been attempting to work out a theory of artistic production which would resolve the dilemma of memory and inspiration. ... This meant that history was not the empirical collection of facts, but the prefiguring of contemporary and future states, a typology of the existent world'.[150] Brecht's focus is superficially dissimilar, in that his use of labour often appears as a negative descriptor. Labour in, for instance, *Mutter Courage* represents that which keeps one wedded to a system of oppression and loss. Likewise, the use of peasant time clearly highlights, and this point is repeatedly driven home, exploitation and expropriation of one's emotional and physical labour. Yet there is another sense in which labour is freeing, and this can be seen in the example of Grusha. In her case, productive labour should never be sectioned off from what it produces: the young and the promise of a new life.

---

148   Plate 2005, p. 22.
149   Plate 2005, p. 29.
150   Whitaker 1999, pp. 104–5.

The experience of creation is tied inextricably to liberation, both of the self as a creative participant in the world and of the community of creators/producers more broadly. And this necessitates a realignment in the relation of the world to our creative fields and also to ourselves. Epic Theatre itself can never be, in this regard, a closed field. By its nature, it requires not merely the activity of the players but the potentially emancipatory labour of the audience's contribution to cultural production. The situated nature of the work requires that, as Sarah Bryant-Bertail argues, 'Epic texts and performances are ultimately concerned with *critiquing their specific historical situation*. They are anything but "timeless", and herein is their strength'.[151] This strength draws both from the work itself and its individual productions through the connections it makes with its audience.

Built into the process of engagement and liberatory practices in theatre, Susan Buck-Morss notes how Benjamin sets out to 'undo the alienation of the corporeal sensorium, to restore the instinctual power of the human bodily senses for the sake of humanity's self-preservation, and to do this, not by avoiding the new technologies, but by passing through them'.[152] In both instances, the use of history to rescue something from the past for the present, and as a source of material for those in the present to learn from, opens the possibility of self-preservation and suggests ways to free ourselves from the current drag on humanity's potentialities.

---

151 Bryant-Bertail 2000, p. 6.
152 Buck-Morss 1992, p. 5.

CHAPTER 6

Conclusion

Over the course of this book, I have sought to bring Blake and Brecht together to show how each developed separate but related aesthetic strategies, and how the work of Benjamin is useful in helping to draw out the processes at work in the two. The first moment dissected is their contemporary period, defined largely by a world of commodified social relations in which a fully formed capitalism exhaustively makes and remakes its subjects in its own image. This was coupled with an analysis of the ways in which one can work around, against and through that system. Both Blake and Brecht construct their own rejections of capitalism by understanding its logics and manifestations: to not do so would produce an ineffective opposition to the systemic nature of the object of their ire. Although the two engage capitalism from different starting points and mediating social and political axes, both comprehend the system's processes and seek, *from that point*, to articulate their oppositional aesthetic politics. In this way, Brecht and Blake begin to develop a politics of experience through the connection to their particular oppressive societies. Capitalism rules by making it impossible to live in a way that is redeemable, fulfilling and compassionate. Masking itself in all those institutions and forms of life that could be potentially life-affirming, capitalism instead provides existential danger and continual exploitation as both reward and punishment for the maintenance of its own system. This process is something that Benjamin understood well, as Michael Jennings notes: 'The essay [The Work of Art] proceeds from the conviction – best articulated in "Experience and Poverty" – that one of capitalist modernity's principle effects is the destruction of the conditions for an adequate human experience'.[1] Once this destructive drive is acknowledged and named, one cannot expect to cast aside all that capital produces without first foraging through its logics and ideologies and using what one can to undermine capital's power. This dynamic – of being opposed to a system while using its logic and processes to oppose it – was a motivator for Benjamin in his examination of the technologies that produce new experience in capitalism. As Jennings continues, '... for Benjamin, technology is at once a main cause of this destruction of experience and its potential solution'.[2]

---

1   Jennings 2016, p. 96.
2   Jennings 2016, p. 96.

Experimentation in the 'now', the moment of the possible, allows one to articulate a new that is creative, while also acknowledging that there is no other space that determines contemporary human experience. Capitalism's various determinations may leave one with little space to operate, but therein is the dilemma of modern oppositional cultural production. There is no escape from capitalist forces' desire to take the oppositional (or that which has an oppositional spirit *in potentia*) and reproduce it in its own image. In some cases, as for instance in the potential in Messianism felt by both Blake and Benjamin, capitalism's nullifying forces are radically blunt.

The co-opting of oppositional impulses involves authorities taking what is life-giving and making and turning it into its opposite. This is a clear form of appropriation and was supported in Blake's historical period down the barrel of a gun, at times literally, as David Worrall's historical study illustrates:

> In Edmonton, Middlesex, a loyalist procession dragooned the church band to accompany a 'triumphal Arch' supported by five men on which a dove held the motto 'No Revolution', while 'the rear was brought up by Women and Children; before night they were *half Seas over* and sang God save the King &c.' Children, songs and socializing were all enlisted in scenes of social conviviality glimpsed at in the text and design of 'Laughing Song' and 'The Little Vagabond' whose 'Ale-house' is not only 'healthy & pleasant & warm' but likely to be a place where political meetings were held.[3]

The daily, grinding problem of capitalism is unavoidable, and one has no option but to go through the system and make the best use of what remains of one's humanity, particularly one's creative intelligence, the best possible outcome, albeit starting from the degraded status that capitalism perpetuates. There is no way out of this prison-house of experience without working with the rubble of existence and experience that one is caught within.[4] Benjamin refers to this dilemma as the 'poverty of experience' in his essay of the same name. He writes: 'This should not be understood to mean that people are yearning for new exper-

---

3 Worrall 1999, pp. 204–5.
4 Edward Larrissy provides a postmodern retort to my argument that the *Songs* are structured to speak to two separate (dialectically contradictory) forms of life and experience. 'Thus, one may concede that there is undoubtedly a strategy in *Songs of Innocence and of Experience* which leads us towards mutual ironizing as constitutive of the relationship between the two "contrary states" ...' (Larrissy 2006, p. 255). This position leads us away from any conception of oppositional forms of life and offers no way out of capitalism's abyss of petrified experience.

ience. No, they long to free themselves from experience; they long for a new world in which they can make such pure and decided use of their poverty – their utter poverty, and ultimately also their inner poverty – that it will lead to something respectable'.[5] For Blake and Benjamin, it is important to know the conditions of one's oppression and exploitation, and then to move toward those experiences that lead into new possibilities.

Brecht and Benjamin's connection to the contemporary moment is not always similar, even though the two learned from each other throughout their collaborations. For instance, Benjamin lauds Kafka's 'depth', meaning the level of Kafka's inquiry into his own historical moment. For Brecht this is insufficient as it misses an attempted resolution, no matter how incomplete. Brecht requires an outcome or direction that comes out of the delving into. Brecht does not object to the examinations themselves, but 'their insufficient *extension*, that they don't emerge on the other side', thus become narcissistic or 'diary-like'.[6] For this reason Brecht begins, particularly in his teaching plays, by taking 'nothing that is based on experience for granted – neither Marxism nor humanity'.[7] Change exists in that space of contradiction between the ability to change oneself in relation to the world, and combatting society's social processes in order to create new experience (not the 'poverty' of the post-World War I economic, social, and political destruction that defined western Europe), in which revolutionary change can begin.

When the momentum behind this new experience cannot be found in the contemporary moment, Brecht and Blake move into history while opposing a realist conception of history that masks or confuses liberatory potential with 'progressiveness'. This realist interpretation, then on the rise in Western social democracy and in the Stalinist distortions of the Soviet Union, waters down a politics of action and ultimately supports, as Brecht puts it, the 'enemies of production'. The engagement with the contemporary moment requires an extra step. It cannot merely be met head on, and therefore history becomes a refuge in which a world of lessening possibilities can be pried open to reveal a moment outside of itself. This allows for the present to reflect on its own position, and prompts change. The retreat into the past cleaves open time's continuum that capital and its enforcers wish to remain closed.

The surrender of the historical terrain is coerced. Nevertheless, Benjamin shows that the past provides something that the present cannot. He writes: 'We have become impoverished. We have given up one portion of the human herit-

---

5 Benjamin 1999, p. 734.
6 McFarland 2013, p. 225.
7 Oesmann 2005, p. 133.

age after another, and have often left it at the pawnbroker's for a hundredth of its true value, in exchange for the small change of "the contemporary".[8] This book's second movement, examining history and historical allegory in Blake and Brecht, has shown that the past is a contested and fraught affair. The moments when this temporality is accessed, and the type of history being engaged, are painful moments, coloured by loss, failure and suffering. As Jameson notes in *The Political Unconscious*, 'History is what hurts'.[9] The periods that Brecht and Blake use here are marked by the dominance of a 'peasant structure of feeling' more generally, even if, in Brecht's case, the structure of feeling is determined by capitalist relations of production and represents capital's drives and imperatives. These are more properly situated at the moment of capitalism's emergence as a hegemonic formation, as we see especially in *Milton, Mutter Courage and Galilei*. Navigating the interstices between feudalism and capitalism involves rejecting the latter's enclosing of historical imagination and an imperative to read history against the grain, while recognising the danger in such an oppositional act, given one's unequal footing versus capitalist power. Reading is not straightforward, and it must be mobilised through oppositional worldviews. Accessing these different temporalities requires an understanding of one's own mediated relation to them. As Robert S. Lehmann notes, history is 'reached only through a certain labour'.[10]

The retrieval of history can neither be an end in itself, nor an end restricted to the artwork itself. The possibility of a better future, or indeed of utopian futures (a requirement that mirrors the breaks that open the history of the present), is achievable through 'just' judgments. Azdak and Blake perform these judgments, reaching beyond the individual and creating community justice. While acknowledging this understanding of the place of community has not been an issue in Brecht studies, the same cannot be said for Blake. It is ironic that, given the revolutionary judgment involved in the retrieval of Milton, revolutionary particularly in its judgment both of forgiving and blame, Blake has been at times 'configured as a soft liberal who was buoyed by the false hopes of a foreign revolution only to soften into respectable quietism in later years when that revolution supposedly revealed its true nature'.[11] Yet Blake was well beyond the 'soft liberals' of his day. As Makdisi notes, 'For most of the radicals of the 1790s – with the notable exception of Blake – individual self-control was the key to

---

8 Benjamin 1999, p. 735.
9 Jameson 1994, p. 102.
10 Lehman 2016, p. 192.
11 Makdisi 2003, p. 19.

Liberty'.[12] The notion of freedom here is one of individual liberty, de-coupled from the responsibility to care for the community.

Blake understands his role in connection with other traditions that put community struggle ahead of individual liberties. In making the links between Blake and Marx, Makdisi argues they were indebted to older communist traditions that were 'principally concerned with questions of being and ontology, and in seeking to ground not just religion but politics (as well as economics and indeed aesthetics) in ontology it differed markedly from a parallel and to a certain extent competitive movement in political thought – democratic liberalism'.[13]

The connection between ontology and an existence grounded in religion, politics and history opens utopian futures, though for Blake his specific form of utopian thought carries the concept of community along with it.[14] David Fallon argues this point using Bloch's distinction between abstract and concrete utopia. He writes: 'Bloch's model of utopia in *The Principle of Hope* is illuminating in relation to tensions in Blake's poems. Bloch distinguishes between "abstract utopia", largely individualistic daydreams which provide refuge from a reality corrupted by ideology, and "concrete utopia", the dimension of present reality which anticipates and reaches towards real future possibilities just beyond the horizon of the present'.[15] This passage rejects a liberal individualism that could not imagine a way out of its own dilemma of desiring an escape but not having the wherewithal to move outside of the individualist frame. In contrast, history, and in particular the history of class struggles, initiated a consideration of the stakes at play in the multiple determinations at work in the present. 'Blake, too, was working at a moment when it seemed essential to preserve a sense of the connection between history and ontology, and to maintain a way of thinking of history itself *as* ontological struggle'.[16] Viewing history as an ontological

---

12   Makdisi 2014, p. 14.
13   Makdisi 2006b, p. 237.
14   In his investigation of Blake's *America*, Makdisi highlights the oppositional nature of the longer-term project that Blake is engaged in, applying what I have termed a brake on history. He writes; 'if this disruption is produced by the prophecy's attempt to blast a hole in what the radicals (and generations of scholars since them) understood to be a continuous and progressive history, it also has the effect of bringing that narrative, and whatever might be understood as the continuum of history, to a sudden and grinding halt' (Makdisi 2003, p. 156). Makdisi notes that he is 'deeply indebted here to Walter Benjamin's discussion of historical time in "Theses on the Philosophy of History"', although his use of Benjamin is not specified as directly as it is here (2003, p. 349).
15   Fallon 2017, p. 18.
16   Makdisi 1999, p. 238.

struggle hints at the danger of leaving it to liberal individualism, or worse. Similarly for Brecht, history is an ontological struggle, yet there is a more pressing note of danger that resounds in his texts. In part this relates to the formation of 'experience' in response to the devastation of World War I, and the impending horror of fascism.

Given these atrocities, it may seem incongruous to discuss history and utopia in Brecht. Yet history's figurative use in Brecht and Benjamin offers a way out of capitalism's crises and wars. 'For Benjamin, the exemplary rhetorical figure for the representation of history is allegory', and I would argue that likewise allegory is similarly prized by Brecht.[17,18] For the two, choosing between socialism and barbarism requires an act outside the presentation of history, wherein experience can be a worthy ontological topic again.[19] In this sense, '... Benjamin establishes a relation between the messianic hope of seeing the "disfigured" world put back in order and the materialist hope for revolution, which was proper to Brecht'.[20]

Putting this 'disfigured' world back in order required a realignment of historical worldviews. Making history open became a precondition for contesting the contemporary. When Brecht and Blake make history unsafe for capitalism, they make the contemporary that much safer in the present. Yet for Brecht, the role of the utopian possibility is to sound out a possible future, which must always be balanced by the two states of history and the present. As Gerhard Fischer notes: 'Brecht's utopian image is thus not based on a supposedly scientific conclusion, a final stage of history as a classless society, but rather emphasizes the contradictory dialectic of past and present as well as the tentative, hesitant, anticipatory and preliminary nature of the political and socio-cultural openness provided by the historical situation'.[21] This tentative approach is sceptical

---

17 Carney 2005, p. 69.
18 In this regard it is interesting to take into consideration Löwy's contention that Benjamin's depiction of Klee's *Angelus* Novus: 'in reality, what it describes bears very little relation to the painting' (Löwy 2005, p. 62). While this may be true, the painting is an allegory that Benjamin connects to history, thus severing our experience of the linear-historical. This allegorical necessity makes Benjamin's reading of history possible.
19 On the notion of severing history from its presentation, Lehmann writes: 'When the allegorical intention is fixed upon epic history – as it is in Baudelaire's lyric poetry as well as in Benjamin's own historical materialism – what is shattered is the temporal continuity of moments. The moments themselves are preserved, them but not as moments, that is to say, not as successive instants in a unidirectional casual chain. What Benjamin calls "allegorical dismemberment" reveals itself in the nineteenth century by cutting (epic) history's temporal joints' (Lehmann 2016, p. 180).
20 Rochlitz 1996, p. 147.
21 Fischer 2008, p. 143.

that utopia can even be spoken. This is similar to Benjamin's 'antifetishism',[22] and it depends on a critical engagement with the 'consciousness of historical man, whose deepest emotion is an insuperable mistrust of the course of things and a readiness at times to recognize that everything can go wrong'.[23] This dual perspective of history and the now defines Brecht and Blake's oppositional aesthetics.

The mistrust in the course of things is well founded in both Blake and Brecht. The notion of danger in early Brecht, and the calamity of history found in his later works, understands life and social processes through the lens of the tyranny of bad social actors. It is in this sense also that Blake's Experience is constructed not merely by unique, despicable actions, but rather as a dominant logic that oppresses all that it encounters. The singular lesson is that capitalism exists to construct misery and war in its pursuit of its own reproduction.

Mistrust in the order of things is in each case double-sided. That is, in as much as there should be a mistrust 'that everything could go wrong', there is an obverse moment, which claims that the ground upon which we stand is far from stable. As Brecht noted, 'so wie es ist, bliebt es nicht / the way things are is not how they will stay'. In this there is potential to create other possibilities and to resist, a space that can be fashioned from within the tyranny of today. Bloch cautions that the desire to have things change can be resolved in 'filled affects or emotions'. These affects, as Jameson explains, 'ask for fulfillment in a world at all points identical to that of the present, save for the possession of the particular object desired and presently lacking'.[24] '[F]illed affects' aim, whether they are desired to or not, is at reproducing the status quo. Given that they desire

---

22 As James R. Martel notes: 'In my own terms, what separates Benjamin from such utopianism is his antifetishism, his suspicion even of the idea of the utopia itself. Without a focus on antifetishism, we get no true antidote, we just get more of the same. Our "dreams" for redemption remain just that' (Martel 2013, p. 57). This does not preclude the hopes and aspirations of a utopian moment. Rather, as Harry D. Harootunian notes, 'Beneath the rubble of reified imagery marking daily life, the world of the early-nineteenth-century Parisian arcades, announcing their seductive lure of consumption and pleasure, was, he believed, a more humane and utopian conception of community, one that the historical materialist was pledged to retrieve ...' (Harootunian 1996, p. 69).
23 Benjamin 1999, p. 542.
24 Jameson 1974, p. 126. Jameson continues, 'Such affects are primitive or infantile to the degree that they amount to magical incantations, a conjuring up of the object in question just exactly as we long for it, at the same time that we hold the rest of the world, and our own desire, magically in suspension, arresting all change and the very passage of real time itself' (Jameson 1974, pp. 126–7).

something other than the faults of the present, but cannot diagnose the lack outside of individuality, they cannot find a way out of their own predicament. They remained frustrated by their inability to operate outside of the language that expresses dominance and control. Bloch contrasts this form of thinking about other possible worlds with what he terms 'expectation-affects'. Releasing the binds constraining our vision of how our world can be remade allows for a radical rethinking of an individualised approach, which tries to remove a particular ill from society's body while leaving others intact. This opens a much broader discussion whereby all previously determined starting points of action are reimagined. Jameson argues that the aim is not so much directed at 'some specific object as the fetish of their desire, than at the very configuration of the world in general or (what amounts to the same thing) at the future disposition or constitution of the self'.[25]

This future disposition is determined by the present conjuncture, and likewise this by the past. Any desire for expectation-affect, in short for a future beyond domination and exploitation, must be cognisant of its own desires and the possible means to achieve a different world. Bloch refers to this as 'educated hope', and it requires both 'knowledge and removal of abstract utopia'.[26] However, it would be inaccurate to present concrete utopia as the abstract utopia 'righted'. A righted form of utopia does not predict or affirm Marxism's supremacy in philosophy, history or the arts. As Ruth Levitas argues, concrete utopia 'can be understood as both latency and as tendency', in that its threads can be identified historically and gesture to an 'emergent future'.[27] This is particularly instructive for Blake. As we have seen, the migration into history he pursues takes place specifically to find that thread that exists in John Milton (less in the person than the poet's relation to his time) and to keep that memory alive and to make it productive for the present. Likewise for Brecht, the peasant past and its lesson for the present provoke discussion for future activity. Grafting the past onto present struggles involves a dialectical montage. This contrast casts light on the present by translating the past onto it.[28] Blake and Brecht fragment reality in order to analyse which aspects can be made use of

---

25 Jameson 1974, p. 127.
26 Bloch 1986, p. 157.
27 Levitas 1990, p. 18.
28 On the question of montage, Gerhard Richter brings Bloch and Benjamin together in the project of historical investigation and redemption. He notes that the two work '... to find in small and obscure objects the seeds of a radically innovative historiography that expresses philosophical rigor through the aesthetic strategies of pastiche or montage ...' (Richter 2007, p. 48).

in envisioning and creating a future that locates all projects as to a greater or lesser degree unfinished. This carries with it a fundamental pursuit of greater justice, wherein the location is always hinted at and struggled over. This is close to Bloch's position within Marxism, in that even 'in its most illuminating form and anticipated in its entire realization, [it] is only a *condition* for a life in freedom, life in happiness, life in possible fulfilment, life with content'.[29] The possibility of arriving at a moment of intervention only exists within this condition. This relies on the moment of 'educated hope', which means training one's mind to notice those gaps that promote forms of life without exploitation. Blake examined this by occupying the space between Experience and Innocence, in order to imagine a world outside of Benjamin's degraded experience. Brecht named this degraded space, and the fact that it cannot offer any fulfilment, in his *Mahagonny Songspiel*, by arguing that 'Something's missing'. Bloch was quite taken by this passage. He writes:

> This sentence, which is in *Mahagonny*, is one of the most profound sentences that Brecht ever wrote, and it is in two words. What is this 'something'? If it is not allowed to be cast in a picture, then I shall portray it as in the process of being (*seined*).[30]

As Peter Thompson notes, 'The *thing* of the *something* is only constituted by the fact that it is missing. Negativity, or the absence of something, is the very means by which that something is constituted'.[31] Yet this missing '*thing*' is also the beginning-point of socialist thought. The cultural materialist positions throughout this text pose what and who could fill this gap, and what and who could make something out of nothing. The who for this question is answered by Bloch himself: '"Processus cum figures, figurae in processu" (The process is made by those who are made in the process)'.[32] Only those who are exploited and oppressed are ultimately agents for change, for their own freedom and the freedom of others. The means of moving through the logics, ideologies and forms of capitalist domination that appear universally in this book's texts originate from those who are themselves made and remade by the process of reproduction. It is for this reason that, in Blake's world, the labour process itself operated as 'a means of revolutionary expression',[33] and that Brecht, fore-

---

29   Bloch 1988, p. 15.
30   Bloch 1988, p. 15.
31   Thompson 2016, p. 450.
32   Bloch in Thompson 2016, p. 443.
33   Linebaugh 1993, p. 174.

grounding materiality, discovered new rudimentary means for the presentation of exploitation. For both writers, artistic discussion began with the theft from and manipulation of workers specifically, and those who labour more broadly. They are never missing, and ultimately create new history and make new worlds.

Bibliography

Ackerman, Alan L. 2006, 'The Prompter's Box: Modern Drama's Allegories of Allegory', *Modern Drama*, 49, 2: 147–154.
Adorno, Theodore W. 1977, 'The Actuality of Philosophy', *Telos*, 31: 120–133.
Adorno, Theodore W., Walter Benjamin, Bertolt Brecht, György Lukács and Fredric Jameson 1998 [1977], *Aesthetics and Politics*, edited by Ronald Taylor, London: Verso.
Ahmad, Aijaz 1994, *In Theory: Classes, Nations, Literatures*, London: Verso.
Alter, Nora M. 2004, 'The Politics and Sounds of Everyday Life in Kuhle Wampe', in *Sound Matters: Essays on the Acoustics of Modern German Culture*, edited by Nora M. Alter and Lutz Koepnick, New York: Berghahn Books.
Alter, Nora M. 2012, 'Composing in Fragments: Music in the Essay Films of Resnais and Godard', *SubStance*, 41, 2: 24–39.
Altizer, Thomas J.J. 2009, 'The Revolutionary Vision of William Blake', The Journal of Religious Ethics, 37, 1: 33–38.
Anderson, Perry 1998, *The Origins of Postmodernity*. London: Verso.
Apesos, Anthony 2015, 'The Poet in the Poem: Blake's 'Milton'', *Studies in Philology* 112, 2: 379–413.
Arjoman, Minou 2016, 'Performing Catastrophe: Erwin Piscator's Documentary Theatre', *Modern Drama*, 59, 1: 49–74.
Ault, Donald 1975, *Visionary Physics: Blake's Response to Newton*, Chicago: University of Chicago Press.
Bahr, Gisela 1971, *Bertolt Brecht: Die Heilige Johanna der Schlachthöfe, Bühnenfassung, Fragmente, Varianten*, Frankfurt a. M.: Suhrkamp.
Bai, Ronnie 1998, 'Dances with Mei Lanfang: Brecht and the Alienation Effect', *Comparative Drama*, 32, 3: 389–433.
Balfour, Ian 2002, *The Rhetoric of Romantic Prophecy*, Stanford: Stanford University Press.
Barndt, Kerstin 2008, 'Aesthetics of Crisis: Motherhood, Abortion, and Melodrama in Irmgard Keun and Friedrich Wolf', *Women in German Yearbook: Feminist Studies in German Literature & Culture*, 24: 71–95.
Barnett, David, 2011, 'Undogmatic Marxism: Brecht Rehearses at the Berliner Ensemble' in *Edinburgh German Yearbook: Brecht and the GDR: Politics, Culture, Posterity*, Volume 5, edited by Laura Bradley and Karen Leeder, Rochester: Camden House.
Barnett, David 2015a, *Brecht in Practice: Theatre, Theory and Performance*, London: Bloomsbury.
Barnett, David 2015b, *A History of the Berliner Ensemble*, Cambridge: Cambridge University Press.
Beech, Dave 2015, *Art and Value: Art's Economic Exceptionalism in Classical, Neoclassical and Marxist Economics*, Leiden: Brill.

Beer, John 1994, 'Blake's Changing View of History: The Impact of the Book of Enoch', in *Historicizing Blake*, edited by Steve Clark and David Worrall, London: St. Martin's Press.

Benchimol Alex 2007, 'Debatable Borders of Romantic Nostalgia: The Redemptive Landscape in Wordsworth and Cobbett', in *Romanticism's Debatable Lands*, edited by Claire Lamont and Michael Rossington, Basingstoke: Palgrave Macmillan.

Benjamin, Andrew (ed.) 2005, *Walter Benjamin*, New York: Continuum.

Benjamin, Andrew 2013, *Working with Walter Benjamin: Recovering a Political Philosophy*, Edinburgh: Edinburgh University Press.

Benjamin, Andrew and Peter Osborne (eds.) 2000, *Walter Benjamin's Philosophy: Destruction and Experience*, Manchester: Clinamen Press.

Benjamin, Walter 1968, *Illuminations*, New York: Schocken.

Benjamin, Walter 1978 *Reflections*, New York: Harcourt Brace Jovanovich.

Benjamin, Walter 1998, *Understanding Brecht*, London: Verso.

Benjamin, Walter 1999, *Selected Writings: Volume 2, Part 1 1927–1934*, edited by Marcus Bullock and Michael W. Jennings, eds. Cambridge: Belknap Press.

Bennett, Benjamin 2005, *All Theatre is Revolutionary Theatre*, Ithaca: Cornell University Press.

Bennett, Michael Y. 2013, *Narrating the Past through Theatre: Four Crucial Texts*, London: Palgrave Macmillan.

Bentley, Eric 1999, *Bentley on Brecht*, New York: Applause.

Bidney, Martin 1988, *Blake and Goethe: Psychology, Ontology and Imagination*, Columbia: University of Missouri Press.

Bidney, Martin 2002, 'Slowed-Down Time and the Fear of History: The Medievalist Visions of William Blake and William Morris', *Journal for Early Modern Cultural Studies*, 2, 2: 100–120.

Birgel, Franz A. 2009, 'Kuhle Wampe, Leftist Cinema, and the Politics of Film Censorship in Weimar Germany', *Historical Reflections*, 35, 2: 40–62.

Blackbourn, David 1997, *Fontana History of Germany 1780–1918: The Long Nineteenth Century*, London: Fontana.

Blackbourn, David 2009, 'The Conquest of Nature and the Mystique of the Eastern Frontier in Nazi Germany', in *Germans, Poland, and Colonial Expansion to the East: 1850 Through the Present*, edited by Robert L. Nelson, London: Palgrave Macmillan.

Blackbourn, David and Geoff Eley 1984, *The Peculiarities of German History: Bourgeois Society and Politics in Nineteenth-Century Germany*, Oxford: Oxford University Press.

Blake, William 1953, *Selected Poetry and Prose of Blake*, edited by Northrop Frye, New York: Random House.

Blake, William 1988 [1965], *The Complete Poetry and Prose of William Blake*, edited by David V. Erdman, New York: Doubleday.

Bloom, Harold 1997, *The Anxiety of Influence*, Oxford: Oxford University Press.

BIBLIOGRAPHY

Bloch, Ernst 1986, *The Principle of Hope*, translated by Neville Plaice, Stephen Plaice and Paul Knight, Volume 1, Oxford: Basil Blackwell.

Bloch, Ernst 1988, *The Utopian Function of Art and Literature: Selected Essays*, translated by Jack Zipes and Frank Mecklenburg, Cambridge, Mass: The MIT Press.

Bodek, Richard 1997, *Proletarian Performance in Weimar Berlin: Agitprop, Chorus, and Brecht*, Columbia, MI: Camden House.

Bohls, Elizabeth A. 2013, *Romantic Literature and Postcolonial Studies*, Edinburgh: Edinburgh University Press.

Bourdieu, Pierre 1993, *The Field of Cultural Production*, New York: Columbia University Press.

Bracher, Mark 1985, *Being Form'd: Thinking Through Blake's Milton*, New York: Station Hill Press.

Bradley, Laura 2006, *Brecht and Political Theatre: The Mother on Stage*, Oxford: Clarendon Press.

Bradley, Laura 2011, 'Introduction' in *Edinburgh German Yearbook: Brecht and the GDR: Politics, Culture, Posterity*, Volume 5, edited by Laura Bradley and Karen Leeder, Rochester: Camden House.

Braskén, Kasper 2015, *The International Workers' Relief, Communism, and Transnational Solidarity: Willi Münzenberg in Weimar Germany*, London: Palgrave Macmillan.

Brecht, Bertolt 1965, *The Mother*, translated by Lee Baxandall, New York: Grove Press.

Brecht, Bertolt 1966, *Galileo*, translated by Charles Laughton, edited by Eric Bentley, New York: Grove Press.

Brecht, Bertolt 1978a, *Brecht on Theatre: The Development of an Aesthetic*, edited and translated by John Willett, London: Methuen.

Brecht, Bertolt 1978b, *The Mother*, translated by Steve Gooch, London: Methuen.

Brecht, Bertolt 1979, *Collected Poems, Poems 1913–1956*, edited by John Willett and Ralph Mannheim, London: Methuen.

Brecht, Bertolt 1987, *Mother Courage and Her Children*, edited by John Willett and Ralph Manheim, translated by John Willett, London: Methuen.

Brecht, Bertolt 1988a, *Gesammlte Werke*, Band 2, edited by Werner Hecht et al., Frankfurt am Main: Suhrkamp Verlag.

Brecht, Bertolt 1988b, *Gesammlte Werke*, Band 21, edited by Werner Hecht et al., Frankfurt am Main: Suhrkamp Verlag.

Brecht, Bertolt 1988c, *Gesammlte Werke*, Band 22.2, edited by Werner Hecht et al., Frankfurt am Main: Suhrkamp Verlag.

Brecht, Bertolt 1988d, *Gesammlte Werke*, Band 23, edited by Werner Hecht et al., Frankfurt am Main: Suhrkamp Verlag.

Brecht, Bertolt 1988e, *Gesammlte Werke*, Band 24, edited by Werner Hecht et al., Frankfurt am Main: Suhrkamp Verlag.

Brecht, Bertolt 1988e, *The Caucasian Chalk Circle*, translated by W.H. Auden, James Stern and Tania Stern, London: Methuen.

Brecht, Bertolt 1991, *Saint Joan of the Stockyards*, translated by Ralph Manheim, Methuen, London.
Brecht, Bertolt 1992, *The Jewish Wife and Other Short Plays*, translated by Eric Bentley, New York: Grove Press.
Brecht, Bertolt 2000a, *Brecht on Film and Radio*, edited and translated by Marc Silberman, London: Methuen.
Brecht, Bertolt 2000b, *Man Equals Man and The Elephant Calf*, edited by John Willett and Ralph Manheim translated by Gerhard Nellhaus, New York: Arcade.
Brecht, Bertolt 2010, *Mother Courage and Her Children*, translated by David Hare, London: Methuen.
Brecht, Bertolt 2012, *Mother Courage and Her Children / Mutter Courage und ihre Kinder*, edited by Tom Kuhn, translated by Tony Kushner, London: Bloomsbury Methuen Drama.
Brecht, Bertolt 2019, *The Collected Poems of Bertolt Brecht*, translated and edited by Tom Kuhn and David Constantine, New York: Liveright Publishing Corporation.
Britt, Brian 2016, *Postsecular Benjamin: Agency and Tradition*, Evanston: Northwestern University Press.
Brooker, Peter 1988, *Bertolt Brecht: Dialectics, Poetry, Politics*, London: Routledge & Kegan Paul.
Brough, Neil, and R.J. Kavanagh 1991, 'But Who is Azdak? The Main Source of Brecht's Der Kaukasische Kreidekreis', *Neophilologus*, 75, 4: 573–580.
Bru, Sascha and Anke Gilleir 2017, 'Red Rosa: On the Gender of the November Revolutions in the German Avant-Gardes', *Modernism/modernity*, 24, 3: 461–483.
Bruder, Helen P. 1997, *William Blake and the Daughters of Albion*, New York: St. Martin's Press.
Bruder, Helen P. and Tristanne Connolly (eds.) 2010, *Queer Blake*, London: Palgrave Macmillan.
Bruder, Helen P. and Tristanne Connolly (eds.) 2012, *Blake, Gender and Culture*, London: Pickering and Chatto.
Bruder, Helen P. and Tristanne Connolly (eds.) 2013, *Sexy Blake*, London: Palgrave Macmillan.
Bryant-Bertail, Sarah 2000, *Space and Time in Epic Theatre: The Brechtian Legacy*, Rochester, NY: Camden House.
Buck-Morss, Susan 1992, 'Aesthetics and Anaesthetics: Walter Benjamin's Artwork Essay Reconsidered', *October*, 62: 3–41.
Buck-Morss, Susan 2000, *Dreamworld and Catastrophe: The Passing of Mass Utopia in East and West*, Cambridge, MA: MIT Press.
Buck-Morss, Susan 1977, *The Origin of Negative Dialectics: Theodor W. Adorno, Walter Benjamin and the Frankfurt Institute*, New York: The Free Press.
Burling, William J. 'Brecht's 'U-effect': Theorizing the Horizons of Revolutionary Theatre', in *Brecht, Broadway and United States Theatre*, edited by J. Chris Westgate.

Calabro, Tony 1990, *Bertolt Brecht's Art of Dissemblance*, Wakefield, NH: Longwood Academic.

Canning, Kathleen 2006, *Gender History in Practice: Historical Perspectives on Bodies, Class, and Citizenship*, Ithaca: Cornell University Press.

Canuel, Mark 2012, *Justice, Dissent, and the Sublime*, Baltimore: The John Hopkins University Press.

Cardullo, Bert 1984, 'A World in Transition: A Study of Brecht's *Mann ist Mann*', *Forum for Modern Language Studies, he German Review: Literature, Culture, Theory*, xx, 3: 263–274.

Carmody, Jim 1990, 'Reading Scenic Writing: Barthes, Brecht, and Theatre Photography', *Journal of Dramatic Theory and Criticism*, 5, 1: 25–38.

Carney, Sean 2005, *Brecht and Critical Theory: Dialectics and Contemporary Aesthetics*, London: Routledge.

Casaliggi, Carmen and Porscha Fermanis 2016, *Romanticism: A Literary and Cultural History*, New York: Routledge.

Caudwell, Christopher 1973, *Illusion and Reality*, New York: International Publishers.

Chai, Leon 2006, *Romantic Theory: Forms of Reflexivity in the Revolutionary Era*, Baltimore: The John Hopkins University Press.

Chandlers, James 2006, 'Blake and the Syntax of Sentiment', in *Blake, Nation and Empire*, edited by Steve Clark and David Worrall, New York: Palgrave Macmillan.

Christensen, Jerome 2000, *Romanticism at the End of History*, Baltimore: The Johns Hopkins University Press.

Clare John 1986, *John Clare, Selected Poetry and Prose*, edited by Merryn Williams and Raymond Williams, London: Methuen.

Clark, Mark W. 2006, *Beyond Catastrophe: German Intellectuals and Cultural Renewal after World War II, 1945–1955*, Lanham: Lexington Books, 2006.

Clark, S.H. 1997, 'Blake's 'Milton' as Empiricist Epic–'Weaving the Woof of Locke'', *Studies in Romanticism*, 36, 3: 457–482.

Clark, Steve 2007, ''There is no Competition': Eliot on Blake, Blake in Eliot', in *Blake, Modernity and Popular Culture*, edited by Steve Clark and Jason Whittaker, London: Palgrave Macmillan.

Clarke, Steve and Jason Whittaker (eds.) 1999, *Blake in the Nineties*, London: Palgrave Macmillan.

Clarke, Steve and Jason Whittaker (eds.) 2006, *Blake, Nation and Empire*, London: Palgrave Macmillan.

Clarke, Steve and Jason Whittaker (eds.) 2007, *Blake, Modernity and Popular Culture*, edited by Steve Clark and Jason Whittaker, London: Palgrave Macmillan.

Clarke, Steve and David Worrall (eds.) 1994, *Historicizing Blake*, London: St. Martin's Press.

Collings, David 1991, 'Coleridge Beginning a Career: Desultory Authorship in *Religious Musings*', *ELH*, 58, 1: 167–193.

Connolly, Tristanne J. 2002, *William Blake and the Body*, New York: Palgrave Macmillan.
Cooper, Andrew M. 1981, 'Blake's Escape from Mythology: Self-Mastery in 'Milton'', *Studies in Romanticism*, 20, 1: 85–110.
Cooper, Andrew M. 2012, *Re-Envisioning Blake*, edited by Mark Crosby, Troy Patenaude and Angus Whitehead, London: Palgrave Macmillan.
Curran, Angela 2001, 'Brecht's Criticisms of Aristotle's Aesthetics of Tragedy', *The Journal of Aesthetics and Art Criticism*, 59, 2: 167–184.
Davies, Keri, and David Worrall 2012, 'Inconvenient Truths: Re-historicizing the Politics of Dissent and Antinomianism', in *Re-Envisioning Blake*, edited by Mark Crosby, Troy Patenaude and Angus Whitehead.
Davis, Jennifer Michael 2006, *Blake and the City*, Lewisburg: Bucknell University Press.
Day, Aidan 2012, *Romanticism*, New York: Routledge.
Deen, Leonard W. 1983, *Conversing in Paradise: Poetic Genius and Identity-as-Community in Blake's Los*, Columbia: University of Missouri Press.
Della Volpe, Galvano 1978, *Critique of Taste*, London: Verso.
Dent, Shirley 2012, 'Thou readst white where I readst black: William Blake, the Hymn 'Jerusalem', and the Far Right', in *Re-Envisioning Blake*, edited by Mark Crosby, Troy Patenaude and Angus Whitehead, Basingstoke: Palgrave Macmillan.
Dent, Shirley and Jason Whittaker 2002, *Radical Blake*, London: Palgrave Macmillan.
Dickinson, Colby and Stéphane Symons (eds.) 2016, *Walter Benjamin and Theology*, New York: Fordham University Press.
Dickson, Keith A. 1978, *Towards Utopia: A Study of Brecht*, Oxford: Clarendon Press.
DiSalvo, Jackie 1983, *War of the Titans: Blake's Critique of Milton and the Politics of Religion*, Pittsburgh: University of Pittsburgh Press.
DiSalvo, Jackie, G.A. Rosso and Christopher Z. Hobson (eds.) 1998, *Blake, Politics, and History*, London: Routledge.
Doherty, Brigid 2000, 'Test and Gestus in Brecht and Benjamin', *MLN*, 115, 3: 442–481.
Du, Weinwei 1995, 'The Chalk Circle Comes Full Circle: From Yuan Drama Through the Western Stage to Peking', *Asian Theatre Journal*, 12, 2: 307–325.
Dworkin, Dennis 2007, *Class Struggles*, London: Harlow.
Eagleton, Terry 1976, *Criticism and Ideology: A Study in Marxist Literary Theory*, London: Verso.
Eagleton, Terry 1979, 'Ideology, Fiction, Narrative', *Social Text*, 2: 62–80.
Eagleton, Terry 1991, *Ideology: An Introduction*, London: Verso.
Eagleton, Terry 1994, *Walter Benjamin, or, Towards a Revolutionary Criticism*, London: Verso.
Eagleton, Terry 1996, *The Illusions of Postmodernism*, Oxford: Blackwell.
Eagleton, Terry 2000, *The Idea of Culture*, Oxford: Blackwell.
Eagleton, Terry 2003, *Sweet Violence: The Idea of the Tragic*, Oxford: Blackwell.

Eaves, Morris (ed.) 2003, *The Cambridge Companion to William Blake*, Cambridge: Cambridge University Press.

Ebert, Teresa L. 2009, *The Task of Cultural Critique*, Chicago: The University of Illinois Press.

Ebert, Teresa L. and Mas'ud Zavarzadeh 2008, *Class in Culture*, Boulder: Paradigm.

Eley, Geoff 2013, *Nazism as Fascism*: Violence, Ideology, and the Ground of Consent in Germany 1930–1945, London: Routledge.

Eley, Geoff 1986, *From Unification to Nazism: Reinterpreting the German* Past, Boston: Allen & Unwin.

Elswit, Kate 2008, 'The Some of the Parts: Prosthesis and Function in Bertolt Brecht, Oskar Schlemmer, and Kurt Jooss', *Modern Drama*, 51, 3: 389–410.

Erdman, David 1969, *Blake, Prophet Against Empire: A Poets Interpretation of the History of His Own Time*, Princeton: Princeton University Press.

Erdman, David V. (ed.) 1990, *Blake and His Bibles*, West Cornwall: Locust Hill Press.

Esslin, Martin 1969, *Bertolt Brecht*, New York: Columbia University Press.

Fairer, David 2002, 'Experience Reading Innocence: Contextualizing Blake's 'Holy Thursday'', *Eighteenth-Century Studies*, 35, 4: 535–562.

Fallon, David 2017, *Blake, Myth, and Enlightenment: The Politics of Apotheosis*, London: Palgrave Macmillan.

Fallon, David 2009, ' ''She Cuts his Heart Out at his Side': Blake, Christianity and Political Virtue', in *Blake and Conflict*, edited by Sarah Haggarty and Jon Mee.

Farrell, Michael 2014, *Blake and the Methodists*, London: Palgrave Macmillan.

Fenves, Peter 2001, *Arresting Language: From Leibniz to Benjamin*, Stanford: Stanford University Press.

Fenves, Peter 2011, *The Messianic Reduction: Walter Benjamin and the Shape of Time*, Stanford: Stanford University Press.

Ferber, Michael 1985, *The Social Vision of William Blake*, Princeton: Princeton University Press.

Fiebach, Joachim 1999, 'Brecht: Gestus, Fable, Attitude-cum-Stance', *Modern Drama*, 42, 2: 207–213.

Fischer, Ernst 2010, *The Necessity of Art*, London: Verso.

Fischer, Gerhard 2008, ' ''Good building': Bertolt Brecht's Utopian Historical Optimism at the End of World War II', *Cultural Studies Review*, 14, 1: 137–146.

Fisher, Jaimey and Barbara Mennel (eds.) 2010, *Spatial Turns: Space, Place and Mobility in German Literary and Visual Culture*, New York: Rodopi.

Fisher, Mark 2009, *Capitalist Realism: Is There No Alternative?*, London: Zero Books.

Foot, Paul 1982, *Red Shelley*, London: Sidgwick & Jackson.

Frye, Northrop 1969, *Fearful Symmetry: A Study of William Blake*, Princeton: Princeton University Press.

Fuchs, Christian 2017, 'Raymond Williams' Communicative Materialism', *European Journal of Cultural* Studies, 20, 6: 744–762.

Fuchs, Elinor 2007, 'Waiting for Recognition: An Aristotle for 'Non-Aristotelean' Drama', *Modern Drama*, 50, 4: 532–544.

Gardiner, Jesse 2015, 'Mother Courage and Political Pragmatism: Sovietizing Brecht during the Thaw', *The Slavonic and East European Review*, 93, 4: 626–654.

Giles, Steven 1997, *Bertolt Brecht and Critical Theory: Marxism, Modernity and the Threepenny Lawsuit*, New York: Peter Lang.

Giles, Steve, and Rodney Livingstone (eds.) 1998, *Bertolt Brecht: Centenary Essays*, Amsterdam: Rodopi Press.

Gilpen, George H. 2004, 'William Blake and the World's Body of Science', *Studies in Romanticism*, 43, 1: 35–56.

Gobert, R. Darren 2006, 'Cognitive Catharsis in The Caucasian Chalk Circle', *Modern Drama*, 49, 1: 12–40.

Goethe, Johann Wolfgang von 1989, *The Sorrows of Young Werther*, translated by Michael Hulse, London: Penguin.

Goldsmith, Steven 2009, 'William Blake and the Future of Enthusiasm', *Nineteenth-Century Literature*, 63, 4: 439–460.

Goodridge, John 2013, *John Clare and Community*, Cambridge: Cambridge University Press.

Gramsci, Antonio 1999 [1971], *Selections from the Prison Notebooks of Antonio Gramsci*, edited by Quintin Hoare and Geoffrey Nowell Smith, New York: International Publishers.

Green, Matthew 2005, *Visionary Materialism in the Early Works of William Blake: The Intersection of Enthusiasm and Empiricism*, New York: Palgrave MacMillan.

Gritzner, Karoline 2015, *Adorno and Modern Theatre: The Drama of the Damaged Self in Bond, Rudkin, Barker and Kane*, London: Palgrave Macmillan.

Gross, Erin M. 2010, 'What is Called Corporeal: William Blake and the Question of the Body', *The Eighteenth Century*, 51, 4: 413–430.

Haacke, Paul 2012, 'The Brechtian Exception: From Weimar to the Cold War', *diacritics*, 40, 3: 56–85.

Haggarty, Sarah 2009, 'From Donation to Demand? Almsgiving and the Annotations to Thornton', in *Blake and Conflict*, edited by Sarah Haggarty and Jon Mee, London: Palgrave Macmillan.

Haggarty, Sarah 2010, *Blake's Gifts: Poetry and the Politics of Exchange*, Cambridge: Cambridge University Press.

Hamacher, Werner 2001, '"NOW": Walter Benjamin on Historical Time', in *The Moment: Time and Rupture in Modern Thought*, edited by Heidrun Friese, Liverpool: Liverpool University Press.

Harootunian, Harry D. 1996, 'The Benjamin Effect: Modernism, repetition, and the Path to Different Cultural Imaginaries', in *Walter Benjamin and the Demands of History*, edited by Michael P. Steinberg, Ithaca: Cornell University Press.

Harris, Susan Cannon 2013, 'Mobilizing Maurya: J.M. Synge, Bertolt Brecht, and the Revolutionary Mother', *Modern Drama*, 56, 1: 38–59.
Hartley, Daniel 2016, *The Politics of Style: Towards a Marxist Poetics*, Leiden: Brill.
Harvey, David 1990, *The Condition of Postmodernity*, Oxford: Blackwell.
Haug, Wolfgang Fritz 1999, 'Rethinking Gramsci's Philosophy of Praxis from One Century to the Next', *boundary*, 26, 2: 101–117.
Hedges, Inez 2006, 'The Aesthetics of Resistance: Thoughts on Peter Weiss', *Socialism and Democracy*, 20, 2: 69–77.
Held, Phoebe von 2011, *Alienation and Theatricality: Diderot after Brecht*, Oxford: Legenda.
Hemingway, Andrew 2017, *Landscape Between Ideology and the Aesthetic: Marxist Essays on British Art and Art Theory, 1750–1850*, Leiden: Brill.
Heynen, Robert 2015, *Degeneration and Revolution: Radical Cultural Politics and the Body in Weimar Germany*, Leiden: Brill.
Hill, Christopher 1977, *Milton and the English Revolution*, London: Faber and Faber.
Hill, Christopher 1991, *The World Turned Upside Down: Radical Ideas During the English Revolution*, London: Penguin.
Hobson, Christopher Z. 1998, 'The Myth of Blake's 'Orc Cycle'', in *Blake, Politics, and History*, edited by Jackie DiSalvo, G.A. Rosso, and Christopher Z. Hobson, New York and London: Garland Publishing, Inc.
Hobson, Christopher Z. 1999, *The Chained Boy: Orc and Blake's Idea of Revolution*, Lewisburg: Bucknell University Press.
Hobson, Christopher Z. 2000, *Blake and Homosexuality*, New York: Palgrave.
Hobson, Christopher Z. 2010, 'Blake and the Evolution of Same-Sex Subjectivity', in *Queer Blake*, edited by Helen P. Bruder and Tristanne J. Connolly.
Hodge, Bob 1995, 'Labor Theory Of Language: Postmodernism and a Marxist Science of Language', in *Post-Ality: Marxism and Postmodernism*, edited by Mas'ud Zavarzadeh, Teresa L. Ebert and Donald E. Morton, Washington, DC: Maisonneuve Press.
Holmes, T.M. 1977, 'Descrying the Dialectic: A Heterodox Line on the Prologue to Brecht's Der Kaukasische Kreidekreis', *Journal of European Studies*, 7: 95–106.
Holmes, Terry 1998, 'The Suppressed Science of Society in *Leben des Galilei*', in *Bertolt Brecht: Centenary Essays*, edited by Steve Giles and Rodney Livingstone.
Honegger, Gitta 2008, 'Gossip, Ghosts, and Memory: Mother Courage and the Forging of the Berliner Ensemble', *The Drama Review*, 52, 4: 98–117.
Horsman, Yasco 2011, *Theaters of Justice: Judging, Staging and Working Through in Arendt, Brecht and Delbo*, Stanford: Stanford University Press.
Horwish, Cara M. 1997, *Survival in Simplicissimus and Mutter Courage*, Bern: Peter Lang.
Hutchings, Kevin 2002, *Imagining Nature: Blake's Environmental Poetics*, Montreal: McGill-Queen's University Press.

Hutton, John 1998, '"Lovers of Wild Rebellion': The Image of Satan in British Art of the Revolutionary Era', in *Blake, Politics, and History*, edited by Jackie DiSalvo, G.A. Rosso, and Christopher Z. Hobson, New York and London: Garland Publishing, Inc.

Ibata, Hélène 2010, 'William Blake's Visual Sublime: The 'Eternal Labours'', *European Romantic Review*, 21, 1: 29–48.

Jameson, Fredric 1972, *Marxism and Form*, Princeton: Princeton University Press.

Jameson, Fredric 1979, 'Reification and Utopia in Mass Culture', *Social Text*, 1: 130–148.

Jameson, Fredric 1991, *Postmodernism, or The Cultural Logic of Late Capitalism*, London: Verso.

Jameson, Fredric 1994, *The Political Unconscious: Narrative as a Socially Symbolic Act*, Ithaca: Cornell University Press.

Jameson, Fredric 1998, *Brecht and Method*, London: Verso.

Jameson, Fredric 2005, "Foreward: A Monument to Radical Instants" in Peter Weiss, *The Aesthetics of Resistance: Volume 1*, translated by Joachim Neugroschel, Durham: Duke University Press.

Jannarone, Kimberly 2009, 'Audience, Mass, Crowd: Theatres of Cruelty in Interwar Europe', *Theatre Journal*, 61, 2: 191–212.

Jay, Martin 1996 [1973], *The Dialectical Imagination: A History of the Frankfurt School and the Institute of Social Research, 1923–50*, Berkeley: University of California Press.

Jeffries, Stuart 2016, *Grand Hotel Abyss: The Lives of the Frankfurt School*, London: Verso.

Jennings, Michael W. 1987, *Dialectical Images: Walter Benjamin's Theory of Literary Criticism*, Ithaca: Cornell University Press.

Jennings, Michael W. 2016, 'The Will to Apokatastasis: Media, Experience, and Eschatology in Walter Benjamin's Late Theological Politics', in *Walter Benjamin and Theology*, edited by Colby Dickinson and Stéphane Symons, New York: Fordham University Press.

Jesse, Jennifer G. 2013, *William Blake's Religious Vision: There's a Methodism in His Madness*, New York: Lexington.

Jones, John H. 1994, '"Self-Annihilation' and Dialogue in Blake's Creative Process: *Urizen, Milton, Jerusalem*', *Modern Language Studies*, 24, 2: 3–10.

Jones, John H. 2010, *Blake on Language, Power, and Self-Annihilation*, London: Palgrave Macmillan.

Jovanovic, Nenad 2017, *Brechtian Cinemas: Montage and Theatricality in Jean-Marie Straub and Daniéle Huillet, Peter Watkins, and Lars von Trier*, Albany: SUNY Press.

Kakel, Carroll P., III 2011, *The American West and the Nazi East: A Comparative and Interpretive Perspective*, London: Palgrave Macmillan.

Kaplan, Jon 2010, 'Preview: The Life of Galileo', *Now Magazine*, May 27–June 3: 39.

Kellner, Douglas 2010, 'Brecht's Marxist Aesthetic: The Korsch Connection', in *Bertolt Brecht: Political Theory and Literary Practice*, edited by Betty Nance Weber and Hubert Heinen.

Kepley Jr., Vance 1983, 'The Workers' International Relief and the Cinema of the Left 1921–1935', *Cinema Journal*, 23, 1: 7–23.

Kinkle, Jeff and Alberto Toscano 2011, 'Filming the Crisis: A Survey', *Film Quarterly*, 65, 1: 39–51.

Kipperman, Mark 1992, 'Absorbing a Revolution: Shelley Becomes a Romantic, 1889–1903', *Nineteenth-Century Literature*, 47, 2: 187–211.

Knapp, Ewout van der 2006, 'The Construction of Memory in *Nuit et Brouillard*', in *Uncovering the Holocaust: The International Reception of Night and Fog*, edited by Ewout van der Knapp, London: Wallflower Press.

Kligerman, Eric 2011, 'The Antigone Effect: Reinterring the Dead of "Night and Fog" in the German Autumn', *New German Critique*, 112: 9–38.

Knopf, Jan 2002, *Brecht Handbuch 1: Stuecke*, Stuttgart: Verlag J.B. Metzler.

Kolb, Alexandra 2009, *Performing Femininity: Dance and Literature in German Modernism*, Berlin: Peter Lang.

Koutsourakis, Angelos 2015, 'Utilizing the 'Ideological Antiquity': Rethinking Brecht and Film', *Monatshefte*, 107, 2: 242–269.

Kovel, Joel 2010, 'Dark Satanic Mills: William Blake and the Critique of War', *Capitalism, Nature, Socialism*, 21, 2: 4–19.

Knudsen, Nicolai Krejberg 2014, 'Redemptive Revolutions: The Political Hermeneutics of Walter Benjamin', *Crisis and Critique*, 1, 1: 167–192.

Kracauer, Siegfried 1966, *From Caligari to Hitler: A Psychological History of the German Film*, Princeton: Princeton University Press.

Kruger, Loren 2004, *Post-Imperial Brecht: Politics and Performance, East and South*, Cambridge: Cambridge University Press.

Kuhn, Tom 2013, 'Brecht reads Bruegel: *Verfremdung*, Gestic Realism and the Second Phase of Brechtian Theory', *Monatshefte*, 105, 1: 101–122.

Kundrus, Birthe 2014, 'Colonialism, Imperialism, National Socialism: How Imperial Was the Third Reich?' in *German Colonialism in a Global Age*, edited by Bradley Naranch and Geoff Eley, Durham: Duke University Press.

Lang, Fritz (dir.) 1943, *Hangmen Also Die*, Arnold Pressburger Films.

Larrissy, Edward 2006, 'Blake and Postmodernism', in *Palgrave Advances in William Blake Studies*, edited by Nicholas M. Williams, Basingstoke: Palgrave Macmillan.

Larsen, Neil 2001, *Determinations: Essays on Theory, Narrative and Nation in the Americas*, London: Verso.

Lavery, Carl 2006, 'Between Negativity and Resistance: Jean Genet and Committed Theatre', *Contemporary Theatre Review*, 16, 2: 220–234.

Lehleiter, Christine 2014, *Romanticism, Origins, and the History of Heredity*, Lanham: Bucknell University Press.

Lehman, Robert S. 2016, *Impossible Modernism: T.S. Eliot, Walter Benjamin, and the Critique of Historical Reason*, Stanford: Stanford University Press.

Lekan, Thomas 2004, *Imagining the Nation in Nature: Landscape Preservation and German Identity, 1885–1945*, Cambridge: Harvard University Press.

Leslie, Esther 2000, *Walter Benjamin: Overpowering Conformism*, London: Pluto.

Leslie, Esther 2007, 'Blake's Lines: Seven Digressions Through Time and Space', *ImageTexT: Interdisciplinary Comics Studies*, 3, 2, available at: http://www.english.ufl.edu/imagetext/archives/v3_2/leslie/.

Levine, Michael G. 2014, *A Weak Messianic Power: Figures of a Time to Come in Benjamin, Derrida, and Celan*, New York: Fordham University Press.

Levitas, Ruth 1990, 'Educated Hope: Ernst Bloch on Abstract and Concrete Utopia', *Utopian Studies*, 1, 2: 13–26.

Lindeperg, Sylvie 2014, *'Night and Fog:' A Film in History*, translated by Tom Mes, Minneapolis: University of Minnesota Press.

Linebaugh, Peter 1993, *The London Hanged: Crime and Civil Society in the Eighteenth Century*, Cambridge, Mass.: Cambridge University Press.

Löwy, Michael 1987, 'The Romantic and the Marxist Critique of Modern Civilization', *Theory and Society*, 16, 6: 891–904.

Löwy, Michael 2005, *Fire Alarm. Reading Walter Benjamin's 'On the Concept of History'*, London: Verso.

Löwy, Michael L. and Robert Sayre 2001, *Romanticism Against the Tide of Modernity*, Durham: Duke University Press.

Lüdtke, Alf 1994, 'The 'Honor of Labor': Industrial Workers and the Power of Symbols under National Socialism', in *Nazism and German Society: 1933–1945*, edited by David Crew, London: Routledge.

Lukács, Georg 1962, *The Historical Novel*, London: Penguin.

Lunn, Eugene 1974, 'Marxism and Art in the Era of Stalin and Hitler: A Comparison of Brecht and Lukács', *New German Critique*, 3: 12–44.

Lunn, Eugene 1982, *Marxism and Modernism: An Historical Study of Lukacs, Brecht, Benjamin, and Adorno*, Berkeley: University of California Press.

Lussier, Mark S. 1996, 'Blake's Deep Ecology', *Studies in Romanticism*, 35, 3: 393–408.

Lussier, Mark S. and Bruce Matsunaga (eds.) 2008, *Engaged Romanticism: Romanticism as Praxis*, Newcastle: Cambridge Scholars Press.

Lyon, James 1975, *Bertolt Brecht and Rudyard Kipling: A Marxist's Imperialist Mentor*, The Hague: Mouton.

Lyon, James 1980, *Bertolt Brecht in America*, Princeton: Princeton University Press.

Macherey, Pierre 1978, *A Theory of Literary Production*, London: Routledge & Kegan Paul.

Makdisi, Saree 1998, *Romantic Imperialism: Universal Empire and the Culture of Modernity*, Cambridge: Cambridge University Press.

Makdisi, Saree 1999, 'Blake and the Communist Tradition', in *Blake in the Nineties*, edited by Steve Clark and David Worrall, London: Palgrave Macmillan.

Makdisi, Saree 2003, *William Blake and the Impossible History of the 1790s*, Chicago: University of Chicago Press.
Makdisi, Saree 2006a, 'Immortal Joy: William Blake and the Cultural Politics of Empire', in *Blake, Nation and Empire*, edited by Steve Clark and David Worrall, New York: Palgrave Macmillan.
Makdisi, Saree 2006b, 'The Political Aesthetic of Blake's Images', in *The Cambridge Companion to William Blake*, edited by Morris Eaves, Cambridge: Cambridge University Press.
Makdisi, Saree 2014, *Making England Western: Occidentalism, Race and Imperial Culture*, Chicago: University of Chicago Press.
Makdisi, Saree 2015, *Reading William Blake*, Cambridge: Cambridge University Press.
Makdisi, Saree and John Mee 2012, '"Mutual interchange": Life, Liberty and Community', in *Re-Envisioning Blake*, edited by Mark Crosby, Troy Patenaude and Angus Whitehead, Basingstoke: Palgrave Macmillan.
Manquis, Robert 1989, 'Holy Savagery and Wild Justice: English Romanticism and the Terror', *Studies in Romanticism*, 28, 3: 365–95.
Markell, Patchen 2018, 'Politics and the Case of Poetry: Arendt on Brecht' in *Modern Intellectual History*, 15, 2: 503–533.
Marks, Cato 2011, 'Writings of the Left Hand: William Blake Forges a New Political Aesthetic', *Huntington Library Quarterly*, 74, 1: 43–70.
Martel, James R. 2013, *Textual Conspiracies: Walter Benjamin, Idolatry, & Political Theory*, Ann Arbor: University of Michigan Press.
Marx, Karl 1990 [1976], *Capital: a Critique of Political Economy, Volume 1*, translated by Ben Fowkes, London: Penguin.
Marx, Karl and Friedrich Engels 1985 [1967], *The Communist Manifesto*, London: Penguin.
Martel, James R. 2012, *Divine Violence: Walter Benjamin and the Eschatology of Sovereignty*, London: Routledge.
Matthews, Susan 2009, 'Impurity of Diction: The 'Harlots Curse' and Dirty Words', in *Blake and Conflict*, edited by Sarah Haggarty and Jon Mee, London: Palgrave Macmillan.
Matthews, Susan 2011, *Blake, Sexuality and Bourgeois Politeness*, Cambridge: Cambridge University Press.
McFarland, James 2013, *Constellation: Friedrich Nietzsche and Walter Benjamin in the Now-Time of History*, New York: Fordham University Press.
McGann, Jerome 1998, 'The Failures of Romanticism' in *Romanticism, History, and the Possibilities of Genre: Re-forming Literature*, edited by Tilottama Rajan and Julia M. Wright, Cambridge: Cambridge University Press.
McKusick, James C. 2016, 'Afterword: The Future of Ecocriticism', in *Wordsworth and the Green Romantics: Affect and Ecology in the Nineteenth Century*, edited by Lisa Ottum and Seth Reno, Durham: University of New Hampshire Press.

McNally, David 2001, *Bodies of Meaning: Studies on Language, Labor, and Liberation*, Albany: State University of New York Press.

McNeill, Dougal 2005, *The Many Lives of Galileo: Brecht, Theatre and Translation's Political Unconscious*, Bern: Peter Lang.

Mee, Jon 1992, *Dangerous Enthusiasms: William Blake and the Culture of Radicalism in the 1790s*, Oxford: Oxford University Press.

Mee, Jon 1994, 'Is there an Antinomian in the House? William Blake and the After-Life of a Heresy', in *Historicizing Blake*, edited by Steve Clark and David Worrall, London: St. Martin's Press.

Mellor, Anne K. 2003, '*Frankenstein*, Racial Science, and the 'Yellow Peril'', in *Romantic Science: Literary Forms of Natural History*, edited by Noah Heringman, Albany: State University Press of New York.

Merriam-Paskow, Jacqueline 1992, 'Brecht's *Leben des Galilei*: The Modern Scientist as Voyeur', *Modern Language Studies*, 22, 4: 42–56.

Midgley, David 2002, 'The Poet in Berlin: Brecht's City Poetry of the 1920s', in *Empedocles' Shoe: Essays on Brecht's Poetry*, edited by Tom Kuhn and Karen Leeder, London: Methuen.

Miklitsch, Robert 1991, 'Performing Difference: Brecht, Galileo, and the Regime of Quotations', *Journal of Dramatic Theory and Criticism*, 6, 1: 15–28.

Milner, Paul 2002, 'Blake's London: Time and Spaces', *Studies in Romanticism*, 41, 2: 279–316.

Miner, Paul 2012, 'Blake: Milton Inside 'Milton'', *Studies in Romanticism*, 51, 2: 233–276.

Morton, A.L. 1966, *The Everlasting Gospel: A Study in the Sources of William Blake*, New York: Haskell House.

Moss, Anne 1998, 'Limits of reason: An Exploration of Brecht's Concept of *Vernunft* and the Discourse of Science in *Leben des Galilei*', in *Bertolt Brecht: Centenary Essays*, edited by Steve Giles and Rodney Livingstone, Leiden: Brill.

Mueller, Roswitha 1989, *Bertolt Brecht and the Theory of Media*, Lincoln: University of Nebraska Press.

Mumford, Meg 2009, *Bertolt Brecht*, London: Routledge.

Murray, Bruce 1990, *Film and the German Left in the Weimar Republic: From Caligari to Kuhle Wampe*, Austin: University of Texas Press.

Nayar, Pramod K. 2014, 'William Blake's 'London' as a Surveillance poem', *The Explicator*, 72, 4: 328–332.

Nussbaum, Laureen 1985, 'The Evolution of the Feminine Principle in Brecht's Work: Beyond the Feminist Critique', *German Studies Review*, 8, 2: 217–244.

O'Connor, Alan 1989, *Raymond Williams: Writing, Culture, Politics*, Oxford: Basil Blackwell.

Oesmann, Astrid 2005, *Staging History: Brecht's Social Concepts of Ideology*, Albany: State University of New York.

O'Regan, Keith 2016, "The View from Below: Film and Class Representation in Brecht and Loach", *Cinema: Journal of Philosophy and the Moving Image*, 8: 88–107.

Orwell, George 1994, *The Penguin Essays of George Orwell*, Penguin: London.

Osborne, Peter 1995, *The Politics of Time: Modernity and Avant-Garde* London: Verso.

Ostmeier, Dorothee 2000, 'The Rhetorics of Erasure: Cloud and Moon in Brecht's Poetic and Political Texts of the Twenties and Early Thirties', *German Studies Review*, 23, 2: 275–295.

Otto, Peter 2000, *Blake's Critique of Transcendence: Love, Jealousy and the Sublime in 'The Four Zoas'*, Oxford, Oxford University Press.

Otto, Peter 2010, 'Politics, aesthetics, and Blake's 'boundling line'', *Word & Image*, 26, 2: 172–185.

Ottum, Lisa and Seth T. Reno (eds.) 2016, *Wordsworth and the Green Romantics: Affect and Ecology in the Nineteenth Century*, Durham: University of New Hampshire Press.

Parker, Stephen 2011, 'Brecht and 17 June 1953: A Renaissance' in *Edinburgh German Yearbook: Brecht and the GDR: Politics, Culture, Posterity*, Volume 5, edited by Laura Bradley and Karen Leeder, Rochester: Camden House.

Parmalee, Patty Lee 1981, *Brecht's America*, Miami: Ohio State University Press.

Patterson, Michael 1981, *The Revolution in German Theatre: 1900–1933*, Boston: Routledge & Kegan Paul.

Peters, Julie Stone 2005, 'Joan of Arc Internationale: Shaw, Brecht, and the Law of Nations', *Comparative Drama*, 38, 4: 355–377.

Pettifer, James 1977, 'Against the Stream–Kuhle Wampe', *Screen*, 15, 2: 49–63.

Piccitto, Diane 2014, *Blake's Drama: Theatre, Performance and Identity in the Illuminated Books*, London: Palgrave Macmillan.

Piccitto, Diane 2018, 'Apocalyptic Visions, Heroism, and Intersections of the Human and 'the Not Human' in Blake's Milton' in *Beastly Blake*, edited by Helen P. Bruder and Tristanne Connolly, London: Palgrave MacMillan.

Pierce, John B. 2000, 'Rewriting Milton: Orality and Writing in Blake's 'Milton'', *Studies in Romanticism*, 39, 3: 449–470.

Pike, David 1985, *Lukacs and Brecht*, Chapel Hill: The University of North Carolina Press.

Plate, S. Brent 2005, *Walter Benjamin, Religion, and Aesthetics: Rethinking Religion Through the Arts*, New York: Routledge.

Polan, Dana 1985, *The Political Language of Film and the Avant-Garde*, Ann Arbor: UMI Research Press.

Pollock, Della 1989, 'New Man to New Woman: Women in Brecht and Expressionism', *Journal of Dramatic Theory and Criticism*, 4, 1: 85–107.

Prager, Brad 2007, *Aesthetic Vision and German Romanticism: Writing Images*, Rochester: Camden House.

Prather, Russell 2007, 'William Blake and the Problem of Progression', *Studies in Romanticism*, 46, 4: 507–540.

Quinney, Laura 2009, *William Blake on Self and Soul*, Cambridge: Harvard University Press.
Rancière, Jacques 2006, *The Politics of Aesthetics: The Distribution of the Sensible*, London: Continuum.
Rancière, Jacques 2007, 'Art of the Possible', interviewed by Fulvia Carnevale and John Kelsey, *Artforum*, March: 258–59.
Rancière, Jacques 2010, *Dissensus: On Politics and Aesthetics*, London: Bloomsbury Academic.
Rancière, Jacques 2011, *The Emancipated Spectator*, London: Verso.
Rawlinson, Nick 2003, *William Blake's Comic Vision*, London: Palgrave Macmillan.
Ray, Gene 2010, 'Dialectical Realism and Radical Commitments: Brecht and Adorno on Representing Capitalism', *Historical Materialism*, 18, 3: 3–24.
Regier, Alexander 2018, *Exorbitant Enlightenment: Blake, Hamann and Anglo-German Constellations*, Oxford: Oxford University Press.
Richards, Robert J. 2002, *The Romantic Conception of Life: Science and Philosophy in the Age of Goethe*, Chicago: The University of Chicago Press.
Richardson, Michael D. 2007, *Revolutionary Theatre and the Classical Heritage: Inheritance and Appropriation from Weimar to the GDR*, Bern: Peter Lang.
Richey, William 1996, *Blake's Altering Aesthetic*, Columbia: University of Missouri Press.
Richter, Gerhard 2002, *Benjamin's Ghosts: Interventions in Contemporary Literary and Cultural Theory*, Stanford: Stanford University Press.
Richter, Gerhard 2007, *Thought-Images: Frankfurt School Writers' Reflections from Damaged Life*, Stanford: Stanford University Press.
Richter, Gerhard 2016, *Inheriting Walter Benjamin*, London: Bloomsbury Academic.
Rippey, Theodore 2007, 'Kuhle Wampe and the Problem of Corporal Culture', *Cinema Journal*, 47, 1: 3–25.
Rippey, Theodore 2009, 'Brecht and Exile: Poetry after Weimar, Poetics during Blitzkrieg', *Monatshefte*, 101, 1: 37–55.
Rix, Robert 2007, *William Blake and the Cultures of Radical Christianity*, London: Routledge.
Robinson, Douglas 2008, *Estrangement and the Somatics of Literature: Tolstoy, Shklovsy, Brecht*, Baltimore: The John Hopkins University Press.
Rochlitz, Rainer 1996, *The Disenchantment of Art: The Philosophy of Walter Benjamin*, New York: The Guilford Press.
Roe, Nicholas 2002, *The Politics of Nature: William Wordsworth and Some Contemporaries*, New York: Palgrave.
Rokem, Freddie 2010, *Philosophers and Thespians: Thinking Performances*, Stanford: Stanford University Press.
Rokem, Freddie 2015, 'The Aesthetics of Learning: Bertolt Brecht's *Die Ausnahme und die Regel* (The Exception and the Rule)', *Theatre Topics*, 25, 1: 57–66.

Roper, Katherine 1998, 'Looking for the German Revolution in Weimar Films', *Central European History*, 31, 1/2: 65–90.
Rosenberg, Jordy 2010, '"Accumulate! Accumulate! That is Moses and the Prophets!": Secularism, Historicism, and the Critique of Enthusiasm', *The Eighteenth Century*, 51, 4: 471–490.
Rosenberg, Jordy and Chi-ming Yang 2014, 'The Dispossessed Eighteenth Century', *The Eighteenth Century*, 55, 2/3: 137–152.
Rounce, Adam 2015, 'John Clare, William Cowper and the Eighteenth Century', in *New Essays on John Clare: Poetry, Culture and Community*, edited by Simon Kövesi and Scott McEathron, Cambridge: Cambridge University Press.
Rupprecht, Caroline 2006, 'Post-war Iconographies: Wandering Women in Brecht, Duras, Kluge', *South Central Review*, 23, 2: 36–57.
Ruprecht, Lucia 2010, 'Ambivalent Agency: Gestural Performances of Hands in Weimar Dance and Film', *A Journal of Germanic Studies*, 46, 3: 255–275.
Said, Edward 1975, *Beginnings: Intention and Method*, New York: Basic Books.
Said, Edward 1979, *Orientalism*, New York: Vintage.
Said, Edward 1994, *Culture and Imperialism*, New York: Vintage.
San Juan Jr., E. 2002, *Racism and Multiculturalist Ideology and the Politics of Difference*, Durham: Duke University Press.
Sandler, Florence 1990, '"Defending the Bible': Blake, Paine, and the Bishop', In *Blake and His Bibles*, edited by David Erdman, West Cornwall: Locust Hill Press.
Schaub, Christoph 2018, 'Labor-Movement Modernism: Proletarian Collectives between *Kuhle Wampe* and Working-Class Performance Culture', *Modernism/modernity*, 25, 2: 327–348
Karl-Heinz, Schoeps 1989. 'From Distancing Alienation to Intuitive Naiveté: Bertolt Brecht's Establishment of a New Aesthetic Category', *Monatshefte*, 81, 2: 186–198.
Schultz, Alexander M. 2009, *Mind's World: Imagination and Subjectivity from Descartes to Romanticism*, Seattle: University of Washington Press.
Schwarz, Roberto 2009, 'Brecht's Relevance, Highs and Lows', *New Left Review*, 57: 85–104.
Setje-Eilers, Margaret 2008, 'A Man's a Man, but What about Woman? Widow Leocadia Begbick in Bertolt Brecht's Play (1926–2006)', *Women in German Yearbook: Feminist Studies in German Literature & Culture*, 24: 96–118.
Shakespeare, David 2013, '"The Sight of All These Thing': Sexual Vision and Obscurity in Blake's *Milton*', in *Sexy Blake*, edited by Helen P. Bruder and Tristanne Connolly, London: Palgrave Macmillan.
Shaw, Leroy 1970, *The Playwright and Historical Change: Dramatic Strategies in Brecht, Hauptmann, Kaiser and Wedekind*, Madison: University of Wisconsin Press.
Shookman, Ellis 1989, 'Barthes's Semiological Myth of Brecht's Epic Theatre', *Monatshefte*, 81, 4: 459–475.

Silberman, Marc 1987, 'The Politics of Representation: Brecht and the Media', *Theatre Journal*, 39, 4: 448–460.
Silberman, Marc 1993, 'A Postmodernized Brecht?', *Theatre Journal*, 45, 1: 1–19.
Silberman, Marc 2008, 'Whose Revolution?: The Subject of Kuhle Wampe', in *Weimar Cinema: An Essential Guide to Classic Films of the Era*, edited by Noah Isenberg, New York: Columbia University Press.
Silberman, Marc 2012, 'Bertolt Brecht, Politics, and Comedy', *Social Research: An International Quarterly*, 79, 1: 169–188.
Siskin, Clifford 1988, *The Historicity of Romantic Discourse*, Oxford: Oxford University Press
Slaughter, Cliff 1980, *Marxism, Ideology and Literature*, London: The Macmillan Press.
Smith, Iris 1991, 'Brecht and the Mothers of Epic Theater', *Theatre Journal*, 43, 4: 491–505.
Smith, Jill Suzanne 2010, 'Just how Naughty *was* Berlin? The Geography of Prostitution and Female Sexuality in Curt Moreck's Erotic Travel Guide', in *Spatial Turns*, edited by Jaimey Fisher and Barbara Mennel, Amsterdam: Rodopi.
Smith, Peter D. 1997, 'German Literature and the Scientific World-View in the Nineteenth and Twentieth Centuries', *The Journal of European Studies*, 27, 4: 389–415.
Sohlich, Wolfgang 1993, 'The Dialectic of Mimesis and Representation in Brecht's 'Life of Galileo'', *Theatre Journal*, 45, 1: 49–64.
Ronald Speirs 2002, ''Of poor B. B.' – and others', *Empedocles' Shoe: Essays on Brecht's Poetry*, edited by Tom Kuhn and Karen Leeder, London: Methuen.
Spiers, Ronald (ed.) 2010, *Brecht's Poetry of Political Exile*, Cambridge: Cambridge University Press.
Squiers, Anthony 2014, *An Introduction to the Social and Political Philosophy of Bertolt Brecht: Revolution and Aesthetics*, Amsterdam: Rodopi.
Squiers, Anthony 2015, 'A Critical Response to Heidi M. Silcox's 'What's Wrong with Alienation'', *Philosophy and Literature*, 39, 1: 243–247.
Squiers, Anthony and Norman Roessler 2011, 'Rethinking Brecht', *Communications from the International Brecht Society*, 40: 119–133.
Steigerwald, Joan 2002, 'Epistemologies of Rupture: The Problem of Nature in Schelling's Philosophy', *Studies in Romanticism*, 41, 4: 545–584.
Sutherland, John H. 1977, 'Blake's Milton: The Bard's Song', *Colby Quarterly*, 13, 2: 142–157.
Suvin, Darko 1984, *To Brecht and Beyond: Soundings in Modern Dramaturgy*, Sussex: Harvester Press.
Suvin, Darko 1994, 'Revelation vs. Conflict: A Lesson from Nô Plays for a Comparative Dramaturgy', *Theatre Journal*, 46, 4: 523–538.
Sprinker, Michael 1987, *Imaginary Relations: Aesthetics and Ideology in the Theory of Historical Materialism*, London: Verso.
Staehler, Axel 2008, 'Writ(h)ing Images. Imagination, the Human Form, and the Divine in William Blake, Salman Rushdie, and Simon Louvish', *English Studies*, 89, 1: 94–117.

Steinberg, Michael P. (ed.) 1996, *Walter Benjamin and the Demands of History*, Ithaca: Cornell University Press.

Tambling, Jeremy 2005, *Blake's Night Thoughts*, London: Palgrave Macmillan.

Taxidou, Olga 2007, *Modernism and Performance: Jarry to Brecht*, London: Palgrave Macmillan.

Thomas, Peter 2010, *The Gramscian Moment: Philosophy, Hegemony and Marxism*, Chicago: Haymarket Books.

Thompson, Edward Palmer 1976, *William Morris: Romantic to Revolutionary*, London: Merlin.

Thompson, Edward Palmer 1982, *The Making of the English Working Class*, London: Penguin.

Thompson, Edward Palmer 1995, *Witness Against the Beast*, New York: The New Press.

Thompson, Edward Palmer 1997, *The Romantics: England in a Revolutionary Age*, New York: The New Press.

Thompson, Peter 1997, *Brecht: Mother Courage and her Children*, Cambridge: Cambridge University Press.

Thompson, Peter 2016, 'Ernst Bloch and the Spirituality of Utopia', *Rethinking Marxism*, 28, 3–4: 438–452.

Thorsteinsson, Vidar 2017, '"This Great Passion for Producing": The Affective Reversal of Brecht's Dramatic Theory', *Cultural Critique*, 97: 56–83.

Tomlins, Christopher 2009, 'Revolutionary Justice in Brecht, Conrad and Blake', *Law and Literature*, 21, 2: 185–213.

Traverso, Enzo 2016, *Left-Wing Melancholia: Marxism, History, and Memory*, New York: Columbia University Press.

Trumpener, Katie 1990, 'Theory, History and German Film', *Monatshefte*, 82, 3: 294–306.

Vaughan, William 1978, *Romanticism and Art*, Oxford: Oxford University Press.

Vine, Steve 2002, 'Blake's Material Sublime', *Studies in Romanticism*, 41, 2: 237–257.

Volosinov, Valentin 1996 [1986], *Marxism and the Philosophy of Language*, Cambridge: Harvard University Press.

von Saldern, Adelheid 2002, *The Challenge of Modernity: German Social and Cultural Studies, 1890–1960*, Ann Arbor: The University of Michigan Press.

Vork, Robert 2013, 'Silencing Violence: Repetition and Revolution in *Mother Courage and Her Children*', *Comparative Drama*, 47, 1: 31–54.

Wang, Orrin N.C. 2011, *Romantic Sobriety: Sensation, Revolution, Commodification, History*, Baltimore: The John Hopkins University Press.

Warley, Christopher 2014, *Reading Class through Shakespeare, Donne, and Milton*, Cambridge: Cambridge University Press.

Weber, Betty Nance 2010 [1982]. '*The Life of Galileo* and the Theory of Revolution in Performance', In *Bertolt Brecht: Political Theory and Literary Practice*, edited by Betty Nance Weber and Hubert Heinen, Athens: University of Georgia Press.

Weber, Betty Nance and Hubert Heinen (eds.) 1980, *Bertolt Brecht: Political Theory and Literary Practice*, Athens: The University of Georgia Press.

Wekwerth, Manfred 2011, *Daring to Play: A Brecht Companion*, London: Routledge.

Welch, Dennis M. 2010, 'Essence, Gender, Race: William Blake's Visions of the Daughters of Albion', *Studies in Romanticism*, 49, 1: 105–131.

Wessendorf, Markus 2016, 'Brecht's Materialist Ethics Between Confucianism and Mohism', *Philosophy East and West*, 66, 1: 122–145.

Westgate, J. Chris 2007, 'Brecht on Broadway: a Dialectical History', in *Brecht, Broadway and United States Theatre*, edited by Chris J. Westgate, Newcastle: Cambridge Scholars Press.

Westgate, J. Chris (ed.) 2007, *Brecht, Broadway and United States Theatre*, Newcastle: Cambridge Scholars Press.

Whale, John 2000, *Imagination Under Pressure, 1789–1832: Aesthetics, Politics and Utility*, Cambridge: Cambridge University Press.

Whitaker, Jason 1999, *William Blake and the Myths of Britain*, London: Macmillan.

Whitaker, Peter 1985, *Brecht's Poetry*. Oxford: Clarendon Press.

White, Daniel E. 2006, *Early Romanticism and Religious Dissent*, Cambridge: Cambridge University Press.

White, John J. 2004, *Bertolt Brecht's Dramatic Theory*, Rochester: Camden House.

White, John J. and Ann White 2010, *Bertolt Brecht's Furcht und Elend des Dritten Reiches: A German Exile Drama in the Struggle against Fascism*, Rochester: Camden House.

Wilke, Judith 1999, 'The Making of a Document: An Approach to Brecht's Fatzer Fragment', *TDR: The Drama Review*, 43, 4: 122–127.

Willett, John 1977, *The Theatre of Bertolt Brecht: A Study from Eight Aspects*, London: Eyre Methuen.

Williams, Nicholas M. 1998, *Ideology and Utopia in the Poetry of William Blake*, Cambridge: Cambridge University Press.

Williams, Nicholas M. (ed.) 2006, *William Blake Studies*, London: Palgrave Macmillan.

Williams, Nicholas M. 2009, 'Blake Dead or Alive', *Nineteenth-Century Literature*, 63, 4: 486–498.

Williams, Raymond 1977, *Marxism and Literature*, Oxford: Oxford University Press.

Williams, Raymond 1980, *Problems in Materialism and Culture*, London: Verso.

Williams, Raymond 1981, *Culture*, Glasgow: Fontana.

Williams, Raymond 1983, *Culture and Society: 1780–1950*, New York: Columbia University Press.

Williams, Raymond 1985 *The Country and the City*, London: The Hogarth Press.

Williams, Raymond 1996, *The Politics of Modernism: Against the New Conformists*, London: Verso.

Williams, Raymond and Merryn Williams 1986, 'Critical Commentary' in *John Clare, Selected Poetry and Prose*, edited by Merryn Williams and Raymond Williams, London: Methuen.

Winstanley, Gerrard 2003, 'A New-Yeers Gift', in *Divine Right and Democracy*, edited by David Wootton, Indianapolis: Hackett Publishing Company, Inc.

Wizisla, Erdmut 2009, *Walter Benjamin and Bertolt Brecht: The Story of a Friendship*, New Haven: Yale University Press.

Wolfreys, Julian 1998, *Writing London: The Trace of the Urban Text from Blake to Dickens*, Basingstoke: Palgrave.

Wolfson, Susan J. 1997, *Formal Changes: The Shaping of Poetry in British Romanticism*, Stanford: Stanford University Press.

Wolin, Richard 1992, *The Terms of Cultural Criticism*, New York: Columbia University Press.

Wood, Ellen Meiksins 1995, *Democracy Against Capitalism: Renewing Historical Materialism*, Cambridge: Cambridge University Press.

Wood, Ellen Meiksins 2002, *The Origins of Capitalism: A Longer View*, London: Verso.

Wootton, David (ed.) 1986, *Divine Right and Democracy: An Anthology of Political Writing in Stuart England*, London: Penguin.

Worall, David 2016 [1999], 'Blake and the 1790s Plebian Radical Culture', in *Blake in the Nineties*, edited by Steve Clark and David Worrall, London: Palgrave Macmillan Limited.

Wright, Elizabeth 1989, *Postmodern Brecht: A Re-Presentation*, London: Routledge.

Wright, Julia M. 2004, *Blake, Nationalism and the Politics of Alienation*, Athens: Ohio University Press.

Wulbern, Julian H. 1971, *Brecht and Ionesco: Commitment in Context*, Urbana: University of Illinois Press.

Youngquist, Paul 1990, 'Criticism and the Experience of Blake's Milton', *Studies in English Literature*, 30, 4: 555–571.

Yousef, Nancy 2013, *Romantic Intimacy*, Stanford: Stanford University Press.

Zavarzaadeh, Mas'ud, Teresa L. Ebert and Donald E. Morton (eds.) 1995, *Post-Ality: Marxism and Postmodernism*, Washington, DC: Maisonneuve Press.

Zimmerman, Marc 1976, 'Brecht and the Dynamics of Production', *Praxis*, 3: 115–137.

Index

abstraction, intuitive 59
Ackerman, Alan 120n
Adorno Theodore 2n, 11n, 19n, 52n, 61, 128n
aesthetics: contemporary trends 3
  deindividualizing 50
  Marxist 38
  materialistic understanding 193
  of resistance 13
  oppositional 1, 8, 10, 63, 68, 196, 202
  political 59, 61
  socio-political 55
agency 182
  of 'emotion' 85
  philosophy of 32
  working class movements 6
agit-prop theatre 60
  Arbeiterhilfe 56
Ahmad, Aijaz 161
Albion 167
alienation technique 60, 125
allegory 120, 201
  historical 199
Alter, Nora M. 51n, 113
alternatives, preventing of 33
Althusser, Louis 15, 182n
Altizier, Thomas J.J. 16n
Anderson, Perry 122n
annihilation, -self 158, 185
Antigone 19
Antinomianism 167
  politics of 81
  tradition of 82, 182
Apesos, Anthony 174, 175n
apocalypse, Milton as spirit of 188
Arendt, Hannah 61, 110
Arjoman, Minou 25n
audience(s), 126: agency 25, 37, 49
  Brechtian 125
  emancipatory labour of, 195 engagement with 12
  meanings producer 15
  productive capacities of 7, 36
Ault, Donald 156–7, 160n
Azdak, character of 147–8, 192

'bad collective' 29, 48
  self-reproduction of 33–4, 44
Bahktin, Mikhail 13n
Bai, Ronnie 23
Balfour, Ian 100n, 155n, 157, 165, 172, 187
Balzás, Béla 56
Barnett, David 110, 119n
Barthes, Roland 12n, 120–1
Baudelaire, lyric poetry 201n
Becher, Johannes 113
Beech, Dave 91n
Beer, John 169n
Benchimol, Alex 173
Benjamin, Walter 2, 19–20, 23, 28, 34, 38, 46–7, 51n, 60n, 61, 101, 107n, 110–12, 121, 128n, 134, 137n, 138, 152, 153n, 154, 171–2, 177, 193, 196
  'antifetishism' 202
  'Author as Producer' 1, 47, 67n
  -Brecht relations 35, 198
  danger notion 160
  hatred of exploitation 118
  history conception 18, 166n, 169
  'jetztzeit' 109n
  Messianism 191
  political decision question 151
  political aesthetic of the now 63
  'poverty of experience' 197
  progress notion opposed 122, 170
  'Theses on the Philosophy of History' 5, 6n, 105n, 112, 152n, 179, 200n
  'What is Epic Theatre?' 30
  work detextualized 179
Bennett, Benjamin 129n
Bennett, Michael 139
Bentley, Eric 12n
Berlin Staatstheater, *Mann ist Mann* production 29
Berlin Volksbühne, *Mann ist Mann* production 25, 29
Berliner Ensemble 110, 114, 141n
Bertail-Bryant, Sarah 195
Bible, the 177, 184
Bidney, Martin 80n, 105n
Birgel, Franz, character of 54, 60n
Bitt, Benjamin 6n

INDEX

229

Blackbourn, David   118n, 127
Blake, William   157–8
  aesthetic strategy   5
  anti-racist poetics   77
  capitalism rejection   196
  cosmology of   64
  'A Cradle Song'   88
  creative grammar   78
  democracy dedication   190
  desires   188
  'Divine Image'   82
  'Excerpt to the Marriage of Heaven and Hell'   70
  historical context of   6
  history use   165, 203
  'Holy Thursday'   85
  imagination conception   72
  innocence conception   81
  justice conception   84
  labour as liberation   194, 204
  'London'   88–9
  Los identity   167
  Marx link   200
  materiality of   71
  Milton   see below
  modernity   102
  mythology of   164
  'On Another's Sorrow'   87
  Orientalism refusal   105
  'philopoesis'   166
  philosophy of living and creating   18
  poetics   173, 187
  privileged location rejection   102
  redemption use   171
  reenergising the present   68
  resistance of   75
  role rethinking   7, 15
  scholars of   155
  sexual imagery   73
  Songs   68
  the bible   184
  'The Chimney Sweeper'   95
  the countryside for   103
  'The Foundation of Empire'   186
  'The Human Abstract'   97
  'The Little Black Boy'   76
  'The Songs' Introduction   63
  utopian thought   200
  visual constructions   91

Bloch, Ernst   14n, 19, 202, 204
  'expectation-affects'   203
  utopia model   200
Bloom, Harold   2n, 168, 190n
body, enjoyment of   69
Bohls, Elizabeth A.   76
Bourdieu, P., concept of forces   2
Bracher, Mark   168n
Bradley, Laura   110, 111n, 129n, 144n
Brandt, Kerstin   55n
Brecht, Berthold: aesthetics of   5, 28, 59
  alternative time   168
  Anglo-American scholarship   22
  Benjamin collaboration, biography   39
  capitalist dynamics addressing   21
  'critical attitude'   41
  Denmark exile   35
  Die Dreigroschenoper novel rewrite   28
  Der Kaukasische Kreidekreis   see below
  Die Heilige Johanna   see below
  distancing techniques   25, 53, 115
  Elisabeth Hauptmann collaboration   49
  exile period   108
  experimentation levels   30
  filmic project   50
  Galileo   see below
  historical context   6
  historisierung   109
  history use   14, 130, 153
  'In Praise of Communism' song   7
  interventionist strategy   33
  Kuhle Wampe   see below
  large work context   47
  Mahagonny Songspiel   204
  Mann ist Mann   see below
  Marxism study   39, 48
  Mutter Courage   see below
  'Of Poor B.B'   102–3
  oppositional culture   151
  poetic works   19
  political theatre   34
  post-USA   149
  pre-1933 work   12
  'Questions from a Worker who Reads'   124
  rising fascism response   37
  teaching plays   31
  theatrical practice   121–2
  the city for   103

'The Threepenny Lawsuit'   50
trajectory of judgment   149
'transportation into the past'   132
use of labour   194
work re-examination   35
Britt Benjamin   6
Brooker, Peter   131n
Brough, Neil   139n
Bru, Sascha   150n
Bruder, Helen P.   74
Bryant-Bertail, Sarah   121
Buck-Morss, Susan   6, 131, 195
   The Origin of Negative Dialectics   5
Bukharin, Nikolai   131
Burke, Edmund   91
Burling, William   108n

Calabro, Tony   150n
Canning, Kathleen   27n
Cannon Harris, Susan   123n
Canuel, Mark   186
capitalism, 197: accumulation logic   87, 95, 102
   cultural logics of   3
   destructiveness of   17, 71
   feudalism interstices   199
   history unsafe for   201
   instantiation of   41
   logics of contemporary   12
   mind impoverishment   186
   monopolising nature of   97
   one-way culture   49
   rejection of   196
   representing in   40
   reproduction of   43, 94
   Weimar   20, 23, 59
   working class remaking   62
Cardullo, Bert   37
care   13, 63–4, 75, 78, 83, 96, 98, 103
   need for   94
   ode to   74
caring: community   19
   gestures of   96
   parental   103
Carmody, Jim   12n
Carney, Sean   146, 201n
Casaliggi, Carmen   66, 67n
Casarino, Cesare   166
Caudwell, Christopher   1n

Chai, Leon   98
Chandlers, James   78n
change, conception of   107
Christensen, Jerome   63n
Church, the, material operation of   132
Clare, John   87, 103n, 169n, 171n
   'Hepstone Green'   86
Clark, Mark   39n
Clark S.H.   179n
Clark, Steve   83n
class: intermediary professional   46
   politics   26
   struggles history   200
   theory of   51
collectivization   142
Coleridge, Samuel   71, 98, 161n, 162, 170n
   Religious Musings   156
collaboration   60
   artistic production   49, 51
   forms of   50
collectives, proletarian   57
Collings, David   156n
Colquhoun, Patrick   90n
comradeship, ideals of   59
Connolly, Tristanne J.   74n, 100
'constellative'   19
contemporary, the, -history contrast   16
Cooper, Andrew M.   184n
Crabb Robinson, Henry   182
creation, experience of   195
criticism: critical gaze production   9
   critique   106
   democratic model of   159
cultural capital   2
Curran, Angela   125

danger: Benjamin notion of   160
   theme of   152
Darmstadt 1926 Brecht production   24–5
Das Rote Sprachcohr   58, 60
Das Wort   111
Davies, Keri   81
Davis, Jennifer Michael   90n
Day, Aidan   66
death drive, Nazi   15
Deen, Leonard W.   158, 164n
Della Volpe, Galvano   108n
democracy, dedication to   190
   dissemination of   100

INDEX   231

Dent, Shirley   95
Der Kaukasische Kreidekreis   15, 141
　Azdak role   147–8, 192
　Grusha, role of   145–8, 151–2, 194
　The Singer, role of   145–6
desperation   67
determination, notion of   65
Dickson, Keith A.   129, 130n
Die Dreigroschenoper, novel rewrite   28
Die Heilige Johanna   23, 40, 95
　ending of   44
　Joan witness role   43, 47
　Mauler, role of   40, 126
　production of scarcity   41
DiSalvo, Jackie   154n
Doherty, Brigid   34, 37
dominant class ideology(ies)   10
　manipulation desire   64–5
Dudow, Slatan   50, 51n, 54, 64, 56, 58n
Dworkin, Dennis   4n

Eagleton, Terry   1n, 10n, 30–1, 35, 123, 126n, 167
　'superstructure' as relational   2
Ebert, Teresa L.   4n
echo, metaphor use   84
'educated hope', Bloch conception   203
education, source of misery   96
Eisler, Hanns   51n, 113–14
Elsaesser, Thomas   172
Eley, Geoff   127, 142n
Elswit, Kate   29n
Engels, Friedrich   67, 112n
English Civil War   161, 184
English Romanticism: experience of   66
　origins of   161
Enlightenment   156
　the English   160
Epic Theatre   27, 30, 32, 34, 41n, 50, 123, 195
　innovative approach   109
　notion of   23
　radical development of   45
Erdman, David   12, 63n, 64, 65n, 78n, 92n, 94n, 105–6n, 156n, 167n, 169–70, 171n, 178, 181
Erpenbeck, Fritz   111
errors   159
Esslin, Martin   12

estrangement effects, political use of   111
eternity   168
experience   79
　as rejection   65
　infrastructure of   97
experiment: experimentation   9, 11, 24, 38, 60
　life as a continuous   13
Expressionism   22
　focus of   10

failing to learn, crime of   119
Fairer, David   94n
Fallon, David   160n, 191n, 200
'false consciousness', notion dispelled   31
fascism   47
　rise of   21
Federal Theatre   26n
'feminization of Culture'   143
Fenves, Peter   107
Ferber, Michael   81n
Fermanis, Porscha   66, 67n
Fichte Sports Club   56, 60
Fiebach, Joachim   15n
film, medium of   50–1
First World War: carnage of   126
　Germany defeat   21
　Social Democrat credits vote   113
Fischer, Ernst   1
Fischer, Gerhard   201
Fisher, Mark, 'Capitalist Realism'   4
Foot, Paul   163n
Frankfurt School   47n
French Revolution   169–70
　England repression period   162
　failures of   6, 161, 173
　hopes destroyed   63
Frye, Northrop   106n, 179
Fuchs, Christian   117
Fuchs, Elinor   123
Fuegi, John   48
future, the, potentials of   30

Gardiner, Jesse   111n
Gay, John, *The Beggar's Opera*   108
gender(s)   27, 124, 186n
　manipulation of   184–5
　politics of   51, 133n
　representation of labour   41n

German Democratic Republic (GDR) 127
  Brecht time in 109–10
German Social Democracy 5
  Social Democratic Party 22, 113
Germany: colonial history 127
  national mythology of 142
  Soviet forces unpopularity 144
gestures 96
gestus 120–2
  Brecht concept of 125
  oppositional practice 122
Giehshe, Therese 119n
Giles, Steve 48n
Gilleir, Anke 150n
Gilpen, George 84n
Gobert, R. Darren 149n
God: as practised thing 80
  benevolence of 165
  Blake conception of 13, 69, 78
  dismissal of as strategic mistake 133
  immanence of 82, 86
  liberatory potential 100
Godard, Jean-Luc, *Contempt* 56
Goethe, J.W. 80n, 90, 174
Goldsmith, Stephen 84, 85n
Goodridge, John 87
Gramsci, Antonio, 'organic intellectuals' 130
Green, Matthew 97n
Grimmelshausen 114
Gritzner, Karoline 11
Gross, Erin M. 69n

Haacke, Paul 152n
Haggarty, Sarah 94n, 161n, 180n, 182
Hamacher, Werner 191–2
Hare, David 114n
Harkin, Peter 111
Harootunian, Harry D. 202n
Hartley, Daniel 116, 117n
Hartung, Guenter 6n
Haug, Wolfgang 132n
headlines, use of 44
heartbeat, metaphor of 168
Hedges, Inez 13n
Hegel, G.W.F, master/slave dialectic 136
Hemingway, Andrew 91–2n
Heynen, Robert 21–2n, 51n
Hiroshima 131

historiography, ruling class models of 147, 192
historical materialism 5, 152
history: 'actual workings' of 59
  'as it was' 169
  as productive memory 111
  Blake recovery of 16, 161
  Blake's conception and use of 155, 171
  Brecht using 21, 108
  compression of 153
  fidelity to 152
  historical failures resurrection 16
  great man theory 139
  migration into 203
  natural 173
  of loss 178
  peasant 140
  prophecy mix 165
  recognition 46
  redemptive politics of 17
  'rewriting' 167
  role of 15
  the present conversation 192
Hobson, Christopher Z 74n, 78, 165n, 186n
Hodge, Bob 4n
Holmes, Terry 130–1n
Holocaust, memory repression 114
Honegger, Gitta 118
Horwish, Cara M. 114
human rights discourse 66
Hutchings, Kevin 89n
Hutton, John 160n

Ibata, Hélène 189
indeterminancy: levels of 92
  structured moments of 6
individual escape, English Romanticism 72
individuality: capitalist refunctioning 48
  constructed notion of 86
inner lives 7
innocence 88
  as rejection 13, 64–5
  Blake conception of 81
  colonisation of danger 71
  cosmological frame of 75
  cultivation of 106
  enacted purity of position 82
  experimentation celebration 104

impulse of 80
potential of 97
religious politics of 79
temporal and spatial co-ordinates 93
'Ironshirts', Gestapo modelled 147

Jameson, Fredric 1, 11n, 14n, 24n, 26n, 38–40, 41n, 49, 53n, 57, 62, 86, 103, 115, 117, 119, 121, 126, 131, 132n, 135, 136n, 144, 148, 199, 202–3
  Brecht and Method 18
  judgment, moment of 149
Jannarone, Kimberly 25n
Jeffries, Stuart 22n
Jennings, Michael 107n, 196
Jesse, Jennifer G. 176
Jesus 178
Johnson, Samuel 99
Jolles, Andre 148
Jones, John H. 8n, 13n, 159n
Jovanovic, Nenad 50, 54, 55n
judgment: figures of 192
  'just' 199
  moment of 147–9
Jutzi, Piel 59

Kafka, Frantz 198
Kakel, Carroll 127
Kant, I. 174
Kasper, Johann 90n
Kavanagh, R.J. 139n
Keats, John 66n, 187
Kellner, Douglas 115n
Kepley Jr., Vance 58
Kinkle, Jeff 54
Kipperman, Mark 163n
Klee Paul, *Angelus Novus* 46, 152, 201n
Kligerman, Eric 113, 114n
Knopf, Jan 26n
Kolb, Alexandra 42n
Korsch, Karl 39
Koutsourakis, Angelos 51n
Kovel, Joel 69n
KPD (German Communist Party) 22
  growth of 56
  Stalinisation of 21
Kracauer, Siegfried 30n, 53n
Kuhle Wampe 11, 23, 45, 48, 50, 53, 55–7, 139, 142

Bönike family focus 53
film production 37
release blocked 58
Kuhn, Tom 114n, 118, 139n
Kundrus, Birthe 127n
Kushner, Tony 114n

labour, as creative 166
  as metaphor 17, 180–1
  Blake on 155, 194, 204
  competing states of being 189
  idea of 190
  movement 57
  Nazi integrity concept 142
Lan-fang, Mei 33n
Lang, Fritz 56n
Larrissy, Edward 197n
Larsen, Neil 7n, 52
Lavater Johann Kasper 91n
Lavery, Carl 145n
Leben des Galilei 129–30, 135
  agency emphasis, 139 idealism-materialism 136
  Little Monk role in 130, 132–8, 151, 193
  numerous revisions of 15
Lehleiter, Christine 174
Lehmann, Robert S. 199, 201n
Lekan, Thomas 113
Leslie, Esther 50, 99, 172
Levine, Michael G. 6n
Levitas, Ruth 203
liberal individualism 200–1
Lindeperg, Sylvie 114
Linebaugh, Peter 205n
literary text, notion of 35
Little, Janet 103n
living, concept of 180
London 90, 106, 190
  'chartered' 94
  'London' 88–9
Los, figure of 163n, 165–6, 168, 177, 181, 188
  Blake identity with 167
loss: depiction of historical 122
  history of 178
love 74
  and Terror 79
  God's 76
Löwy, Michael L. 64–8, 84n, 85, 99, 154, 156, 165n, 170, 193, 201n

Lüdtke, Alf 142, 143n
Lukács, Georg 1n, 11n, 52, 126n
  Brecht critique of 7
Lunn, Eugene 32n, 35–6n, 58
Lussier, Mark 67n, 185n
Lustspiel 37
Luxemburg, Rosa 71, 150
Lyon, James 151n

Macherey, Pierre 30
Makdisi, Saree 13n, 64n, 70n, 71–2, 73n, 77, 82, 84n, 90–2, 97n, 102, 105–6, 155n, 165–6, 172–3n, 178, 181n, 183–4, 187–8, 191n, 199–200
'William Blake and the Communist Tradition' 18
Manhattan Project 131
manipulation: theory 26n
  paternalistic 99
Mann ist Mann 21, 24, 45, 136, 139
  'bad collective' 29, 33–4, 44, 48
  Begbick role 27, 33
  Galy Gay, role 27–31, 36, 47, 63
  1931 production 34
  productions history 26
  radio version 36
  rewrites 36
Manquis, Robert 63n
Markell, Patchen 110n
Martel, James R. 6n, 202n
Marx, Karl 61, 67, 112, 147, 182n, 187
  Capital Volume I 144
  Marxism 1, 22, 31, 65
materiality: foregrounding of 28, 32
  historically placed 135
  materialist ontology, experience of 72
Matsunaga, Bruce 67n
Matthews, Susan 74n, 88n
Mayakovsky, Wladimir W. 149
McFarland, James 198n
McGann, Jerome 163n
McKusick, James C. 193
McNally, David 3, 122, 128n, 153, 170n
McNeill, Dougal 124n
'Me-Ti', *Book of Changes* 51
meanings, recreation of 194
meat, as metaphor 42–3
Mee, Jon 74n, 81n, 105, 166n, 182n
Meiksins Wood, Ellen 131n

Mellor, Anne K. 77
Merriam-Paskow, Jacqueline 135n
Messianism 16, 191, 197
  potential in 197
metaphor: base/superstructure 28
  chalk circle as 149
  echo 84
  heartbeat 168
  labour 180–1
  meat as 42–3
  nature 73, 187
Midgley, David 103n
Miller, Arthur 120n
Milton 16, 19, 154, 157n, 161–3, 172, 174, 182, 191
  Blake as character 175
  judgment in 199
  Milton summoned 158, 176–8
  Oothoon 176
  redemption text 155
  Satan characterised 167, 175, 180, 188
  The Elect 183
  Urizen 156
Milton, John 156, 159, 163, 165, 171, 203
  as character 185
  as spirit 173
  era of 184
mind, impoverishment of 186
Miner, Paul 164n
Mitchell, Stanley 121n
modernity: capitalist 10
  dialectical analysis 68
  modernist experience of 172
  rejection of 67
montage, use of 50
Morris, William 9n
Morton, A.L. 81n
Moss, Anne 137n
Mueller, Roswitha 10
multiaccentuality 37
Mumford, Meg 140n
Murray, Bruce 53, 56
Mutter Courage 14, 57, 115, 119, 121, 125, 151
  GDR production 111
  historical background 113
  Kattrin self sacrificing role of 124, 128
  Paris production 120
  Swiss Cheese death 118
  theme of loss 114

INDEX

Nagasaki 131
Natural Religion, critique of 160
nature, metaphorical use 73, 187
naturphilosophie 173-4
Nayar, Pramod K. 88
Nazis 120
   attitudes hold of 144
   classics use 143
   early signs of 28
   ideologies of 127
   rise of 63
   rule 126
Nero Films 56n
'new man' 37
'new Woman', figure of 10n
Newton, Isaac 154, 185
   Blake criticism 156
   English Enlightenment figure 160
   'Phantasm' 158
   worldview 157
Novotny, Stephen 141n
now, the: experimentation in 197
   moment of 12, 16-17
   politics of 18, 21, 25
   theatre of 32
Nuit et Brouillard 114
Nussbaum, Laureen 41-2n

O'Connor, Alan 119n
Oesmann, Astrid 31, 40, 41 n, 122n, 198n
older order, idealised 67
Oppenheimer, J. Robert 131
oppositional movements, problems of 10
Orc 63n
organised knowing 45
Orientalism, Blake rejection 105
Orwell, George 82-3
Osborne, Peter 17, 18n
Otto, Peter 100n, 156n
Ottwalt, Ernst 50

Pabst, G.W. 42n, 56
'packer', significance of 24
Paine, Thomas 92n
parable 37, 141n, 147
   use of 142
Paradise Lost 163

Paradise Regained 159
Parker, Stephen 111n
Parmalee, Patty Lee 39-41n
past the: Benjamin's notion of 175
   liberating potentialities of 72, 112
   present relation 113
   retrieval of 64
Patterson, Michael 25
peace, abstract category of 138
   Peace of Augsburg 132
peasant(ry), the 135, 144, 147, 194
   exploitation of 115, 117
   history silence 118, 140
   'structure of feeling' 199
   suffering of 151
   time of 148
Peters, Julie Stone 45n
petit-bourgeois intellectuals, position rejection 48
philosophy, aesthetic 32
Piccitto, Diane 9n, 171n
Pierce, John B. 178n
Pike, David 35n
Piscator, Erwin 25
   Proletarian Theatre 22
Plate, S, Brent 194
pleasure-making processes 73
Polan, Dana 59-60
politics, formal aesthetic of 20
Pollock, Della 10n
positionality, social 31
Prager, Brad 173
precision 38
   foregrounding of 28
production: aesthetics of 1
   belief in 8
   cultural 2
   enemies of 104
progress, notion of 122
   Benjamin opposition to 122, 170
progressive cultural expression, traditions of 22
Prometheus Company 58n
proportion 185
'quantification of Life': as disenchantment 67
   opposition to 66

race: colonial narratives 76

Nazism appeal to   113
   racial superiority   127
radio, *Mann ist Mann* production   36
Rancière, Jacques   8, 49
Ranters, the   161n
rationalism, mechanical   99
'real', the   30, 126n
   practical relation to   31
realist poetics   1
Red Megaphone   142
Red Revues   23
redemption   191
   as ecstasy   163
   Blake viewpoint of   19
   possibility of historical   184
reenchantment of the world   67
regeneration, possibility of   188
Regier, Alexander   91n
religion   43, 132
   distortions of   63
   emphasis on, 45 redemptive   181
rent, oppressive   57
repression, fault-lines   160
'residual culture'   14, 167
resistance, aesthetics of   13
Resnais, Alain   113
restructuring, of modern workers   11, 34, 62
Reynolds, Sir Joshua   91
   dominant discourse of   92
Richards, Robert J.   174
Richardson, Michael   126n
Richey, William   159n
Richter, Gerhard   203n
Rimbaud, Arthur   108n
Rippey, Theodore   54, 108–9n
Rix, Robert   64n
Robinson, Douglas   116n
Rochlitz, Rainer   201n
Roessler, Norman   11n
Rokem, Freddie   136
romanticism   65, 99, 165n
   capitalist modernity rejected   67
   origins of English   161
   theories of   66
Roper, Katherine   58n
Rosenberg, Jordy   87, 168
Rounce, Adam   169n
Royal Academy of the Arts, elitism of   91
Royal Society   99

ruling class lack of lasting hegemony   21
   innocence colonising   71
Rupprecht, Caroline   149n
Ruprecht, Lucia   34n
Russian Revolution   20–1
   failure of   6
   implausible successes of   22

Said, Edward   69n
   Culture and Imperialism   186
Saint Joan figure   40n
San Juan Jr, E.   3
Sandler, Florence   157n
Satan, in *Milton*   167, 175, 180, 188
   Milton battle   189
Sayre, Robert   64n
   65–7   84n, 99, 156, 165n, 170
Schaub, Christoph   57
Schelling, Friedrich   173
Schlutz, Alexander M.   161n
Schoeps, Karl-Heinz   40–1n
Scholem, Gershon   101, 107n
Schwarz, Roberto   41n
sedition laws   162
self-reflexivity, continual   35, 134
Setje-Eilers, Margaret   27
sex   74
   imagery   73
   sexism   55, 70
   sexuality   27n, 55n, 64, 74, 96n, 140n, 186n
Shakespeare, David   184, 185n
Shaw, Leroy   26n
Shaw, George Bernard   45n
Shelley, Mary, *Frankenstein*   77
Shelley, Percy B.   66n
   'A Defence of Poetry'   186
   poetry concept   187
   'The Masque of Anarchy'   163
   'The Triumph of Life'   98
signature, 'private property' of   49
Silberman, Marc   34n, 37, 39, 40n, 50n, 60n, 124n, 147n
Siskin, Clifford   64n
slaughterhouse   42
sleep   74
Smith, Peter   132n
social democracy, Western   198
   German   2, 22, 113

INDEX

socialism: building of   140
   Soviet socialist realism   51
social sciences, linguistic turn   3
society: determinism   117
   reenergised   68
   social experience primacy   49
Sohlich, Wolfgang   133n
Solomon, biblical story of   15
Soviet cinema   50
Sozialistische Einheitspartei Deutschlands   111
Speirs, Ronald   103n, 109n
Sprinker, Michael   15n
Squiers, Anthony   11n, 12, 125
Staehler, Axel   72, 73n, 106
Stalin, Josef   110, 141n
   literacy policy   35
   orthodoxy wariness   150
   show trials   131
   intellectuals under   134
stasis as protection   77
Steadman, Richard   80n
Steffin, Margarete   46n
Steigerwald, Joan   173
Sternberg, Fritz   39n
subjectivities, engineering of   51
suffering for the cause, theme   138
suicide   54–5, 58
surplus extraction, historical forms   144, 194
suspense-building, negation of   53
Sutherland, John   177
Suvin, Darko   43, 46–7, 128, 134n, 148
'sympathetic identification'   75

Tambling, Jeremy   80n
Taxidou, Olga   33n
theatre: constant updating need   32
   incomplete   25
   Marxist political   23
   radical agitprop   22
Thelwall, John   162
Thirty Years War   118n
Thanksgiving for the Peace of Utrecht   94n
Thomas, Peter   130n
Thompson, E.P.   8, 9n, 13n, 15n, 16, 17n, 64n, 79, 81, 105n, 106, 120n, 154, 156n, 160n, 161–2, 167, 177, 182
Thompson, Peter   204
Thomson, Samuel   103n

Thorsteinsson, Vidar   22n
time   183
   alternate conception of   167
   as a resource   171
   historical   179, 192
   'messianic'   107
   peasant   194
Tomlins, Christopher   90n
Toscano, Alberto   54
tradition   177
tragedy, drama avoidance   123
Traverso, Enzo   171
Tretjakov, Sergei   35
Trotsky, Leon   141n
Trumpener, Katie   55
'Tuis'   46

unemployment, individual workers impact   52
uniaccentuality   36
USA (United States of America) Brecht in   108n
   stage, Stanislavsky dominance of   109
USSR (United Soviet Socialist Republics):
   collectivization process   140n
   funding from   56
   Stalinist distortions   198
utopia, conceptions of   203
   Blake's   200

value, abstracted   43
van der Knapp, Ewout   113n
Vaughan, William   66
Vine, Steve   187n
Volosinov, Valentin, *uniaccentuality*   36
von Saldern, Adelheid   143
Vork, Robert   14, 124
vulnerability, child's   84

Wang, Orin N.C.   85
Warley, Christopher   159
Weber, Betty Nance   109n, 129
Weigel, Helen   118
Weimar Republic: Berlin alternative organisations   52
   feminism   27n
   post-1929 crash   21
   radical art   22

Weiss, Peter 13–14n
Wekwerth, Manfred 141n
Welch, Dennis M. 64n
Wessendorf, Markus 146n
Westgate, J. Chris 141n, 150n
Whale, John 98
Whitaker, Jason 95, 194n
Whitaker, Peter 103
White, David 162
White, John J. 108, 109n
Wilke, Judith 25n
Willett, John 12n
Williams, Merryn 171
Williams, Raymond 2, 8n, 9, 12n, 14, 15n, 66n, 68n, 72n, 90n, 92n, 116–17, 119n, 171n, 186
   Marxism and Literature 65
   'residual culture' notion 167
Williams, Nicholas 69n, 157, 182n
Winstanley, Gerard 81n
Wizisla, Erdmut 14n, 30n, 39n, 47n, 61, 101, 102n, 110, 121n, 152n
Wolf, Friedrich 119
Wolfreys, Julian 89n
Wolfson, Susan 162, 163n
Wolin, Richard 4n
women 74
   Blake representation of 184

Brecht theatre roles 48, 133, 140n
   experience of 27n
   proletarian 42n
   right to choose 55n
   sexuality 140n
Wordsworth, William 66n, 71, 162, 170n, 173
   'Tintern Abbey' 85
   'The Prelude' 75
working class, capitalist remaking 11, 62
   agency of movements 6
working people, situation of and the church 134
World War, devastation of 201
Worrall, David 81n, 197
Wright, Elizabeth 124n
Wright, Julia 179n
Wulbern, Julian H. 123n

Yang, Chi-ming 87
Youngquist, Paul 174
Yousef, Nancy 75

Zavarzadeh, Mas'ud 4n
Zhdanov, Andrei 126n
Zimmerer, Jürgen 127n
Zimmerman, Marc 116n
Zoergiebel, Karl 39n